RISKY
BUSINESS

RISKY
BUSINESS

Corruption, Fraud, Terrorism
& other Threats to Global Business

Stuart Poole-Robb & Alan Bailey

**KOGAN
PAGE**

Publisher's note

Every possible effort has been made to ensure that the information contained in this handbook is accurate at the time of going to press, and the publishers and authors cannot accept responsibility for any errors or omissions, however caused. No responsibility for loss or damage occasioned to any person acting, or refraining from action, as a result of the material in this publication can be accepted by the editor, the publisher or any of the authors.

First published in 2002
Reprinted 2002

Kogan Page Limited
120 Pentonville Road
London N1 9JN
www.kogan-page.co.uk

© Kogan Page and Contributors 2002

British Library Cataloguing in Publication Data

A CIP record for this book is available from the British Library.

ISBN 0 7494 3817 7

Typeset by Saxon Graphics Ltd, Derby
Printed and bound in Great Britain by Biddles Ltd, *www.biddles.co.uk*

Contents

Contents

Contents

Foreword

A lifetime of involvement in the fight against crime has taught me the value of intelligence; carefully gathered information that is corroborated, analysed and used to good effect. The same value attaches to intelligence that corrects the often-held misconceptions about the influences on commercial investment in overseas markets.

The word 'globalization' has a particular meaning for the large multinational corporations; as it has for those of us who recognize that crime and terrorism now cross frontiers apparently with relative ease. Crime and terrorism are not the only enemies of those with international commercial enterprise in mind. The concept of Grey Area Dynamics™ described in this book lists other influences such as bureaucracy, corruption, unfair competition, unfair trading, counterfeiting and the effects of cultural, political and religious differences that impinge on commercial decision-making. The concept covers all of those legal and illegal, passive and active influences that can affect success. The range of those influences is wide and, frankly, disturbing.

Since the tragic events of 11 September 2001 in New York and Washington, there is a new awareness of the risk of action by extremists of all types. Serious though that threat may be, the long list of *threats* or *risks* to commerce is equally serious; and demands greater board attention and, perhaps, a non-conventional approach to due diligence appraisals. Sadly, there is a degree of arrogance, naivety and certainly ignorance in some international boardrooms. There is, of course, defence against the risks and the first line of that defence is awareness among the decision-makers and those they employ. To ignore the risks could be fatal – to both the business and to individuals as experience has shown. This book provides a health warning, and awareness and intelligence in abundance.

The Rt. Hon. Sir John Wheeler, PC, JP, DL, Chairman, Service Authorities
for the National Criminal Intelligence Service and National Crime Squad

Foreword

Make no mistake: the intelligent executive of a multi-national company knows that there's no panacea for eliminating risks in extra-national activities. The global situation is too complex to allow that. No matter how enticing the opportunities, there are so many imponderables that risk is the order of the day.

Risky Business is a practical guide to recognizing risks and thereby minimizing some of them. The authors of this book make no facile claims or promises. What they offer is a sensible, highly pragmatic guide to identifying and assessing the risks that can defeat foreign operations. Their experiences warrant your attention.

Stuart Poole-Robb and Alan Bailey have developed through many years of experience an almost all-encompassing geopolitical, due diligence operation that accounts for a sober myriad of vital factors. I consider their programme complementary and supplementary to other necessary components of information-gathering. In translating information into corporate intelligence, they have a way of looking at risky solutions and dealing with them with lowered risk. That's as much as we can ask.

Dan C Pinck served in the Office of Strategic Services, the forerunner of the Central Intelligence Agency. He is the author of 'Stalking the History of the Office of Strategic Services'. *A memoir of his work behind enemy lines will be published in 2002. He is a member of the Special Forces Club.*

Acknowledgements

Many people have contributed to the creation of this book. First, there are the sources of the information that the book contains – nearly 3,000 of them across an increasingly violent and risk-laden world. Then there are those who make up the board and permanent staff of the Merchant International Group (MIG) – and, particularly, Dr Rashna Writer, the Group's Head of Global Risks, whose skilful pen makes sense of the mass of material received at MIG every day. There are those who contributed handsomely to the early years of MIG and shared some of the hairier moments – Ian Henderson, Franc Milburn and a host of others.

There are many more. Maria Muñoz who strung everything together, the contributions of Major Mike Coldrick, MBE, GM, DSA, and Gregory Craig, RIBA, on the structural security of buildings, Mike Hussey and Tony Partington of Canary Wharf Group plc and the editorial hand of Jonathan Reuvid of Kogan Page which guided all of us towards early publication – our thanks are due to all of them.

Stuart Poole-Robb and Alan Bailey
Belgravia
January 2002

Introduction

The tragic events of 11 September 2001 in New York and Washington, and their aftermath, have brought into sharp focus the risks to businesses and employees in international markets. The risks are not confined to the actions of a few fanatical terrorists. They encompass a range of activity arising from different cultures and attitudes. They stem from the willingness or otherwise of governments to strengthen weaknesses in policing, judicial systems and anti-terrorism and to stamp out organized crime, corruption, unfair trading, counterfeiting, cronyism, bureaucracy and civil unrest.

All of these things exist to some degree in every country of the world. Through its international network – both official and clandestine – the Merchant International Group has developed, and continues to develop, an unparalleled knowledge of the risks facing international businesses and those employed by them. The group publishes regular fortnightly, monthly and annual risk updates and analyses of 'invisible risks' in specific countries from its own unique perspective (details of which can be found at the back of this book). In addition, the group acts for many major international corporations in identifying, analysing and evaluating risks before and after investment and determining likely threats to success and safety well beyond the norms of due diligence.

Risk is a word in common use. Its definition includes hazard, danger, exposure to mischance or peril – and, more particularly, the chance or hazard of commercial or personal loss. Risk is, of course, a matter of perception – and perception is, too often, clouded by expertise and by the narrow limits of professional specialization. Today, we are making more significant decisions in an even more perilous market knowing far less than ever before – and that cannot be right. The optimistic entrepreneur, the finance director, the security consultant, the lawyer – all will perceive and measure risk from different standpoints. Their views are influenced by current news and media opinion – often totally subjective – and the traumas and experiences of their personal and working lives from the time they were 'mewling and puking in the nurse's arms'.

It follows that total agreement on commercial strategy and risk assessment is often hard to reach – even after the most careful standard due diligence analysis. Some contributors to the process of strategic decision-making will discount the risks that their colleagues may regard as significant. In the past, there was, too often, an assumption that differences in history, culture and religion mattered little. The tragic events of 11 September 2001 in New York and Washington will have weakened that former assumption. But there is rather more risk than those three basic differences might suggest.

The Merchant International Group (MIG) has a simple tag line – 'We look at the world differently'. Through a network of nearly 3000 informants and operatives – both official and clandestine – in more than 140 countries, MIG gathers information. It then seeks corroboration and, after analysis, that information becomes intelligence. From that solid base, MIG developed Grey Area Dynamics™ – a method of risk assessment and measurement well beyond standard due diligence.

There are over 100 headings in MIG's listing of Grey Area Dynamics™ – covering legal, illegal, active and passive influences on risk. They include risk to investment, buildings, stock and personnel. This book deals with each dynamic and each risk in detail and measures the degree of risk in terms of world geography, culture, religion, politics and economies. It seeks to be comprehensive because the first defence against risk is *total awareness*.

Total awareness must be followed, in some respects, by training, particularly in relation to employees and their families who may be at serious and continuing risk in some locations.

There are defences against risk that are possible to build – some in relation to the structures in which people work and live, others in defence of stock, the security of personnel and their families and then the whole range of influences on success covered by what MIG calls its Grey Area Dynamics™. All of this is explained in detail on the pages that follow. These pages contain current intelligence as at the date of publication. We must all recognize that the world in which we live and work is affected by shifting influences – influences which intensify or change in other ways all too frequently to bring and sustain varying degrees of risk in different locations and affecting different commercial enterprises.

There is a standard list of threats that can be applied to every country or, indeed, to every commercial venture. Standard due diligence has, in the past, not been diligent enough – and, because the world since 11 September 2001 will never be the same again, there has to be a new emphasis on commercial intelligence. The word 'intelligence' must not be confused with 'information'. Before it becomes reliable intelligence, information must be collated, corroborated, analysed and applied to a given set of circumstances, each measured against the yardsticks of risk. And risk is not always related to what was known yesterday. An unthinking statement by a politician can echo round the world in an hour and intensify immediate risk to commercial and industrial interests. It is, sadly, that kind of world.

Religious fanaticism and political extremism are clearly a vital part of risk assessment – part of the weighting applied to global and national risk through MIG's measurement of Grey Area Dynamics™. Political extremism can often be transient although long-lasting – the problems of Northern Ireland are a mix of religious and political intolerance. Religious fanaticism is likely to be with us forever. Islam, for example, is currently the world's fastest growing religion whereas Christianity, in all of its forms, is allegedly in serious decline. But there is another dimension to both religious and political extremism – the criminal dimension through theft, extortion, kidnap and a range of activities that line the coffers of whatever sect or group is involved. Today, countries' special forces, trained by the special forces of US and UK, freelance and act for drug cartels, organized crime and for themselves. Kidnap and ransom have become a profit-making business.

It is not, therefore, surprising to find some political groups still making a good living out of criminal activity. Good livings are not easy to give up – and, whatever political accommodation is made to meet the stated aims, there is unlikely to be an end to the criminal activity that has bolstered incomes for twenty years or so. Some religious groups are of the same mind whatever their professed ideals – and their methods are just as efficient.

Terrorism and crime are the headline-grabbing activities – but there are other, more insidious, risks capable of inflicting damage to an investment. Bureaucracy – the gagging inefficiency of red tape – is one. Cronyism – favouritism in political appointments and the letting of contracts – is another. Bribery and corruption – sometimes on a massive scale – are endemic in many parts of the world. All of these things are part of Grey Area Dynamics™, which the commercial strategists ignore at their peril.

The war declared on international terrorism after the events of 11 September 2001 is both a physical and a political one. However long that war may last, the commercial war will last for much longer – the war against commercial risk in international markets through extremism, corruption, crime, cronyism, counterfeiting and all those influences logged under MIG's Grey Area Dynamics™.

Read on – it's a serious business.

Part One

Invisible Risk and its Impact on Investment

1
Operating in overseas markets

Business strategy and operations in non-domestic markets involve risks. Indeed, all non-domestic investment and associated activities are risky business. The markets concerned are attractive because they offer opportunities for rapid growth, lower production costs and potentially higher returns. At the same time, these markets expose companies to risks outside normal day-to-day commercial experience and conventional due diligence.

Effective corporate risk management demands the successful and timely identification and evaluation of threats to the achievement of corporate strategy. Successful strategy requires the correct organizational configuration of resources within a changing environment. Non-domestic markets are very much a changing environment, in terms of what one knows and is used to. To understand both the operational (micro) and strategic (macro) environments, companies need reliable and objective intelligence.

The globalization of markets and the pressure continually to produce healthy returns for the shareholder while keeping costs down have meant that more and more executives are daring to enter new markets without adequate due diligence or research. Losses incurred by US and UK companies in non-domestic markets in 1999 exceeded $70 billion and these are not trade losses. This was a considerable proportion of global foreign direct investment (FDI) of $827 billion in 1999. The global FDI figure for 2001 fell to $760 billion (Source: *UNCTAD*) – but, as yet, losses have not been calculated. As an aside, the immediate cost of the events of 11 September in material and financial terms is estimated to be over 1 per cent of US gross domestic product. It is interesting to note that, in the first full week following 11 September, the level of unemployment in New York alone rose from 50,000 to 450,000. Losses across the board for 2000 are about $105 billion. Following the events of 11 September 2001, annual losses could well exceed $200 billion.

Merchant International Group (MIG) estimates that over two thirds of the 1999 losses are directly attributable to Grey Area Dynamics™ (GADs). The concept of GADs was formulated by MIG as a collective description of passive and non-passive, legal and illegal factors, of which corruption, bureaucracy and unfair market competition are but a few. The identification and evaluation of GADs is extremely difficult when decision-makers and others often do not know what to look for or how to look for it.

In attempting to manage the 'risk/reward' relationship, most executives make the 'arrogant' mistake of assuming that the illusory safety of the corporate womb provides all the protection necessary to safeguard assets and to ensure healthy returns. Others equate risk management with security for their investment, wrongly assuming that they have the skills and resources to deal with such matters. That is a catastrophe of misconception. Much of the vital corporate intelligence seldom reaches down to the operational level in time for the on-the-spot decision-makers to make the correct choices.

When intelligence does reach the 'arena', it is generally more by luck than by judgement. By this time, it has been watered down to what others believe to be pertinent. In the process, unpalatable truths are kept from management, especially if they reflect adversely on senior personnel. At the same time, personal and departmental agendas are served at the expense of the 'big picture' and, in the long run, this costs the corporate much more.

Without adequate budgets or access to all the information and fearing that non-performance or withdrawal will reflect badly on them and their chance of promotion, people dare to gamble on risks costing millions. What they have succumbed to is an 'intelligence gap' between what they think they know and what they perceive to be the risks on the one hand and what they need to know and what the real risks are on the other. This is the difference between perception and reality.

Traditional forms of research and due diligence no longer suffice in the non–domestic arena. The information provided by sovereign risk and credit rating is lacking in terms of the invisible risks lurking below the corporate waterline. Risk is a gigantic iceberg with the most dangerous parts of it hidden by the waves of misconception, ignorance and naivety. The identification and evaluation of GADs can provide the decision-maker with access to all the risks, weaknesses and threats to enable informed planning.

This book serves to introduce the concept of GADs and to highlight all the pitfalls that confront investments and company activities in non–domestic markets. It is aimed at board-level directors, presidents and middle management alike. It is intended to be both informative and useful to those engaged in executive decision-making in the non–domestic arena and those advising others in such a role.

Most of the corporate examples used in this book are taken from the experience of MIG and its clients. Names, industry sectors, dates and markets have been changed where necessary to ensure continued confidentiality for all concerned.

To all those prepared to tackle risk from this perspective, we wish you luck and ask you to remember the following:

It isn't the critic who counts,
or the one who describes how the strong may have stumbled,
or how the doer of deeds could have done better.

The credit goes to the man in the arena,
who, if he wins, knows the triumph of achievement,
and who, if he fails, fails while daring greatly.

(Anon.)

2
Invisible risks

To be conscious that you are ignorant is a
great step to knowledge.

Benjamin Disraeli

As global competition increases, large companies from different states and regions, and operating across different industry sectors, rush to achieve strategic positioning in markets across the world. The leaderships of these companies operate on the assumption that the large developing and newly industrialized states are crucial to their long-term survival (as, of course, are the developed countries). Global foreign direct investment (FDI) has increased from $660 billion in 1998 to $827 billion in 1999. Much of this is attributable to the growth in cross-border mergers and acquisitions (M&A) which had an announced value of $1,100 billion in 1999 (Source: *UNCTAD*).

In fact, global FDI declined by 40 per cent in 2001. In the year 2000, it reached $1,300 billion but fell to $760 billion in 2001. Cross-border mergers and acquisitions amounted to just $600 billion in 2001 (far less than 6,000 deals) compared with $1.1 trillion covering 7,900 deals in 2000.

Nevertheless, despite the falls in both FDI and M&A, large and small corporations, as well as other investors, cannot ignore any non-domestic market. The whole rationale of investment is high profits if done at the right moment. However, the Latin American debt crisis of the 1980s,

Mexican devaluation in 1994 and the Asian crisis in 1997 meant that the term 'emerging markets' became a much-tarnished phrase. This applied to both FDI and Foreign Portfolio Investment (FPI).

That was a big stigma, with emerging market companies being seen as a real risk for investors. US or European companies are subject to US or European law as regards stock market valuation, accounting standards, transparency, risk management and corporate governance. Therefore, they are perceived to be less of a risk than their emerging market counterparts. This may partly explain why the industrialized world received $609 billion of 1999's FDI (Source: *UNCTAD*), with the USA remaining the largest single recipient.

People do have short memories, however, and were soon back in Russia with their money just as Western corporate vultures hovered over South Korea following the Chaebol's troubles. FDI to South Korea increased by US $3 billion to $8 billion in 1999 (Source: *UNCTAD*) and rose to $15.7 billion – a record high – in 2000. The inward flow of investment to the 'developed' world was over $1,000 billion in the year 2000 but had fallen to $500 billion in 2001 – the USA remaining the largest single recipient in 2001. China is now the developing country receiving the most FDI – rising from $41 billion in 2000 to $46.8 billion in 2001, although it is expected to fall from that level in 2002.

The Enron scandal is likely to have a serious impact on corporate America. Confidence in the system (in particular the part played by major accountancy firms) has taken a severe jolt – and underlines the seriousness of 'conflict of interest' as a Grey Area Dynamic™.

But why did foreign investors make mistakes in the first place? It is clear, with hindsight, that the Asian emerging markets were ill-equipped to deal with the high growth that they experienced and that, while they may have had a competitive manufacturing base, their financial institutions were unable to deal with sudden and massive inflows and outflows of capital. State governments had often directed national banks to lend without proper risk or credit analyses and these banks were able to hide bad loans through lack of transparency to outside scrutiny.

Many Asian companies and governments seemed unaware of how to borrow prudently in global financial markets, failing both to analyse and manage risk. Corrupt members of the ruling elites in these countries, such

as the Suharto family in Indonesia, used banks and international development money for their own wealth creation activities in business ventures
that were often financially unsound.

As the crisis bit, Asian governments were forced to raise interest rates to
prevent money outflows. They saw major development projects halted
while stock markets and currencies fell in value. Most turned to the IMF
for help. All were told that they would have to restructure financial systems
and be better supervised with openness and transparency. The cosy relationships between politicians and bankers would no longer be tolerated and the
ruling elite could no longer guide lending and investment.

To most Westerners, these types of reform are a logical part of corporate
culture, alongside standardized accounting procedures, sound principles of
corporate governance and sensible risk management. For the states in
question, such principles represent an enormous change from some Asian
business cultures, where the national economy was, and is, run by a
monopoly of corrupt officials, businessmen and military officers – without
public or parliamentary scrutiny. Many of the problems of East Asia related
directly to issues of transparency, accountability, cronyism and corruption.

Yet foreign investors are still making the same mistakes and suffering
losses in non-domestic markets. Over 75 per cent of overseas joint ventures
and acquisitions fail to meet either their time-scale objectives or projected
profits, resulting in direct loss and shareholder dissatisfaction (Source: *MIG*).
For many multinationals, 90 per cent of their overseas profits come from
just 10 per cent of their foreign operations. This puts corporations in a
precarious position if even only one of these key markets becomes unstable or a negative environment for business. As we have said, US corporations lost an estimated US $60 billion in 1999 and UK companies lost in
excess of $16 billion (Source: *UNCTAD*). Over two thirds of these losses
are directly attributable to Grey Area Dynamics™ (GADs), according to
MIG.

Grey Area Dynamics™

Non-domestic markets frequently offer opportunities for rapid growth,
lower production costs and potentially higher returns but expose

companies to risks outside their normal day-to-day experience. The problem in all non-domestic markets is how to make sense of the myriad factors that govern sensible investment decisions at both macro and micro levels. There are different definitions of country risk analysis depending on who you ask and what that person does professionally. Lawyers, bankers, management consultants, economists and others involved in the overseas strategy formulation will all have different perspectives, agendas and advice to give.

This publication attempts to look at country risk from the broadest possible perspective. Some definitions of country risk are:

- **political factors**: an assessment of a state's stability and regulatory regime;
- **economic factors**: GDP growth rates, interest rates, balance of payments, industry sectors, threat of new entrants etc;
- **sovereign risk**: the ability of a country to meet its obligations in hard currency;
- **benchmarks**: the risk and investment weighting that investment banks and large scale investors give to markets in areas such as bonds and equity;
- **security factors**: the internal and external security environment and the physical threat to corporate assets, operations and personnel;
- **potential partner/customer/acquisition appraisal**: an assessment of the creditworthiness, viability and suitability of a potential customer, partner or acquisition target;
- **Grey Area Dynamics™**: a collective description of passive and non-passive, legal and illegal risk factors not generally evaluated in conventional due diligence and risk assessments.

Any of these categories will provide useful information regarding operations and strategy in non-domestic markets but, to see the whole picture, analysts and decision-makers need to be aware of all the factors actually in and around the market in question that could have a bearing on the key objective of success. The general reliance on visits by 'qualified' executives has had the effect of generating subjective and limited information of doubtful value and quality. The recent economic and political crises have clearly demonstrated the downside of failing to take such factors into account.

Grey Area Dynamics™ are the factors that affect the return on assets and performance and which can threaten the success of a foreign investment project. The gravest danger is that these factors not only cause under-performance but also threaten cessation of performance altogether.

The GADs framework is made up of country-specific factors that cause assets or investment to under-perform. There are over one hundred different GADs but the ten key headings are:

- corruption;
- bureaucracy;
- counterfeiting and theft;
- cultural issues;
- legal safeguards;
- organized crime;
- unfair trade;
- unfair competition;
- asset security;
- extremism.

Each of the ten major GAD headings listed in Figure 2.1 is scored out of a possible total of 10 points.

MIG's ten GADs and their sub sections

1. **Corruption**
   - 1.1   Bribery
   - 1.2   Blackmail
   - 1.3   Patronage
   - 1.4   Disguised beneficial ownership
   - 1.5   Nepotism
   - 1.6   Cronyism (including old boys network)
   - 1.7   Political coercion/corporate hospitality/gifts
   - 1.8   Political and economic corruption

1.9 Sponsorship

1.10 Vested interests

2. Bureaucracy

2.1 Red tape

2.2 Vested interests

2.3 Deliberate/enforced delay

2.4 Political influence

2.5 Cultural habits

2.6 Local and regional interference

2.7 Perceptions of bureaucratic rules vs reality

2.8 Local/central government domestic action

2.9 Extortion

2.10 Agents/distributors action (eg Mr Fixit, etc.)

3. Counterfeiting and theft

3.1 Fraud

3.2 White-collar theft

3.3 Blue-collar theft

3.4 Piracy

3.5 Tribal action (eg tribes in Africa damaging oil pipes to steal and resell oil)

3.6 Product adulteration

3.7 Product diversion

3.8 Official/unofficial customs action

3.9 Payment to slack workers for easy jobs, 'consultancy services' (eg halyava in Russia)

3.10 False accounting

4. Cultural issues

4.1 Country culture

4.2 Corporate culture (including local staff motivation and training)

4.3 Religious differences

4.4 Tradition

4.5 Customs/ethics (eg attitude towards child labour)

4.6 Civil unrest

4.7 Language/dialects

4.8   Public hostility/distrust
4.9   Integration
4.10 Xenophobia

5.   Legal safeguards
5.1   Industrial action
5.2   Trade unions influence
5.3   Government policy
5.4   Nationalization
5.5   Environmental hazards
5.6   Customs or other duties
5.7   Corporate governance
5.8   Regulations
5.9   Tax
5.10 Hidden political agenda

6.   Organized crime
6.1   Kidnap
6.2   Ransom
6.3   Extortion
6.4   Drugs/arms/people trafficking
6.5   Smuggling
6.6   Cyber crime
6.7   Protectionism
6.8   Money laundering
6.9   Secret societies
6.10 Criminal/union activity

7. Unfair trade
7.1   Parallel trading
7.2   Product diversion
7.3   Dumping
7.4   Hidden barriers to entry
7.5   Sponsorship
7.6   Government policy
7.7   Pricing
7.8   Minority, right or left-wing, groups (hired to damage competitor's reputation)

7.9 Nepotism

7.10 Vested interests (lobbying from corporations to government)

8. Unfair competition

8.1 Commercial espionage

8.2 Vested interests

8.3 Media relations

8.4 Lobbying

8.5 Corporate secrecy (unavailability of information)

8.6 Embargo

8.7 Local government interference

8.8 Plants (when employees are planted to disrupt the business of a competitor)

8.9 Litigious culture (if a court case is initiated in order to damage the reputation of a competitor)

8.10 Boycott

9. Asset security

9.1 Pilferage

9.2 Product contamination/alteration

9.3 Disgruntled employees

9.4 Computer and IT issues (hacking)

9.5 Threat to management/staff/premises

9.6 Extremists (such as the Animal Liberation Front)

9.7 Minority groups (like Greenpeace)

9.8 Civil unrest

9.9 War

9.10 Natural disasters (floods, volcanoes)

10. Extremism

10.1 Tribalism

10.2 Minority activist groups

10.3 Environmental groups

10.4 Terrorist activity – religious (eg Al Qaida)

10.5 Extreme right and left-wing groups

10.6 Religious fanaticism

10.7 Terrorist activity – political (eg FARC)

10.8 Extreme industrial action

10.9   Sectarianism

10.10 Genocide

'Intelligence' about each GAD heading is measured for a particular country. The higher the score, the greater the problem as represented by the GAD factor. A score of 9.0 or higher for corruption, for example, would indicate that corruption was endemic in a particular country. A score of 1.0 would indicate that it was a negligible factor in business operations. Each country is evaluated against the ten principal GAD headings. The scores from each of the ten headings are then added together to give a total possible country score of 100 points. The higher the number of points, the greater the risk

Passive/legal
- Language and dialects
- Local customs and traditions
- Local staff motivation and training
- Tribalism and integration
- Regulations, taxes and duties
- Currency and capital exposure
- Payment methods and banking practice
- Environmental hazards
- Pressure groups
- Media relations

Non-passive/legal
- Industrial and labour relations
- Absence or effectiveness of legal safeguards
- Governmental policy and nationalization
- Disguised beneficial ownership
- Bureaucracy and local government
- Public or media hostility
- Protectionism
- Nationalism/xenophobia

Grey Area Dynamics™

Passive/illegal
- Bribery and corruption
- Vested interests and cronyism
- Patronage
- Product diversion
- Parallel trading
- Hidden barriers to entry
- Dumping
- Red tape
- Bureaucracy

Non-passive/illegal
- Counterfeiting and fraud
- Pilferage
- Unfair market competition
- Product piracy
- Ethics and corporate espionage
- Organized crime
- Threats to physical assets
- Kidnap and extortion
- Terrorism/religious extremism
- Civil unrest
- Product contamination

Source: MIG

Figure 2.1 The main Grey Area Dynamics™ that cause assets to under-perform

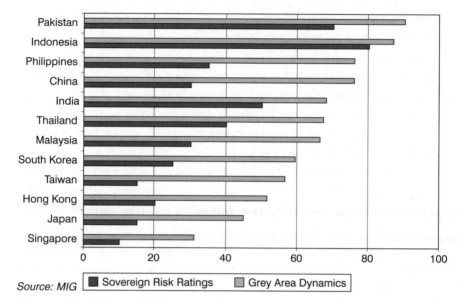

Figure 2.2 Asia and the Far East: Sovereign Risk Ratings vs Grey Area Dynamics 2001

posed by the GADs. Operating in a country with a score of 75 points or more would be highly problematic, while a country with a score of 30 points or less would be a relatively benign environment for business.

According to the specifics of the market and situation, certain GADs may never arise at all or may be so commonplace that there is no choice but to accept them. What they share in common is that they are usually obscure to decision-makers at the time of contractual or financial commitment and, in many cases, for a long time afterwards.

The iceberg

As many of these GAD factors are invisible to the untrained eye or because they are ignored or 'brushed under the carpet' for various reasons (perhaps because they might spoil a deal), they do not feature in most credit ratings or investment and banking reports. Many of these reports focus only on sovereign risk factors or country benchmarks. It is significant that the major credit rating agencies were caught out by the Asian crisis, as were most of the leading investment banks in the Asian and Russian crises. Hundreds of millions of dollars were lost as a result.

An investment banker, whose organization lost vast sums in Russia and who saw many of his colleagues lose their jobs, commented: 'The fact that so many international banks all got caught out by Russia shows that there is just not enough knowledge in Western investors' minds on that point. They are not doing the amount of research that they should do with respect to understanding the psyche of the authorities in that country if things go wrong. It's all very well when things are going fine, but what happens when the **** hits the fan?'

Sovereign risk ratings relate to the likelihood of a sovereign state defaulting on its official debt obligations but do not adequately portray the real risks for investment. Sovereign risk ratings do not take account of GAD factors. These are hard to track and assess from a strictly sovereign risk or country political/economic viewpoint. They remain, however, a significant problem for businesses. They affect returns at one end of the scale and have impact on the corporate image and on people's safety at the other.

The differences between sovereign risk ratings and GADs can be clearly seen if one takes an average of the sovereign ratings given by the two major ratings agencies, and compares them with Grey Area Dynamics™. It could also be called the 'difference between the real risk and the perceived risk'.

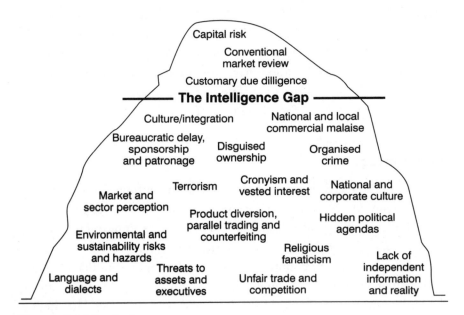

Figure 2.3 The Iceberg

The way that GADs correspond to sovereign risk ratings is shown in Table 2.1

Table 2.1 Comparison between sovereign risk ratings and GADs

Standard & Poors's	Moody's	MIG GAD score	Risk level
AAA	Aaa	10	Low
BB	Ba2	50	Medium
C	C	90	High
D		100	Highest

Grey Area Dynamics™ are invisible risks that can catch the unwary, just as an iceberg is a risk to a ship because it is invisible and deadly below the waterline.

In the non-domestic arena, the success of a given business undertaking – whether it be entry, exit, joint ventures, acquisitions or day-to-day operations – depends upon an ability to comprehend, in-depth, the various Grey Area Dynamics™ that exist in a market. The greater the level of ignorance, the greater the vulnerability to both commercial and non-commercial risks.

The non-domestic market is an alien playing field, driven by alien dynamics, operating within a different cultural context, with different rules and, therefore, different determinants of success. A British company operating in the US may assume familiarity with US conditions, based on cultural misconceptions (discussed later in the book).

Traditional due diligence, risk assessment and strategic analysis are not up to the task of identifying risk in the non-domestic arena. They ignore the salient issues that may be visible, if you know what you are looking for, or (more likely) invisible, if you do not. People involved in non-domestic market strategy, both within and outside the organization, may acknowledge the existence of some GADs, but do not necessarily incorporate these into their risk assessments. Furthermore, any analysis or advice will be subject to perceptions, personal agendas and politics.

All of the above lead, deliberately or inadvertently, to an intelligence gap between what the decision-makers think they know and what they perceive to be the risks and what they actually know and what the real risks are. This intelligence gap needs to be bridged in order to make informed decisions.

Still, many companies and financial institutions are either unaware of or only pay lip service to GADs, and therefore do not include them in their assessment of operating risks or potential returns. The exceptions are certain types of company, such as international mining corporations or oil concerns, which are regularly exposed to corrupt practices, political instability and operations disrupted by military conflicts, by virtue of the business they are in and the locations in which they operate. Even *they* do not always get it right.

It is vital to assess and quantify the risks associated with GADs and then, in combination with sovereign risk, identify the total risk exposure associated with a particular business strategy, investment or operation. Chapter 3 looks at some of the problems associated with information gathering and the corporate strategy process. The remaining chapters examine the various elements of Grey Area Dynamics™ in detail, using real-life case studies to illustrate problems encountered in non-domestic markets, and include advice on how to avoid the common pitfalls.

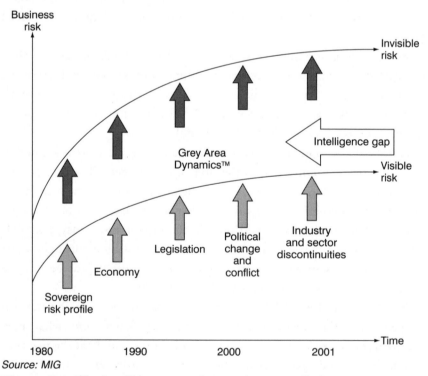

Source: MIG

Figure 2.4 The intelligence gap (perception vs reality)

3
The problem with strategy

*In business as on the battlefield, the object of strategy is to
bring about the conditions most favourable to one's own side,
judging precisely the right moment to attack or withdraw, and
always assessing the limits of compromise correctly.*

Kenichi Ohmae, 1992

Before embarking on an examination of the various Grey Area
Dynamics™ and their real and potential impacts in greater detail, it is
necessary to understand the corporate strategy process with regard to non-
domestic markets. There are usually several problems associated with strategy formulation, and not just those resulting from the interplay and impact
of GADs. If these can be successfully ironed out, then an organization is
likely to obtain a much better approach to dealing with the problems
presented by the non-domestic environment.

It is useful to break down the strategy process into a number of stages so
as to be able to analyse each one and discover where problems can occur.
For the purposes of this study, the strategy process will be broken down
into five stages. Each can then be examined in detail:

- **Direction** – the directive given by the board or executive vice-
  president of a strategic business unit (SBU) for formulation of a strategy
  for market entry, exit, target acquisition, etc. This may filter down to a
  smaller business unit (BU).

- **Information collection** – the gathering by the strategy team or others of the information necessary to carry out their analysis.
- **Analysis and planning** – the interpretation of the information collected, which turns it into intelligence for use in strategy formulation.
- **Bargaining** – the evolution of the strategy based upon bargaining and interplay within the organization.
- **Decision-making** – acting on the intelligence and strategic plan.

Direction

Companies are expected to have rational business strategies and these are supposed to be directed and mandated by the senior management, either at board level or at business unit level. If senior management is parochial and narrow-minded, this is reflected at middle-management level. If senior management has preconceived notions about the financial, technological and investment environments, this will determine the kind of direction it gives to subordinates as to the organizational strategies it wants to adopt.

A common reason for deciding to embark on a market entry strategy, for example, could be as follows: 'The competition is there, we need to be there and, if we analyse all the risks, we'll simply convince ourselves that we shouldn't be there.' Senior executives could decide to enter a market for this reason alone, even if a non-subjective analysis indicated that there was no real economic rationale for doing so or strong reasons why they should not.

No one lower down the corporate ladder will try to sabotage a superior's pet project or cause disruptions, when it has already been decided higher up the chain at board level. This is because many large corporations lack the culture that allows the individual to express doubts openly. Most people do not have the will or ability to say what they think of a particular course of action or situation for various reasons; they will generally tend to concur and agree with their superiors and peers. Family and career considerations come into play, so the end result is that people tend to acquiesce to direction from above without really questioning it.

There is the danger that the board level executive, with his sights set on expansion overseas, will instruct his team to prepare a strategy where the analysis justifies the executive decision, rather than accurately portraying the external environment. The decision has often already been made before the market intelligence is available, where the final decision justifies the analysis, rather than the analysis justifying the final decision. If the SBU and BU fail in the market concerned, they may well play it down and keep it 'under wraps', so that no one at company headquarters finds out; or, at least, not until the people concerned have moved on, leaving the mess for their successors to clean up. This is a recipe for disaster.

The senior management bears direct responsibility to shareholders when it fails to exercise sound risk management of the activity in question. Shareholders may not be the only ones affected. A failure to appreciate the risks may bring the unwelcome attention of the media, pressure groups or regulators. In extreme situations, lives can be lost.

Sound risk management requires a situation where: 'the aims of corporate strategy are understood, the threats to successful achievement of that strategy are identified, the aspirations and risk appetite of stakeholders are taken into account, and an appropriate level of controls is in place' (Ohmae, 1992).

The key word here is 'threats' because, without identification of the factors likely to impact on a particular course of action, the whole game plan may unravel with all the attendant consequences.

Information collection

Cost cutting and downsizing have become embedded in Western business culture and the allocation of piecemeal resources, usually due to cost pressures, necessitates taking short cuts. In the home or traditional markets, such practices may suffice as corporate analysts and decision-makers utilize existing experience and resources efficiently. It is inadequate for acquisition of intelligence in an overseas market environment or intelligence about a company or individuals.

In most companies, there is a shortage of people with the necessary international experience to analyse risk and evaluate return. Often those with little or no overseas knowledge are expected to undertake research, risk assessment and strategy formulation in completely alien environments.

If they do not do this themselves, then they are forced to rely on facilitators and middle-men whose own motives are open to question and who may be working for other companies, foreign intelligence organizations or organized crime groups. The result is that many or most of the underlying potential risks are either missed or ignored.

There exists the ever-present danger of taking appearances at face value. International travel, overseas housing and multilingual ability are commonplace for leading businesses today, yet there is still a level of ignorance and arrogance, especially among Western European and American firms operating outside Western markets. Some companies try to overcome these cultural differences through training, education and by having culturally and racially diverse personnel.

The 'illusion of familiarity' is the, usually subconscious, act of perceiving a current situation in the light of a previous experience. When operating outside home markets, it is quite tempting to fall back on points of familiarity, while skimming past the unpredictable and unfamiliar. People are forced to simplify the complexity of the environment that they face and give it selective attention. Given this complexity, even if the person concerned has a very good understanding, it is unlikely that this will hold true for all decisions in all situations. What people tend to do is selectively access the knowledge that seems most relevant for a given situation.

Someone sent abroad on a fact-finding mission with scant knowledge of the local environment will not usually send back quality information. Passing information back will be a risk in itself, as inter-human communication problems manifest themselves. Trying to reproduce acquired perceptions in the mind of another is difficult enough, and is increased when the subjects of communication are intangibles or abstractions such as aspirations, intentions, purpose, motivations or local business culture. None of these will be especially clear to the fact-finder, so the chances of misconception by the receptor are greater.

Analysis and planning

The increased uncertainty of non-domestic markets leaves decision-makers subject to the ability of their organizations to collect information on these environments. They then have to analyse it and use it successfully in their decision–making to take that organization in a desired direction, if indeed objectives can be clear cut and emphatic. According to Kenichi Ohmae: 'Analysis requires considerable skill and experience, and can be undertaken seriously only when there is constant access to accurate market information

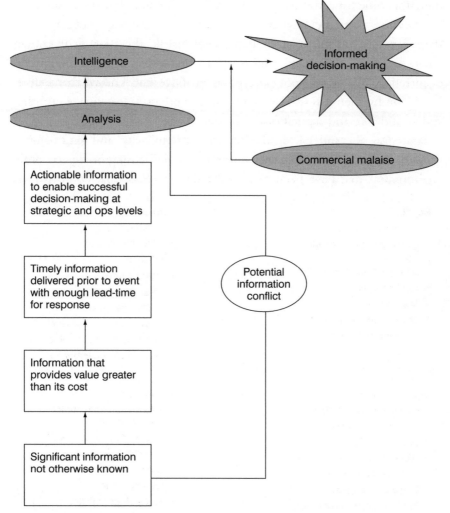

None of the above is of any consequence if the decision-makers suffer from what we call the commercial malaise – arrogance, ignorance or naivety.
Source: MIG

Figure 3.1 Corporate intelligence criteria (the executive sickness)

… No proper business strategy can be built on fragmentary knowledge or analysis'. (Ohmae, 1992: 34)

Understanding a situation depends on information about it, as well as the perception of that information. The analyst will rarely have direct access to the information on which he must rely. For non-domestic markets, one can assume that information will be poor, unless the company has been working there for some time and has local know-how, contacts and risk awareness.

The non-domestic environment cannot be analysed properly when starved of critical information that might 'break' the strategy if known. There are many people who have said to themselves after an unexpected occurrence: 'We would not have gone in if we had known that before-hand', but by then it is too late, with capital and assets lost, image tarnished and confidence and reputations in tatters.

Strategists also suffer from the 'illusion of familiarity' and tend to over-simplify the complexity that they come across by focusing on aspects of the environment that have been historically important or that confirm prior

Political
- Government stability
- Industry regulations/social legislation
- Deregulation/liberalization
- Tariff controls
- Taxation policy
- Employment law
- Environmental protection

Economic
- Business cycles
- GNP trends
- Inflation
- Interest rates
- Unemployment
- Exchange rates
- Disposable income levels
- Single currency impacts
- Trading alliances/barriers

Socio-cultural
- Population growth/shift
- Income distribution
- Social mobility
- Work/leisure/quality of life
- Health/education/welfare
- Lifestyle changes
- Public opinion, expectations and values
- Media opinion

Technological
- Information/communications breakthroughs
- Substitute technologies
- Emerging technologies
- Digital economy
- Obsolescence
- Technology transfer

Source: MIG

Figure 3.2 PEST analysis: conventional considerations

views and assumptions. Analysis can easily become myopic and biased towards traditional economic and financial factors.

Coping with uncertainty is one of the main problems of corporate strategy and it is surprising how little attention is paid to 'on the ground' operational risks. Strategists might argue that they are not interested in the micro level, despite the fact that problems here will unravel the strategic plan or prove it is flawed.

Strategists try to identify potential business 'discontinuities' or changes in the business environment by focusing on economic and industry factors such as business cycles, income levels, industrial regulations, taxation policy and the like. These types of factor fit much more readily within the traditional strategist's mindset than do tribalism, corruption, vested interests and organized crime. This is reflected in the analytical tools that the strategist uses. By failing to identify the potential risks involved, the analysis becomes flawed, however brilliantly the other factors are interpreted.

Michael Porter's 'five forces' (see Figure 3.3) are a classic means of examining the competitive environment in a particular market with regard to competitive rivalry, new entrants, relative power of buyers and suppliers and threat of substitute products. It does not, however, take account of hidden barriers such as unfair market competition, lack of legal safeguards, cronyism or bureaucracy, which are all formidable obstacles in non-domestic markets. This conventional analytical approach suits the needs of business schools and corporate headquarters, rather than the requirements of non-domestic research and analysis.

Analysis of a market's competitive environment should also include an appraisal of the GADs facing competitors. This would give a more accurate picture as to the attractiveness of competing in a market where certain GADs may apply to the detriment of one competitor, while the other manages to operate effectively in spite of them, or even because of them. One only has to consider how many tenders are won by bribery of corrupt government officials or by knowing the 'right' people.

SWOT analysis (strengths, weaknesses, opportunities, threats) is a popular way of combining analyses of an organization's resources, competencies and strategic capability with analysis of the external environment. It is used to identify the extent to which the organization's current strategy and its strengths and weaknesses are capable of dealing with changes in the

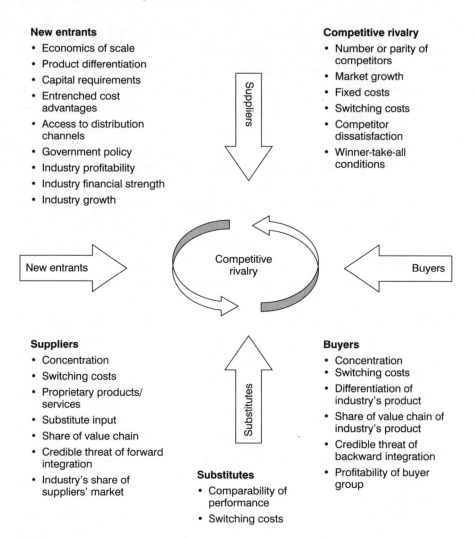

New entrants
- Economics of scale
- Product differentiation
- Capital requirements
- Entrenched cost advantages
- Access to distribution channels
- Government policy
- Industry profitability
- Industry financial strength
- Industry growth

Competitive rivalry
- Number or parity of competitors
- Market growth
- Fixed costs
- Switching costs
- Competitor dissatisfaction
- Winner-take-all conditions

Suppliers
- Concentration
- Switching costs
- Proprietary products/ services
- Substitute input
- Share of value chain
- Credible threat of forward integration
- Industry's share of suppliers' market

Substitutes
- Comparability of performance
- Switching costs

Buyers
- Concentration
- Switching costs
- Differentiation of industry's product
- Share of value chain of industry's product
- Credible threat of backward integration
- Profitability of buyer group

Adapted from ME Porter

Figure 3.3 Porter's five forces

business environment. It is also used to assess whether there are opportunities to exploit company core competencies and resources for competitive advantage.

In general, threats as represented in the SWOT matrix (see Figure 3.4) must be overcome before opportunities can be grasped. The 'energy' required to overcome threats derives from the organization's relative strengths and weaknesses. Much of the energy available will be used in

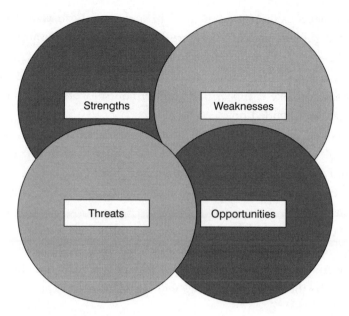

Figure 3.4 A SWOT matrix

coping with the threats, often leaving little or nothing to take advantage of the opportunities. SWOT is a fairly limited tool because the traditional mindset of most analysts will preclude awareness of Grey Area Dynamics™, making the analysis largely irrelevant. Evaluating the critical success factors for a particular strategy will then be affected by the foregoing SWOT analysis.

Strategists will simplify the environment using generic terminology, referring for example to a dominant competitor rather than a list of competitive attributes. In their minds, they compete with the French and Germans, rather than specific companies, or perceive one particular company as 'the competition'. Over time, these simplifications of reality predominate.

The risk is that this mindset dictates which signals from the environment are chosen to match with this selective representation of reality, and therefore which information is used for strategy formulation. Information that confirms Company X being the main competitor is absorbed, while contradictory information is not.

Sometimes, competitors will compound cognitive problems in a deliberate attempt to deceive. Using the example of mergers and acquisitions, it is not unusual for companies engaged in such activity to want to keep it confidential (unless, perhaps, they are looking from the wrong end of a hostile takeover). Techniques range from restrictions on outflows of corporate information to the outside world to deliberate dissemination of false information, to make it appear that another course of action is to be taken rather than the intended one.

Analysts and decision-makers in other companies may reject the possibility of being deceived because they see no evidence of it. If deception is well planned and properly executed, then one should not expect to see any evidence of it at all, because surprise and security are the key objectives of deception plans.

However, the possibility of deception should not be rejected until it is either disproved or until a systematic search has been made for evidence of deception and none has been found. Most people will not think along these lines. To their detriment, they will see what they expect or want to see.

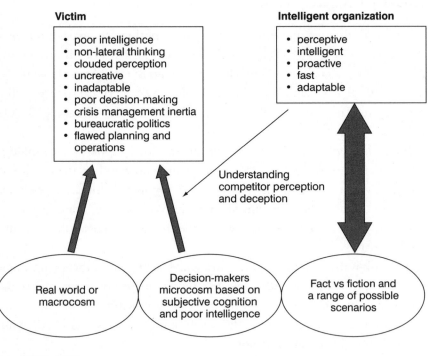

Source: F Milburn/MIG

Figure 3.5 Organizational perception of the external environment

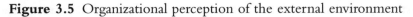

Perceptions of the environment are doubly important in non-domestic markets. Firstly, they are alien and beyond the understanding of those without extensive experience of them. Secondly, the illusion of familiarity means that people will interpret the environment incorrectly and come up with totally inappropriate responses to it. Non-domestic markets present different risks and challenges, which need to be successfully identified, evaluated and prepared for. Decision-making based on strategic analysis cannot be successful in the absence of the correct information.

Grey Area Dynamics™ also present special problems when it comes to cost analysis – of both the organization's costs in a certain market and that of a competitor. Estimating the key cost drivers which impact at each stage of the value chain is hazardous, because hidden factors like bureaucracy, cronyism and corruption can change the costs dramatically from one market to another and between competitors in a market. In a Muslim country, for example, does one add cultural factors to a competitor's labour costs, which will be higher than those of other markets because men and women have to be transported separately to the workplace? Catering costs will similarly be higher because of food sensibilities. Can one adequately estimate how labour costs might increase in a highly unionized environment such as the US? Can costs account for bribery or unforeseen security problems caused by organized crime or political instability?

These types of issue are likely to throw estimates widely out so that the true organizational and competitor costs remain obscure. This obviously has an implication for profit and loss figures. Tools such as Activity Based Management (ABM) will not help to identify the hidden costs in a complex business environment that are necessary to identify whether or not the business is likely to be profitable. Bribery may not even be a

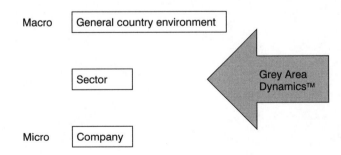

Figure 3.6 Research model for non-domestic markets

recognized activity. A group of products in the business portfolio may be profitable in one market and unprofitable or even non-viable in another because the invisible risks mask the true cost of doing business. Typically, taking account of GADs will increase the perceived risk of a particular market as expressed by sovereign risk ratings by as much as 20–50 per cent and reduce the rate of return of a project by 10–30 per cent.

Many companies have lost money when they could have identified the problems and mitigated them. Going beyond GADs, focused analysis needs to be done for different types of business. A consumer goods producer will face quite different GADs in a non-domestic market than, for example, a financial services company.

In addition, the nature of the proposed venture – franchise, licence agreement, partnership, joint venture, acquisition or start-up – will affect the impact of GAD factors on the project. Just as potential returns increase as involvement deepens, so, too, do the associated GADs. The national

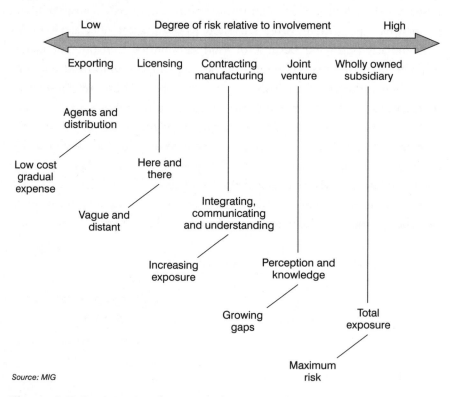

Figure 3.7 Business involvement relative to risk

country of origin of the business will also have a bearing on the GADs encountered in country. A US company operating in Iran, for example, will have a completely different risk profile from a German one.

Bargaining

The final outcome of the strategy planning process is likely to be problematic because of the bureaucratic and departmental characteristics of most large organizations. Corporate strategy will often be determined by a bureaucratic approach that recognizes the different aims and objectives of business units and departments, often with unequal influence within the organization. This is the narrow-minded parochial outlook mentioned above. In recommending actions, participants will be guided not just by what they perceive to be in the company's interest in relation to a particular market but also by the interest of their particular business unit, expectations about their personal performance and their personal and career concerns.

The interplay among participants from which a decision emerges will be affected by many factors: the nature of the market; the quality of bargaining skills; the nature of information gathering and support; the existence or otherwise of an accepted hierarchy among the participants; the clarity or otherwise with which the competencies and interests of participants are defined; the relative importance of the issue and what kind of trade-offs are available – all those as well as what friendships or antipathies exist. Different departments and business units will perceive things differently.

At board level, this will boil down to whose interest the foray into a non-domestic market represents. Is it a pet project of the Vice President for Asia, which he knows will conflict with the interests of the Vice President Middle East and Africa? This might be reflected further down the line, with actors in a high profit-making strategic business unit (SBU) resenting the diversion of resources to a loss-making SBU, just because the potential return on investment (ROI) for that SBU's activities in a new market is high.

Decisions that emerge from the bureaucratic process, the result of interplay and bargaining by different sections and interests, are very often conditioned by what happens at each stage of the process. It may be difficult even for the participants to determine how the final decisions came to be made.

Decision-making

This is where the strategy process comes back full circle, once the strategic plan is in the hands of the senior decision-makers. A lot of decision-makers acting in relation to uncertain environments will be driven by the nature of their competition. Organizations often look to peer groups for comforting signals to justify their own actions. If one corporation moves into Country X, then that is often a good enough reason for a rival to make a similar move. Following on from this, the rival might then justify not carrying out thorough due diligence, which is costly and time-consuming. It does so on the premise that, if others are already in the market, then they must have already done their risk assessments and that, therefore, the market has to be relatively safe. If a good blue chip company has moved into a particular market, then others will follow.

An organization might be willing to suffer losses by engaging a competitor in a non-domestic market, just to prevent the competition from dominating that market. Accordingly, companies go into a market in order to deprive their rival of profits, even though it entails losses for themselves.

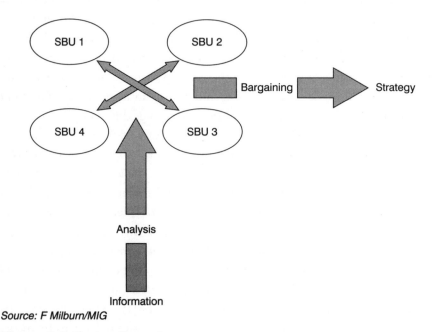

Source: F Milburn/MIG

Figure 3.8 Rationality vs bureaucracy

Corporate decision-makers willing to take gambles may often get away with more than an objective analysis of the situation would suggest. To do business in non-domestic markets is to take risks, which are generally greater and less well understood than those in the domestic environment. It would be advantageous if senior decision-makers understood all the reasons why they were becoming involved overseas and how decisions relating to non-domestic markets came to be made. This would create the conditions for a far more effective and rational strategy. Understanding the interplay of Grey Area Dynamics™ is a crucial step in this process.

4
Understanding culture

*Yet across the gulf of space, minds that are to our minds as
ours are to those of the beasts that perish, intellects vast and
cool and unsympathetic regarded this earth with envious
eyes, and slowly and surely drew their plans against us.*

H G Wells, *The War of the Worlds*, 1898

To understand non-domestic actors (companies, governments, potential
partners etc.), one has to understand their assumptions and values as well as
their own misconceptions. Otherwise, interpreting their decisions or future
actions is tantamount to partially informed speculation. Often, some aspects
of foreigners' behaviour could seem irrational or even 'not in their best
interests', while the rest of their behaviour seems normal. If this happens,
then the person making these observations is projecting his or her values
on to foreign decision-makers and entities. This is misunderstanding the
logic of the situation as the foreigner sees it.

It is no good relying on the dictum that 'business is business' and that this
applies everywhere. A common mistake is the failure to differentiate
between the home and the non-domestic market, either categorizing them
together, thus denying any difference at all, or treating all markets in the
same way. Problems occur as the organization underestimates the cultural
diversity it faces. Of course, non-Western companies and individuals have
the same problems. A Middle-Eastern or Indian company would have a
wide variety of GADs to deal with on entering the UK or US markets.
Their misconceptions would also be shaped by cultural differences.

This type of analysis, 'mirror-imaging', is a potential cognitive trap. No matter how much expertise someone applies to interpreting the value systems of foreigners and foreign entities, the tendency is to project the interpretations of one's own mind once hard evidence is exhausted. A different approach would be to role-play, and actually act out the role of the other decision-maker or actor with assistance from others, perhaps as part of a corporate 'war-gaming' exercise (this is discussed in the closing chapter). It is only by living out the role that one can break mindsets and relate to facts or ideas in ways outside habitual patterns or experience.

It is still difficult to interpret issues such as 'face' for the Chinese, which, for them, is a quality from which a person's stature is derived. If one has 'face', then it is an indication of honesty and good character, which is lost through shameful transactions, such as reneging on deals, and gained through improvements to personal standing or for help given in times of difficulty.

It is easy to be complacent when nearly the entire world has adopted Western business dress and when 75 per cent of global business is conducted in English. Problems also extend into the non-verbal sphere as body language conveys different messages to different cultures. For English people, eye contact is important and lack of eye contact can imply dishonesty or suspicion. The Japanese lower their eyes when speaking to a superior as a sign of respect. There is a lot of room for misconception, which can harm business dealings.

Different parts of the world also have different attitudes to time. In the UK, meetings are held at set times and it is rude to be late or even not turn up at all. This contrasts with the 'siesta' mentality in parts of Latin America and the time flexibility that exists in the Middle East. Western businessmen need to be careful not to impose their timeframes on others, just as those others need to be aware of Western attitudes to time. Visible, invisible, verbal and non-verbal differences can all lead to misunderstanding when attempting to bridge cultural barriers.

Westerners also tend to attribute cultural stereotypes to regions such as East Asia when, culturally, they are very diverse. 'Confucian' values have been attributed to business in East Asia when this is clearly not the case. Indonesia, with almost 200 million people of whom around 90 per cent are Muslim (the largest Muslim population in the world), is clearly an exception to this rule. East Asia is quite simply not one homogeneous mass.

Taking a topical and recurrent area of corporate activity, mergers and acquisitions (M&A), as an example, how difficult is it to gauge the reactions of the foreign board to the prospect of merger or to assess the difficulties of the human elements or the post-merger integration process? (Hubbard, 1999.) In M&A, there are three types of cultural differences to be experienced: cross-national, inter-company, and across business units or functions.

Inter-company and cross-business unit/functional differences are difficult enough, but cross-national differences can be manifested in work legislation, language, employee attitudes and behaviour, working practices, company procedures and management styles and philosophy. Other issues include tribalism, religion and national, as well as corporate, culture. Those constitute a plethora of potential opportunities for misconception of the situation as it is.

Cross-national, cultural differences are usually acknowledged when the two companies speak different languages but the use of translators brings with it a risk that what you say is not translated in a way or tone that you desire. This makes it doubly difficult to gauge the mindset or perceptions of the other side. It is hard enough when one speaks the language fluently. Even then, there are enough cultural and linguistic differences between the British and Americans to cause perceptual problems.

Try this exercise. Place a world atlas in front of you, open at a map of Russia. Imagine that you are the Russian President or one of his closest advisors, sitting in a cabinet meeting in the centre of Moscow. As you do this, place your forefinger on the spot where Moscow is marked on the map. With your free hand, rotate the map so that the European countries bordering Russia to the west are uppermost, i.e., facing away from you. Try to imagine what your Russian character might feel about these countries, in terms of culture, threats, business opportunities and the like. Try to imagine what you might think about foreign firms operating in your country. Try to imagine what a Russian may think that a foreigner might think about Russia.

Now rotate the map counter-clockwise so that the countries bordering Russia to the south are uppermost. Make the same mental considerations. Continue doing this until you have been all the way around the map and, hopefully, with some knowledge of Russia, you might see things differently and be able to look out rather than look in. Try this for any other country or imagine yourself as a businessman or chairman of a potential acquisition target. Put yourself in someone else's shoes.

Business integration

Business integration pertains to the cultural fit of a particular company within a non-domestic market. Firstly, how do the corporate *modus operandi* and attitude to business compare with the cultural norms and practices of a particular market? Secondly, to what extent is a company going to be affected by cultural divisions within that market itself? The question of how cultural differences impact on business operations leads on to issues such as workforce motivation, initiative and market-orientation, which will differ widely from market to market. Global standards inevitably fail unless they are flexible enough to be adapted to local conditions and managers have the insight to make the fit happen.

To achieve this, it is useful to consider not just how a business will be perceived but which forces shape cultural issues within the society itself. A company that has a well-publicized history of successful operations in Israel, for instance, may face extensive difficulty in finding a suitable partner in Saudi Arabia or the Gulf States. Problems of this kind relate more to the goings-on within the marketplace itself than they do to the corporate culture of the company. There is the case of the over-worked UK manager nearly causing an international incident because he was bullied by a director into introducing an Israeli company to his firm's product range – and so he put the Israelis in touch with the main Middle East distributor – an Arab.

Local attitudes can be particularly important in the selection of senior management for non-domestic ventures in ways that are neither fair nor pleasant. An example is the existence of deep-rooted anti-Semitism in Poland. In one case in 1998, a leading European retailer was shocked by the poor first-year performance of its new venture in Turkey. It had not realized that choosing an extremely capable Greek to be the venture's chief executive might negatively impact on relations with the company's Turkish managers or the negotiation of terms with suppliers and distributors.

Integration issues such as these are critical to the long-term success of a non-domestic enterprise. Unfortunately, the term 'integration' is a bit vague

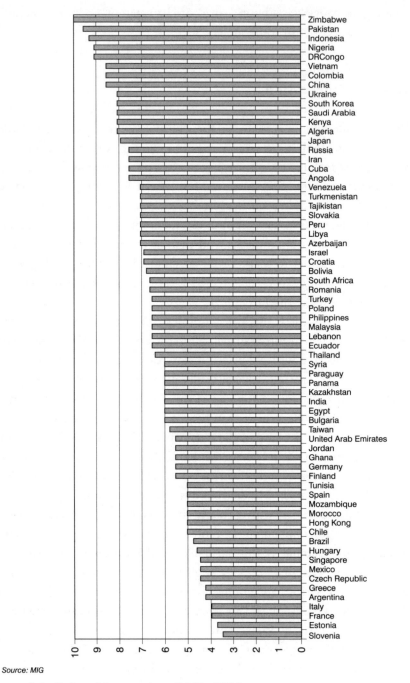

Source: MIG

Figure 4.1 Cultural integration GADs 2001

and can be applied to a variety of different factors without providing a clear guide for action. It is not surprising that business and cultural integration are frequently subsumed into even more general terms of management and are rarely formally or structurally addressed by companies. Certainly, the tools of risk assessment and strategic analysis do not take account of them. Executives taking up posts overseas are not often well briefed on their new environment and especially the potential hazards it may offer, both to businesses and the person.

Time spent in reconnaissance is seldom wasted: there is no substitute for experience and first-hand exposure to integration issues. But not everyone can go overseas. Even when they do, most executives see only the insides of airports, hotel rooms and offices. Some of the key areas where differences may exist between a company's or individual's outlook and what is encountered in the non-domestic environment are suggested below:

- **Capitalism and market orientation**
  - To what extent are local companies, businesspeople and employees motivated by market-based standards of competitive performance?
  - How do your company's and your own attitudes towards capitalism and the free market differ from the attitudes in a non-domestic market?
  - How might misunderstandings and misconceptions arise as a result?

- **Cultural differences in values**
  - What differences in morality, ethics and acceptable behaviour are there between the non-domestic environment and the one(s) with which you and your company are familiar?
  - What assumptions might be made based on the local value system that might clash with assumptions based on familiar values?
  - Is an effort being made to clarify these differences, in order to prevent conflict or to resolve conflicts if they arise?

- **Language**
  - What linguistic challenges need to be overcome to operate effectively in a non-domestic market?
  - How widespread is the use of a single language as opposed to local dialects?
  - Does the local population have any understanding of your language and vice versa?

- How much effort is made to understand and use local language(s) by expatriate personnel?
- Is the use of a third language, non-native to both sides, necessary for the conduct of everyday business?
- Do linguistic differences regularly give rise to misunderstandings?

- **Pressure groups**
  - To what extent are pressure groups (such as, human rights, environmental protection, trade union, aid, religious and other non-governmental organizations) active, and are their activities likely to affect corporate activity?
  - How well are they organized?
  - How much influence do they wield – politically, financially and in terms of public opinion – in the non-domestic market and internationally?
  - What stance do the local authorities adopt towards them?
  - What sort of relationship might exist between them and your business?
  - Is it necessary to win over, or at least avoid antagonizing, key elements?
  - How is this relationship to be managed?

- **Social/ethical issues**
  - What social divisions exist in the non-domestic market?
  - To what extent do poverty, class or caste divisions and ethnicity feature in business relationships?
  - How sensitive will business operations be to these divisions?
  - To what extent are businesses perceived to take sides in favour of some positions and against others?
  - Can the business avoid becoming labelled?
  - Would such labelling render the business vulnerable to hostility from pressure groups?
  - How should the business respond if forced to take a stand on controversial social or ethical issues?

- **Xenophobia**
  - What historic antagonisms exist within the non-domestic market between different regions, races and linguistic groups?

- What antagonisms condition local people's and authorities' attitudes toward foreigners?
- How negative are the effects of these prejudices?
- To what extent may xenophobic, nationalistic or factional interests affect a business's choice of location, commercial relationships and personnel?
- How might falling foul of these factors affect performance?

● **Competitors/other foreign firms**
- What is their experience and history of operating in the market/country concerned?
- What difficulties have they encountered and why?
- To what extent have they succeeded in overcoming them?
- Do they have an advantage over other foreign firms operating in the market in terms of cultural/integration issues (does a French firm, for example, find it easier to operate in Iran than an American one)?
- How does the competition perceive your likelihood of successful integration into a particular market?
- How can you leverage their cultural/integrational weaknesses against them?
- Can they do this to you?

Case study: South Korea

Principal GADs

● local customs and traditions;
● nationalism/xenophobia;
● corruption.

South Korea is an alien culture, even to others in the region, and the South Koreans can be very insular. The Republic of Korea is a country where a business network flourishes and which has to be cultivated carefully. They are not particularly fond of foreigners and Westerners are particularly alien to them.

A large Western consumer goods corporation was interested in taking advantage of the decline in business in the Asia Pacific region in 1997/8, when many markets were in decline following the Asian Crisis. South Korea was especially hard hit. The Chaebol had over-stretched themselves and now they, in turn, were in trouble due both to the macro and micro economic environments, and their own corruption, mismanagement and nepotism.

One Western executive pushed in such an aggressive way that the South Koreans agreed to a meeting. When the Western company's senior director flew in, there was no one to meet him at the airport so he took a taxi and went straight to the offices of the South Korean company. There to meet him was the entire board. They were polite but not chatty and the atmosphere was stiff. They just said, 'Hello, we understand that you wish to talk to us'.

He made his presentation indicating his interest in aspects of their business. They said, 'We have told you the situation but you were not prepared to listen. As a courtesy, we listened to you but we have nothing more to say'. The boardroom lapsed into total silence. After some time, the Western executive, feeling very embarrassed, got up and left without saying a word, took a taxi back to the airport and flew back home. They have not spoken since.

The Western company had wanted to take advantage of the decline in a particular business of one of the Chaebol. It was impatient and keen to close a deal and pushed too hard in its negotiations; as a consequence, the company was seen as extremely rude. To a Westerner, it would not have seemed so but the South Koreans had a different response. They saw the Westerners as 'cherry picking' when the country was weak and the company down on its luck. This created resentment. The South Koreans were desperate for the money that would come with a deal, but the Western company could have found that, by acquiring this business, it actually had a 'cuckoo in the nest', if indeed it had succeeded in buying the company at all.

Several European governments have pushed their companies to invest in Asia in general and South Korea in particular, where European companies are seen as lagging behind the Japanese and Americans. The Japanese do not have an easier time, as the South Koreans see them as culturally arrogant

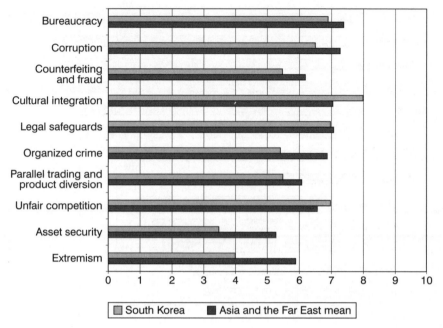

Source: MIG

Figure 4.2 South Korea vs Asia and the Far East GADs 2001

and unwilling to provide local technology transfer. The Japanese, for their part, are more willing to accept local constraints than their American or European counterparts, partly because of the bitter legacies of Japanese imperialism.

The Japanese government has not been able to take an active role in pushing East Asian governments to open up to FDI compared with the Americans. Again, this is because of Japan's cultural image and past history, but they got around this problem. Japanese aid flows are biased towards the interests of large Japanese companies, which are engaged in prioritizing the kind of aid projects that the Japanese government will support, involving Japanese firms in bidding and agenda setting. The Japanese have taken a lower profile but possibly a more effective one.

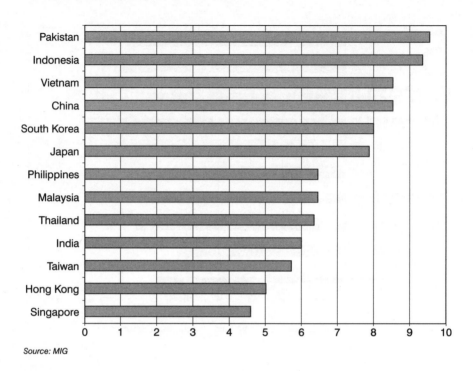

Source: MIG

Figure 4.3 Asia and the Far East: cultural integration GADs 2001

5
Bureaucracy, corruption and Foreign Direct Investment

We are accused by regulators in developed countries who have different standards and guidelines compared to developing countries, and this can be quite prohibitive for us. We get our licences revoked and the screws tightened by international regulators. We've got reputation risk, which is a problem for a firm that's supposed to have a certain quality of business, a certain code of conduct and a decent bona fide operation. Our holding company doesn't like to see headlines where they believe that we are being accused of acting improperly. A lot of these issues we can't touch upon publicly.

Investment Banker

Bureaucracy is a special GAD because it can itself involve both legal and illegal activities and encompass other GADs too. Bureaucracy is a feature of most large organizations and is especially applicable to governments. Bureaucracies in the Third World have the worst reputations, although there are signs of increasing bureaucracy emanating from EU states.

This spectre of corruption (discussed below) is added to the problems of bureaucratic delay and complexity. In many cases, serious efforts are being made to address bureaucracy, because international investors, credits and IMF assistance are generally easier to attract and retain if bureaucratic efficiency pertains to a particular state. However, any foreign firm operating in a non-domestic market will have to deal with bureaucracy to some extent.

Every business operating overseas must consider the delay it will face in obtaining the appropriate documentation and authorization to conduct business. Companies must also consider what obstacles may be erected before them and how best to overcome them. The impact of these factors on time frames and costs will also need to be considered. Obtaining licensing and permits for start-up, business development and also for changing

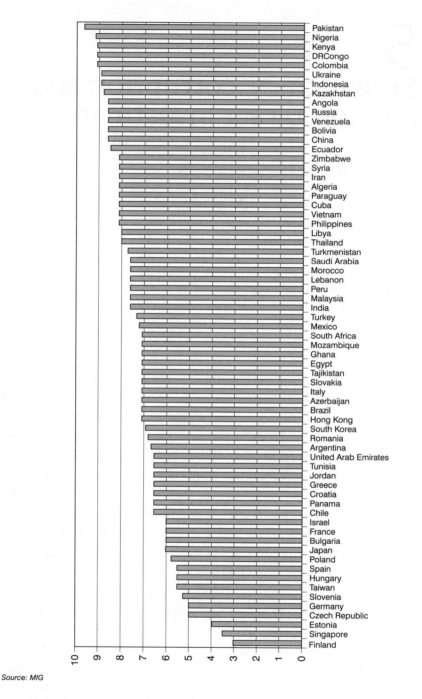

Source: MIG

Figure 5.1 Bureaucracy GADs 2001

the nature and scope of business activity is a time-consuming process, even in the hands of rapid, efficient bureaucrats. This is true even before illegal GADs like corruption, bribery, vested interests and patronage enter the equation.

The key feature of bureaucracy is that it raises more complicated issues than that of 'red tape' alone. Bureaucracy can be actively and deliberately obstructive to foreign investors in response to political pressures, vested interests and special lobbies. Ominously, it can be actively deployed against companies by their competitors in a number of ways. This may be legal – such as drawing authorities' attention to a competitor's failure to fulfil a regulatory requirement – or it may be illegal – such as arranging for officials, through bribery, to stall, harass or interfere in order to disrupt a company's operations. This leads to issues of unfair competition, which are examined in depth in Chapter 9.

To determine the extent that bureaucracy affects business operations, it is useful to consider aspects of its size and efficacy in relation to the particular sector and form of activity.

- **Accountability of public officials**
  - What official/legal or unofficial recourse would be possible in the case of incompetent or unfair treatment at the hands of bureaucracy?
  - What sanctions exist to ensure that officials perform their roles impartially and responsibly?
  - What governmental and public controls exist over bureaucratic appointments and operations?
  - To what extent is it possible to ensure that problems do not recur?

- **Calibre of officialdom**
  - How well trained and paid are the personnel?
  - What kind of status are they accorded in society?
  - How common is the practice of supplementing official income with a second job or through graft?
  - Is graft the product of greed or necessity?
  - How do these issues affect the competence, morale, dedication and honesty of public servants?
  - To what extent are they under national or international scrutiny?

- **Discretionary power of officials at different levels**
  - Who are the appropriate officials to cultivate?
  - To what extent would good relationships smooth progress and poor relationships create hindrances?
  - If there is corruption in the system, from where is it likely to originate and how does it operate?

- **Politicization of bureaucratic departments**
  - Are there political rivalries between departments and ministries?
  - Might good relationships with one department lead to problems with other sections of state officialdom?
  - Could the company become caught in a crossfire of any kind?

- **Regulatory credibility and enforceability**
  - Does the bureaucracy have clear responsibilities and a reputation for carrying them out properly and systematically?
  - How easy and common is it for companies to side-step regulations?
  - Are *ad hoc* arrangements between individual companies and officials typical practice?
  - Does this encourage bribery for special treatment?

- **Size of the public sector**
  - How large are the various bureaucratic structures with which companies regularly interact?
  - What effect does size have on the complexity of regulations?
  - How long does it take to process requests and permits?
  - How does size impact on the effectiveness of officials?

- **Transparency of decision-making**
  - When a decision is taken, is it clear who has made it and what the reasons are for it?
  - How responsive is the bureaucracy to requests for information?
  - Is the development of new regulations traceable and clearly explained?
  - What level of access to senior officials do companies have?

- **Political control**
  - What is the level of political control by the executive over the bureaucracy?

– Is the government weak or prone to frequent change, leaving the civil servants in a strong position, or is the reverse true?
– Is political control based on ethnic, religious or doctrinal factors?

● **Competitors/foreign firms**
– Who are they close to in the bureaucracy/elite and how is this facilitating business for them?
– How can you exploit these relationships?
– What does the competition know about your own relationships and how can they exploit these?

Bureaucracy and liberality of investment regimes

Bureaucracy and liberality of investment regimes are closely tied because, generally, it is the government of a state and bureaucracy that facilitate or hinder foreign investment. There is only a very general correlation between FDI inflows and the degree of liberality of the regime. China's investment regime is currently highly protectionist; its legal framework is not very transparent and corruption is rife. Yet firms are aware of this and continue to engage in business there because they feel that they have to be in the Chinese market. In other words, the perceived benefits outweigh the perceived risks. During WTO accession talks, Chinese negotiators hinted that American companies could be denied access to the huge Chinese market, a prospect that no global company would wish to countenance. Companies are, therefore, generally willing to ignore the more difficult issues for the sake of access to a large market.

Countries with lower FDI inflows will sign liberal bilateral investment regimes giving exclusive market access to foreign companies. They do not impose local content and hiring requirements because they are desperate for FDI. Governments of larger markets like China can refuse to sign these types of agreements because they are so attractive to FDI. Market size, growth potentials and strategic considerations mean that certain states can get away with much more than others.

For most companies, the risk is in being denied access to the sectors in which they wish to invest, foreign exchange controls and the ability to repatriate profits. They are much less concerned by local requirements on content, technology transfer or hiring in large markets, because flexibility is far more likely to win them approval from local bureaucracy. China has been able to reap the benefits not only of FDI but also of sensitive technology transfer, while trying to prevent foreign firms owning more than a 50 per cent stake in certain key sectors.

One could suggest that countries that engage in industrial policy intervention are highly corrupt or engaging in other bureaucratic meddling and will simply lose FDI to more liberal regimes. Of course, there is a negative relationship between corruption and economic growth in some states, but most developing countries are in the position of being able to say, 'If you don't like it, tough. Your competitor will.'

Corruption

> *It is difficult for large firms with business and clients in a country to write about sensitive issues involved, such as bribery. In any case, if it (corruption/bribery) is at a certain level, we would be incriminating ourselves. In the course of our own business in the country, we have to abide by the customs of that country. Sometimes, of course, those customs might not be acceptable in the international arena – that's a very sensitive issue.*
>
> Investment Banker

Corruption is primarily considered a public sector phenomenon. Government and bureaucratic structures tend to be the organizations most commonly accused of corruption because, unlike many businesses, they are expected to be impartial in their actions or idealistic in intention, existing to serve the interests of the governed (in democratic states). Though not limited to particular societies, corruption is a classic feature of countries where there is widespread poverty and inequality and, typically, where public sector jobs are one of the major sources of social and financial advancement. Corruption is a feature of any large organization, public or private sector, where a scarcity or need can be most swiftly met by illegal means.

Some years ago, there was a serious earthquake in Turkey. Representatives of international aid agencies meeting in London were appalled to be told that 80 per cent of the first pay load of aid flown to Turkey had failed to reach those for whom it was intended. The Turkish authorities did not at the time (and may still not) pay their soldiery very much – and it was the soldiery who unloaded the relief aircraft.

Corruption can be loosely defined as the use of a public office, or other position of responsibility, in which an individual is accountable to others for conduct and performance, to further private interests. Culture and context often define what constitutes corrupt behaviour. It is also open to individual interpretation to a large degree. The same behaviour is likely to be perceived very differently, depending on the location and the people involved.

It is common to cite the giving of gifts and other marks of respect as examples of activities that can stray easily into corruption. There is a very fine line between a gift and a bribe. Most Western companies would deny being involved in any kind of corrupt practice, whether giving or receiving inducements or payments. Certainly, direct financial inducements to secure deals tend to be frowned upon. Europeans are not averse to offering inducements to secure deals, offering future reductions, goods vouchers or even holidays.

Paying a government official to ensure that a deal is influenced in favour of a certain party would certainly be considered corrupt. Paying a private agent to lobby with that same official in exchange for payment and, frequently, a post-deal commission that constitutes a proportion of the total value of the deal may or may not be corrupt, depending on the specifics of the situation.

Bribery is the most obvious form of corruption, such as offering and accepting payments in return for certain favours. The favours may involve securing a contract, delaying an investigation or suppressing a critical report. Bribery could be used to create obstacles for a competitor, by leaking vital information, deliberately delaying permits, freezing assets or launching a probing inquiry. Patronage and cronyism – the deliberate favouring of certain individuals over others on the basis of special relationships rather than merit – are forms of corruption. They are also fairly common in non-domestic markets.

Corruption is commonly acknowledged to have contributed to the structural weaknesses behind the Asian financial crisis and subsequent

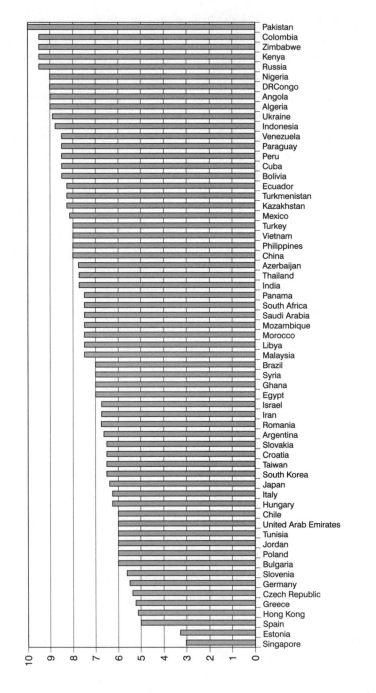

Source: MIG

Figure 5.2 Corruption GADs 2001

economic slump. There is no doubt that, in the early and mid–1990s, many deals and loans in Asia were facilitated by corruption. In many cases, the links between government officials, their families and business people were simply too close, orientated towards mutually beneficial private commercial arrangements instead of open and free competition. In the case of Indonesia, firms were so focused on growth and market size prospects that they massively underestimated the risks, thinking that the Suharto regime would last for ever. Many people therefore underestimated just how fragile some political and economic systems were.

Clearly, the best guides to assessing corruption in any given location and situation are national laws and the rules of conduct for members of particular organizations. The latter, which must include industry-specific forms of regulation common to firms in a sector, are particularly important if there are breaches of the rules. The ethical positions that underlie them may be considered corrupt even if they do not go against the letter of the law. It may not be illegal under local laws to pay a third party to lobby for a particular outcome or smooth the path of the company. This may, in fact, be critical to the success of an enterprise. Yet, if revelation of such activity creates a suspicion of corruption by the company in the minds of the public or stakeholders, the damage inflicted on the company's reputation and its business can be significant. The potential fallout from this ethical minefield is examined in Chapter 8. Companies are commonly implicated in corruption simply through involvement of any kind with corrupt and illegitimate regimes. Most of the time, although such allegations may become public knowledge, they are less likely to lead to legal problems.

Until 1998, only US companies were legally compelled to follow their national laws while operating in overseas markets under the conditions of Foreign and Corrupt Practices Act (FCPA), originally instituted in 1977 and extensively amended in 1988. Non-US competitors previously faced no such constraints (apart from knowing which key player(s) to bribe). Now, at least 20 countries have similar laws and more are enacting them. Countries that prohibit payment of bribes to overseas officials include: Austria, Belgium, Canada, Germany, Japan, Korea and the UK. They do so under the OECD 'Convention on Combating Bribery of Foreign Public Officials in International Business Transactions', ratified by the UK in December 1998. Wilful ignorance of corrupt practices by corporate executives is no longer a defence in cases of ethical breaches. The Organization of American States' 'Inter-American Convention against Corruption' was signed in 1996 and also requires signatories to criminalize transnational corruption.

The UK is also planning to go further by introducing a single offence of corruption to cover Members of Parliament, public officials and the private sector. Current proposals will extend the jurisdiction of the courts in England and Wales to prosecute corruption offences committed abroad by UK citizens and UK incorporated companies. Jurisdiction would also be extended to cover non-UK nationals, so long as part of the offence occurred in the UK. MPs would no longer be able to claim parliamentary privilege.

The FCPA shares much of the substance of the newest international developments. In some markets where US political influence may be limited and where GADs distort the competitive environment, the FCPA can be a disadvantage. For this reason, it is worth considering precisely what limitations it imposes. Under the FCPA, all US companies and individuals are criminally liable if they bribe any foreign official to obtain or retain business. For the purposes of the FCPA, a 'foreign official' is defined as a person with discretionary authority. Certain accounting standards are laid down to ensure that the disposal of all funds can be accounted for.

The FCPA applies to any US citizen, national or permanent resident, and any organization principally based in the US and subject to US law. US companies are responsible for the actions of all subsidiary firms in which they hold a stake of more than 50 per cent. If the holding is 50 per cent or less, all that is necessary is to try to make recommendations reasonably and in good faith. The company governed by the Act is criminally liable if it provides funds to a third party to bribe any foreign official.

Criminal liability in these cases applies only if the companies and individuals acted 'knowingly'. A state of knowledge is deemed to exist if the actor is aware that he/she is making an improper payment; that the circumstances for an improper payment exist; that there is a substantial certainty of an improper payment being made or if the actor holds a firm belief that any one or more of these situations is true. Criminal liability also applies, therefore, to actions that show evidence of wilful disregard or deliberate ignorance of circumstances.

The FCPA does not prohibit all payments to foreign officials. Payments made to expedite a routine governmental action are not considered bribes, though the officials accepting such payments would almost certainly be considered corrupt. Routine governmental actions include: obtaining licences/permits, processing documents, providing (legal) police protection, mail delivery and cargo loading and unloading. In many cases, making such payments actively fosters corruption within bureaucracies (though it is unlikely that any new precedents would be set but, without them, routine business operations would be intolerably delayed or entirely impossible).

The FCPA also offers two forms of affirmative defence from criminal liability. Firstly, if no laws of the foreign country have been breached, then companies or individuals may pay, give gifts and make promises to foreign officials. Secondly, if payments or gifts are considered to be reasonable and *bona fide* expenses directly related to the product promotion or the execution of a contract with a foreign agency, then they do not count as bribes.

It appears that what is and is not a bribe is a matter of presentation and perception in much the same way as the concept of corruption itself. The FCPA provides significant hedges for US companies to operate unethically but not in breach of the Act. It should be expected that other legislation adopted elsewhere will take a similarly pragmatic approach, deliberately providing loopholes large enough for companies to press home what advantages they can.

When dealing with a grey area like corruption, it is important to remember that what is perceived to occur, domestically and non-domestically, can affect a company's situation as much as what actually occurs. Assessing the level of corruption in a particular market, and positioning a company in relation to it, can only be properly accomplished on a case-by-case basis. Some of the issues that should be considered include the following:

- **Location**
  - To what extent does corruption form a part of the everyday business environment at national/regional/local levels?
  - If bribes are paid in one country, will the company develop a reputation as a bribe-payer elsewhere?

- **Accounting standards**
  - What sort of accounting practices are conventionally adopted and how do they match up to accounting standards in the home market?

- Would it be possible to conceal evidence of corruption from auditors?
- What level of complicity might there be from auditors themselves?

- **Anti–corruption policy credibility and enforceability**
  - What does the law consider corrupt?
  - Is corruption recognized as a problem and, if so, what steps are being taken to deal with it?
  - What legislative measures are in place to define, deter and punish corruption?
  - Are there anti–corruption police units or government agencies?
  - What powers of oversight and access to information and enforcement do they have?

- **Cronyism, nepotism and vested interests**
  - Is there an open culture in the selection, appointment and promotion of personnel and to key government and private sector positions?
  - Is the assignment of public sector contracts based on the competitive merits of company tenders, rather than the identity of the company's principals and political allegiances?
  - How much influence can key individuals wield over political and commercial appointments of this kind?
  - To what extent do relationships with political elites affect the success of a business in the marketplace?

- **Cultural differences**
  - Relative to the domestic market, what activities and forms of remuneration are considered acceptable?
  - Is the giving of gifts a feature of business relationships?
  - To what extent is the value of the gift linked with the value of the deal/relationship?
  - How is 'whistled' viewed – the laying of information that corruption has been practised?

- **Judicial independence**
  - How much freedom from interference does the legal system have in processing corruption cases?
  - Is the judiciary itself vulnerable to corruption?

- How and how much is political pressure brought to bear in order to protect suspects or conceal information from investigations?
- Are the police and other investigatory agencies corrupt?

● **Political leadership**
- To what extent are anti-corruption initiatives led and sponsored from the top levels of government?
- How corrupt are political and bureaucratic echelons perceived to be?
- Are anti-corruption measures allowed to touch personnel at the upper levels as well as those lower in the hierarchy?
- What balance do the country's leaders strike between idealism and pragmatism on the issue of corruption?

● **Political change**
- If a company is bribing a senior bureaucrat, member of government or political elite, how susceptible is the current business 'arrangement' to political change (eg a military coup or change of cabinet)?
- How will this affect new 'business' relationships?

● **Transparency of decision-making**
- Is it clear how decisions are reached and who is responsible for making them, in both public and private sector affairs?
- How obvious would it be if a key decision-maker were to succumb to some form of corrupt influence?
- How could the risks of being disadvantaged in this way be minimized?

● **Competitors/other foreign firms**
- What is their experience and history of operating in the market country concerned?
- What difficulties have they encountered and why?
- To what extent have they succeeded in overcoming them?
- Do they have an advantage over other foreign firms operating in the market in terms of corruption issues?
- Who are they bribing?
- How much are they paying?
- Are corrupt activities aimed at facilitating business for the company?

- – Are corrupt activities aimed at enriching individuals (without their firm's knowledge)?
- – Are corrupt activities aimed at preventing the entry of other companies into the market, disrupting activity in country or to prevent market exit?
- – How can knowledge of any corrupt practices by competitors be leveraged against them?
- – How can a competitor's knowledge of others' corrupt practices be leveraged against them?

- **At home**
  - – What impact would an action taken in a non-domestic market have on opinions closer to home?
  - – Would that action be viewed as corrupt in the home market?
  - – How would this impact on stakeholder relationships?
  - – How would authorities at home react?

Case study: Indonesia (1)

Principal GADs

- Bribery and corruption
- Bureaucracy
- Vested interests and cronyism
- Governmental policy
- Unfair competition
- Patronage
- Hidden barriers to market entry

A leading Western car manufacturer tried to penetrate the Indonesian market but failed to appreciate the most important aspect of Indonesian business culture. The company executives made it clear that they did not want to deal with the then President Suharto or his family who had the last say in whether FDI flourished in the country through their patronage in large deals.

The executives were aggressive and arrogant in their approach, on the basis that they were a foreign direct investor, that they would do as they pleased in the market and that they did not need anyone's help. They failed to appreciate that the prevailing business culture was patronage through corruption and the contempt with which they viewed the Indonesian government was a 'slap in the face' to Suharto. This meant that, once they had made the initial investment and started to get business moving, Suharto was going to react adversely.

Suharto's youngest son, Tommy, was involved in a joint venture with an Asian car manufacturer and, when those cars started to enter the market, Suharto had the tariff increased on the Western company's products and raw materials, making the end product unprofitable and therefore uncompetitive. At the same time, he exempted the Asian manufacturer from a 35 per cent luxury tax. As a result, the Asian product was on the market at a price of around $10,000 – half the cost of its rivals. The Western manufacturer lost money – but this has not prevented its quick return to the Indonesian market post-Suharto, despite political, economic, religious and security problems.

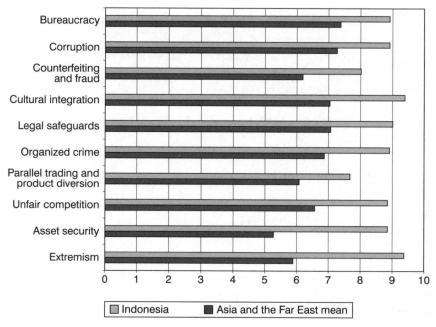

Source: MIG

Figure 5.3 Indonesia vs the Far East 2001

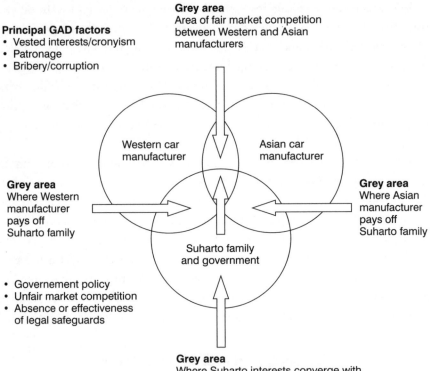

Principal GAD factors
• Vested interests/cronyism
• Patronage
• Bribery/corruption

Grey area
Area of fair market competition between Western and Asian manufacturers

Western car manufacturer

Asian car manufacturer

Grey area
Where Western manufacturer pays off Suharto family

Grey area
Where Asian manufacturer pays off Suharto family

Suharto family and government

• Governement policy
• Unfair market competition
• Absence or effectiveness of legal safeguards

Grey area
Where Suharto interests converge with Asian manufacturer's and where Western manufacturer loses $s

Source: MIG

Figure 5.4 The automotive conundrum – Indonesia

Case study: Indonesia (2)

Principal GADs

- Vested interests and cronyism
- Patronage
- Bribery and corruption
- Governmental policy
- Bureaucracy and local government
- Absence or effectiveness of legal safeguards
- Civil unrest
- Religious extremism/terrorism

A large Western company won an Indonesian contract to upgrade and improve an Indonesian utility's infrastructure over a period of 25 years and with a proposed investment by the Western company and others of over US $150 million. The contract was secured through a 75:25 per cent stake joint venture with a local company controlled by one of former President Suharto's family. That family member was to receive 20 per cent of the profits from the venture for 25 years.

With the fall of the Suharto government in May 1998, the company had its contract cancelled by the 'new' Indonesian authorities, during a period of intense civil unrest in the Indonesian capital, Jakarta. The contract was cancelled because of the participation of the Suharto family member and because of widespread criticism of the deal, as well as public demonstrations against corruption and nepotism in general.

The authorities claimed that the contracts had been unfairly awarded without a proper tendering process after the former president had intervened on behalf of the Western company. This was a serious setback for the company's attempts to establish an international business, having previously written off over US $150 million in other bad overseas investments.

During three decades in power, Suharto became notorious for the lucrative favours that he bestowed upon his family and close circle of business cronies. Local banks would give easy credit to those companies and individuals enjoying his patronage. The Western company lost its contract as part of the campaign to strip away the assets of the Suharto family acquired through nepotism.

A company spokesperson was quoted at the time as saying, 'It is a country where the way to do business involves influence – and the influencing lines have now changed. It was a fact of life that you had to have a partner company and there would always be a member of the Suharto family attached to it in one way or another.' In this case, the company was lucky. Having gone to Indonesia and having got into bed with Suharto and son, they were fortunate to get away with it when the situation changed. Their assumptions were based on economic and political data that were flawed because they took no account of the grey issues that ran beneath the surface. They were then completely unprepared for Suharto's fall and the messy aftermath.

There must have been extreme anxiety on the board back home, as they pondered over the amount of money that they had invested and about what might happen to the company if they lost this contract and were not allowed back into the marketplace. Their problems boiled down to inadequate research. A non-conventional appraisal of the factors affecting political and economic stability and of the people on whom they were pinning their hopes would have enabled them to avoid these problems. They thought that they were saving money by running research budgets with minimum expense to achieve the objective, using professional disciplines normally employed or used in a Western market. In the event, these proved totally inadequate and demonstrated extreme naivety on the part of the company's leadership.

With the survival of the contract at stake and with the physical threat to their assets as civil unrest escalated in Jakarta and other parts of Indonesia, they were lucky that Suharto's successor, Habibie, wanted to see Indonesian infrastructure improved and a stable climate for investment restored. If there had been a military coup, the company would not have got its contract back, or even access to the Indonesian market, without paying substantial sums of money.

Indeed our latest forecasts predict further problems in Indonesia. Another Western company in the same line of business suffered the same treatment at the hands of the new Indonesian authorities for its 60:40 per cent stake joint venture with a close Indonesian associate of Suharto. Many other foreign companies have also been anxious that their business dealings with the old regime would jeopardize current and future investments. It is worth noting that the businesses that thrive in such a hostile environment and market involve the Chinese and the Dutch.

In 1990, the American telecommunications company AT&T and Japan's NEC and Sumitomo were all competing for the right to supply $300 million of telephone equipment to Indonesia. The hidden costs of Suharto's patronage were estimated at 25–30 per cent of a contract, so the Americans and Japanese acted quickly to buy the support of his children. The Americans engaged as their agent his eldest daughter, Tutut, while the Japanese hired his son, Tommy. Faced with the dilemma of having to choose between the president's two offspring, Indonesian officials came up with a novel solution. They doubled the size of the contract and awarded the prize jointly.

Michael Camdessus, then IMF president, said of the Indonesian contracts: 'Under the nice façade of market economics, there was a high degree of inappropriate government intervention, including lending based on personal connections. When the structure of ownership is not transparent, when too many *ad hoc* decisions are taken and when market forces are prevented from playing their normal discipline role, serious imbalances and deadly inefficiencies can build up'.

In 1996, the CEO of Merchant International Group commented in a survey released by MIG: 'Although Indonesia has an increasingly reputable credit standing and has started to score well on most quantitative studies, our project research, however, indicates that it has a higher level of corruption and bureaucratic delay than any other country in direct contradiction of the credit reports of such companies/agencies as S&P and Moody's.

The Suharto era Indonesian contracts have come back to haunt foreign investors with the presidency of Abdurrahman Wahid. Local authorities asserted their influence and demanded contract revisions as power was devolved. At the same time, a number of Indonesian companies tried to take advantage of the legal uncertainty to gain the upper hand over foreign

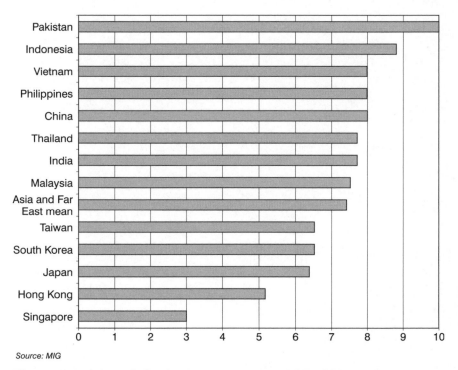

Source: MIG

Figure 5.5 Asia and the Far East corruption GADs 2001

partners. Japanese businesses hinted that Indonesia would lose FDI if contracts were not respected.

The foregoing analysis does not support the use of bribery to ensure that a company enters a market successfully. In foreign territory, however, companies need to play by local rules and, to do so, they need to understand the business culture, including the culture of patronage and corruption. If one knows where the problems are, then there is every chance of being able to operate freely and effectively with the minimum of harassment. At the very least, a company should be able to walk away without further loss or other adverse consequences.

6
Legal safeguards

*We can go to legal counsel in a country to carry out business
and it can still blow up in our faces, because the country
might decide to change the rules and then we run into difficulties.*

*Do you know what these people are going to do? Once they've
got you in, they can keep you there — you are at their mercy —
what's to stop them acting in their own self interest?*

Investment Banker

A major concern for companies operating in non-domestic markets is the
level of protection their operations, personnel and assets are given under
local laws. The performance of an enterprise, in terms of the timeframe for
returns and the rate of return itself, may be hostage to legal obstacles or the
absence of sufficient recourse to the law. Companies need to know that
their investments receive as much legal protection as possible and that they
are able to repatriate profits home.

It is important to remember that the Western legalistic approach to
business, especially in corporate law, is less evident elsewhere. The problem
of an absence of legal safeguards does not always arise because there simply
is not enough of a legislative framework in place. More often than not, the
problem lies with the inability — for whatever reason — for that framework
to be used in an impartial and reliable fashion, if indeed it is used at all.

It is useful to consider how these problems may arise and what damage
they will inflict on a business. Even in cases where a legal difficulty can be
solved with relative ease, the costs associated with finding the solution can
be painfully high. Fees for corporate legal representation are rarely low.

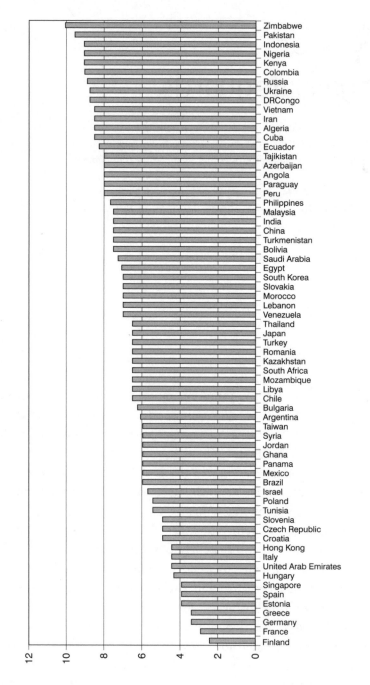

Source: MIG

Figure 6.1 Legal safeguards GADs 2001

Many less-developed markets will have backlogged and corrupt judicial systems, which both increases costs and lengthens the time required to reach verdicts.

A government decree might block a substantial investment overnight, or expropriate assets, causing trading to cease or take place only erratically. Government failure to enforce contracts may result in huge losses. The absence of legal tools that a company is accustomed to deploying elsewhere may make it difficult to compel uncooperative debtors to service their obligations. Archaic bankruptcy laws in many non-domestic markets have prevented the recovery of enormous value from insolvent companies.

Before assessing whether or not legal measures will be effective in a particular case, there is an important previous step that most people contemplating legal action go through – questioning whether resorting to the law is the best response at all and what other options are available.

People accustomed to settling problems in the courts or having the backing of an army of legal advisors may not consider other options in sufficient depth. They may assume that the best course of action is to play safe, but how they do so may be shaped by expectations that do not fit comfortably into their current frame of reference – such as being able to rely on due process of law to attain their goals. They may also be aware that legal victory can be extremely costly, in ways that they may not even have considered.

Taking another company or individual to court may lead to the deterioration of a broad spectrum of relationships, irrespective of the outcome of the court case, to the extent that an out-of-court settlement may look more attractive with hindsight. This is particularly the case in markets where successful businesses, foreign and domestic, rely on the development of long-standing ties.

There are several ways in which launching a legal action can plausibly lead to loss and poor performance, even in the case of victory. Where the opponent is politically and commercially well-connected, a company may find itself burdened with grudges from powerful government bodies, companies and individuals for years afterwards. Opponents may feel goaded into bringing other pressures to bear. These are certainly not limited to counter-suits. Links with organized crime could be exploited, for example, to disrupt a company's operations and threaten its personnel. In addition, and not least, even a victorious legal battle may involve the revelation of details about the company's operations and attitudes that negatively impact public and official opinion (an obvious example of this being the 'McLibel' trial in the UK). It may be useful to consider some of the following:

- **Elite interests**
  - How far do corporate legal affairs and disputes in a particular sector reflect, and have effects on, local political and economic elites?
  - Are there areas of activity and actors that enjoy special forms of protection?
  - By contrast, are other sectors and actors vulnerable?
  - What conditions decide levels of protection and vulnerability?
  - Where do your operations fit into the equation?

- **Judicial independence and effectiveness**
  - Are legislative provisions enforced properly by law enforcement agencies and judicial bodies?
  - To what extent can the legal process be interfered with or distorted to serve particular interests?
  - To what extent are the authorities disposed to favour indigenous interests over foreign companies in cases of legal dispute?
  - To what extent are they subverted by organized crime?
  - Do cases involving government authorities, whether as plaintiffs or defendants, receive impartial treatment from the judiciary?
  - How long do different kinds of cases tend to take and by what methods are they pursued?

- **Legal culture**
  - To what extent does legal action form a recognized means of redress?
  - How frequently is it used?
  - How effective is it perceived to be?
  - Are legal safeguards used proactively or do they exist simply as formalities?
  - How do government departments, competitors and pressure groups vary in their use of criminal and civil prosecution?

- **Legislative sophistication**
  - What legal safeguards exist for particular kinds of activity?

- What inferences might be drawn from less specific statutory provisions if a legal dispute in that area arose?
- How do corporate legislation and corporate governance compare with domestic market legislation?
- What is the legal balance of power between creditors and debtors?
- Are there strong well-maintained ownership and bankruptcy laws?
- Are the legal representatives, available locally, sufficiently skilled to handle a company's needs?
- Are foreign legal advisors competent to deal with local issues?

- **Potential for counter-action**
  - What potential impact would resorting to legal action have on the company's relationships and position in the market?
  - How vulnerable is the company to counter-attack, in the conventional legal sense and in non-conventional ways (grudges, dirty tricks, criminal activity, political pressure etc.)?
  - In what ways could pursuit of a judicial solution compromise the company, domestically and non-domestically?

- **Competition**
  - To what extent are competitors viewed favourably by legal authorities?
  - Who are they paying?
  - What are the connections and why?
  - How can you exploit this knowledge to your advantage?
  - Do competitors know of your own legal connections?
  - How could they exploit these against you?

Case study: Poland

Principal GADs

- Government policy
- Absence of legal safeguards
- Environmental hazards
- Local government and regulations

A global chemicals company bought a business in Poland from the Polish government. They carried out their standard pre-acquisition due diligence, which convinced senior management that everything was fine. Six months post-acquisition, the local authorities sent officials to the plant acquired by the foreign company and closed them down. Waste seepage from the plant's drains had affected the surrounding area. The Polish government told the foreign management that they had to clear up the surrounding area and install equipment to make sure that it did not happen again. It cost the foreign firm around US $4 million to do this, as well as losing production for six months.

The foreign company had failed to carry out due diligence – not just on the proposed acquisition but on the environmental question. There was no environmental audit pre-acquisition. They should, with hindsight, have checked the plant more thoroughly beforehand. They should have spent time looking at the questions concerned and factoring them into their negotiations with the national government from the start. This probably would have increased the acquisition price overall but would have saved trouble later. Their objective, however, was to buy the business cheaply and,

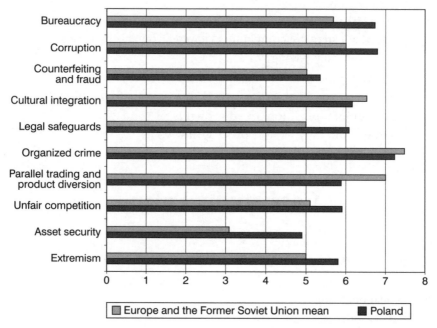

Source: MIG

Figure 6.2 Poland vs Europe and the Former Soviet Union GADs 2001

in doing so, they thought they had a bargain. It rebounded on them when the authorities saw an opportunity not only to 'clean house' but also to extract further payment for 'the local community'. The foreign company lost money and production time due to inadequate due diligence – all because of the somewhat contemptuous and arrogant attitude of an organization that straddles the world and thinks that it knows better.

Case study: CIS/Ukraine/Russia

Principal GADs

- Absence or effectiveness of legal safeguards
- Government policy
- Bureaucracy
- Corruption
- Organized crime
- Vested interests

Western utilities contemplating their exit strategies from countries of the Commonwealth of Independent States (CIS) have had some real problems. Many of these companies jumped into these markets on the basis of rapid returns, low labour costs and certain promise of success. When the USSR was still in existence and first considered relatively open, it was the energy, communications and construction companies that went in first. Their research and due diligence, however, was totally inadequate. The USSR then broke apart into dissimilar countries with different cultures, political factors and GADs that impacted those businesses.

Many of these companies have expended fortunes to gain entry. The problem was that, once they realized the extent of the problems confronting them, it was too late. In the CIS, one cannot just up and leave the country, as one might close down an unprofitable business in London or New York. The reaction of the locals to one's assets and people can be severe because, by pulling out, one is further damaging their economy, livelihood and 'special' interests.

The countries of the CIS, those FSU members who retain links with the Russian Federation, are all experiencing varying degrees of economic turmoil, making them uncertain places to invest in or exit from. They mostly have unacceptably high GAD ratings. Coupled with this is the fact that outside firms have used joint ventures and partnerships to reduce and spread their risk exposure. As corruption, organized crime, bureaucracy and lack of legal safeguards are all endemic in these states, it is essential that prospective business partners are investigated thoroughly before the contract is signed, in addition to the regular country/market risk analysis and due diligence.

The Ukraine has, since its independence, become the victim of an organized crime and corruption epidemic. Nine out of ten Ukrainian companies are in contact with corrupt officials, who, with government pay in arrears, may derive up to 60 per cent of their income from bribes. It would be naive for a foreign investor to expect to conduct business without exposure to corruption, which may represent as much as 20 per cent of the total cost of a project. Elements of the police, military and intelligence services are actively involved with organized crime groups, OCGs, which we examine in the following chapter – and they actively manage some gangs. It is highly likely that prospective local business partners will be linked with OCGs, which protect their investments and are not averse to using illegal or violent means to ensure that their profit objectives are met.

Among the government and bureaucracy, there is a preference for dealing with a small number of large firms that preserve and foster close links between government, business and crime. Contact networks became the standard routes to success in business and politics during the final decades of the Soviet era. This continues to be the case in the less controlled business environment of today. Deregulation and liberalization can only be broadly successful if a basic respect for the rule of law is present; in the Ukraine, it manifestly is not. It is this lack of legal safeguards that is now, arguably, the main threat to businesses in the Ukraine. Such are the levels of corruption within the Ukrainian government that only those with strong local links have a chance to foster relations with those in power. When faced with such a situation, corporations need to be equipped with knowledge of their opponents and their business objectives, when the dynamics which are working against foreigners are all the more volatile and dangerous.

Vested interests and red tape also affect expected returns. In the Ukraine, bureaucracy and vested interests may actually pose more of a problem than the local Mafia. When faced with bureaucratic obstacles or vested interests, it is essential that the relationship interplay between key principals is charted. Without this, time and valuable resources will be lost following dead ends and in 'gifts' going to the wrong people.

Occasionally, the fine hand of the conman has been replaced by the knuckle-dragging exploits of Neanderthal man. In one case, a serious dispute resulted in the company's executives being harassed, framed for petty crimes, beaten up and, in short, edged out of the country altogether. Needless to say, recourse to law did not prove successful.

'Blat' (meaning exchange in Russian) is now an accepted way of life for the former communist regimes. It arose out of the need, driven by shortages of many goods and services, to barter favours and acts of goodwill that could later be repaid in kind. This has become endemic within the bureaucratic process and where it meets the world of business. These favours were

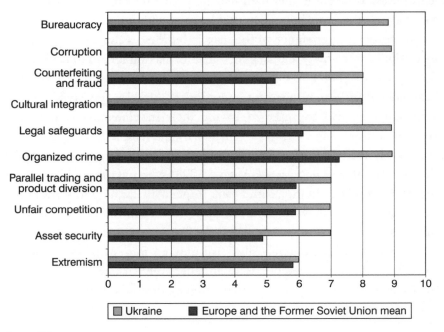

Source: MIG

Figure 6.3 Ukraine vs Europe and the Fromer Soviet Union GADs 2001

linked either directly to the individual or, more usually, to the company or civil service department that they represented. Many of these debts of honour were gathered up and later used by both organized crime and unscrupulous businesses. It is important to be aware of the existence of *blat*, the need for favours done to be commensurate with the service provided. They remain in force as a form of off-balance sheet debt until they are repaid. Such favours are useful ways of bypassing legal and bureaucratic problems.

Russia is still a risky place in terms of legal safeguards. Western concepts of business are virtually non-existent and many Russian business people have trouble with the most basic concepts, such as honouring a contract. Russian business practice can, at times, appear extremely bizarre to the outsider. Armed guards have featured regularly in Russian contests for management control, because those in control of a plant can quickly strip assets and capital for financial gain. Armed management take-overs seem to be the preferred method for establishing control of assets, in preference to legal means. Western businessmen seeking payment from Russian distributors and other debtors have been met by men with guns.

The constant interference of the state in business is also a concern. New legislation is often hasty and lacking in depth, making it hard to understand for all parties. Foreign business people are also hard-pressed to find independent lawyers. In one case, 'independent' local lawyers contracted by a foreign firm had to agree to having their travel restricted and their communications subjected to surveillance by the state.

Probably the best known instance of lack of legal safeguards was during the Russian financial crisis of August 1998, when Russia defaulted on foreign bank loans and the central bank stopped intervening to support the rouble, effectively allowing it to devalue. Western investment banks lost hundreds of millions of dollars when the Russian government ruled that the currency hedge contracts they had entered into with local Russian banks were unenforceable. The Russians effectively changed the rules after the event and there was nothing that could be done about it.

7
Criminal activities

*Organized crime in America takes in over forty billion
dollars a year, and spends very little on office supplies.*

Woody Allen

The INTERPOL definition of organized crime, as adopted by the General
Assembly of INTERPOL member countries in 1998, is as follows:

*Any enterprise or group of persons engaged in continuing illegal activity that has, as
its primary purpose, the generation of profits irrespective of national boundaries.*

Organized crime groups (OCGs) include, but are not restricted to, Chinese
Triads, Japanese Yakuza, the Italian Mafia, American Cosa Nostra, South
American Cartels and organized groups from the Former Soviet Union.
Organized crime is one of the fastest growing problems for international
business as well as governments. As business has globalized, organized crime
has done the same, taking advantage of the spread of capitalism and new
technologies.

To give some idea of the scale of the problem, it is variously estimated
that between US $50 billion and $500 billion from illegal activities is
laundered each year, that is, given the appearance of having come from a
legal source. Exact figures are hard to pin down. The scale of the problem
is huge and money-laundering operations have become increasingly

sophisticated. Advances in technology have aided the criminal, particularly in money transfers. An organized crime group put in place a sophisticated hacker – operating from Russia – who targeted American banks. The 1999 Bank of New York scandal revealed that some US $7 billion had been illegally transferred from Russia abroad, involving a total of approximately 160,000 transactions over a four-year period. This, the largest money laundering case ever, is, nevertheless, just the tip of the iceberg.

The main activities of OCGs are:

- racketeering;
- fraud;
- car theft;
- robbery;
- armed assault;
- drug dealing;
- trafficking in weapons and radioactive material;
- trafficking in human beings and endangered species;
- prostitution;
- smuggling of precious goods and antiquities;
- extortion;
- gambling;
- embezzlement;
- control of black markets;
- product diversion and parallel trading;
- money laundering.

Geographically, there is a tendency for OCGs to appear and flourish where there are opportunities for quick profits and where rule of law is weakest. To legitimize the wealth from their illegal activities, they have to channel money into other investments, diversifying into every sector imaginable. Organized crime is present in every market and country that is attractive to legal business, in addition to many that are not.

The problem for international business is that, to the naked eye, organized crime is very often indistinguishable from legitimate business. The term 'money laundering', for example, comes historically from the investment in legitimate laundry businesses by US OCGs, as a legal front to process their ill-gotten gains. The grey areas between crime and commerce are populated by unscrupulous people who move from the legal to the illicit and back again, as circumstances and opportunities dictate. Many joint ventures and investments involve OCGs or their money, which, for the business concerned, can cause criminal liability and loss of reputation, quite apart from loss of assets or capital.

Conventional due diligence is inadequate for dealing with companies and individuals that may have links to OCGs. The large global accounting firms have been setting up big forensic accountancy practices, but these are normally called in after the event, when money has disappeared and it is too late. What is needed, in order to mitigate the risk posed by OCGs, are thorough and specific background investigations into individuals, companies and other relevant entities. This should be done before entering into any commitment and before any paper is signed, and should be done for any type of involvement.

Even if no evidence of OCG involvement or unsavoury facts are uncovered, the time spent in extra research is seldom wasted. New opportunities can be discovered, unforeseen risks brought into the open and better negotiating positions established. If threats are uncovered early enough, then the business has more lead-in time for an adequate response and will stand a much better chance of walking away from a potentially damaging situation.

Organized criminal activity extends into other GADs because of the nature of their business. Activities such as counterfeiting and fraud, corruption, asset security, parallel trading and product diversion may all have OCG involvement to some extent or other. Bureaucracy is an especially grey area for foreign businesses, as many will be infiltrated or co-opted by OCGs to varying degrees. In Russia, for example, it is acknowledged that large parts of the military, security and intelligence apparatus are involved with or corrupted by organized crime. This occurs at all levels of the organizational hierarchy, from top to bottom. In China, foreign businesses can unwittingly contract with Triad-controlled business or corrupt and criminal elements of the People's Liberation Army (PLA). With the Chinese take over of Macao in 1999, local Macao Triads themselves were concerned that mainland Triads with links to, or controlled by, the PLA would usurp them, with connivance from mainland officials.

Invisible risk and its impact on investment

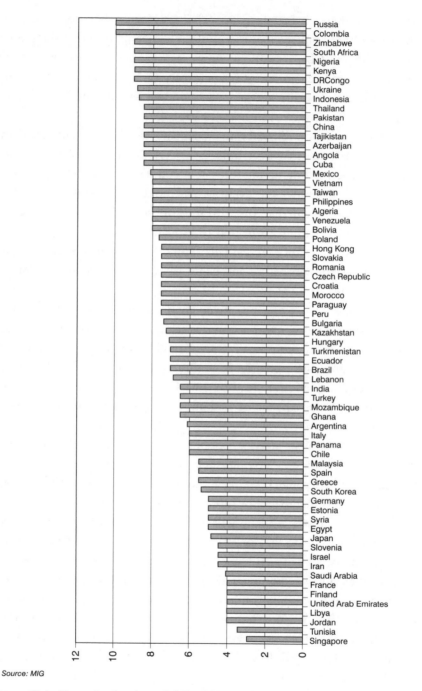

Source: MIG

Figure 7.1 Organized crime GADs 2001

Mexico has had problems with corruption, organized crime, kidnapping and political and economic instability in recent years. With the advent of the North American Free Trade Agreement (NAFTA) and Mexican growth, American and other foreign firms have seen the country as a springboard into Latin America. In Mexico, several powerful families control the major businesses. Some have been involved in drugs like the Tijuana Cartel, but all actively seek out new business, especially in privatizations. While the Mexican government seeks FDI, these families manoeuvre themselves, through their web of influence, into a position where they are partners with incoming investors. The Mexican government has tried to create transparency but these families wield enormous influence and will always try to corrupt the incorruptible. They have done so before. Embarking on a business venture in Mexico cannot be done with traditional due diligence, otherwise foreign businesses could find themselves intimately involved with drug cartels.

Legitimate businesses fall victim to the practices of OCGs listed above, but the most direct way they make money is through extortion in return for 'protection' of premises, personnel, deliveries etc., or for kidnap ransoms. Failure to comply meets with escalating violence and damage to property such as arson. The other problem is rising insurance premiums. This, together with loss of investor confidence and reputational issues, ensures that most foreign firms in such situations will keep quiet. Even if they went to the police, it is likely that the OCG will have influence there too, compounding the lack of legal safeguards.

Business may not be the direct target of OCGs but can be caught in the crossfire of competition between different groups in bombings and physical attacks. They can also be caught in the battle between OCGs and government agencies. As a prelude to the Second Chechen War, Moscow saw several bombings aimed at civilians, which were blamed on Chechen 'terrorists/gangsters', and which may or may not have been the work of Russian government personnel, acting as *agents provocateurs*.

When thinking about organized crime, it may be useful to consider the following:

- **Encountering organized crime**
  - What relationships does your company have, or seek to develop, that could be linked with organized crime?

- Have thorough background checks been made?
- How would the company react if approached by a suspect individual or organization?
- What means are available to check and verify?
- What counter-measures can be put in place to minimize risks to assets, personnel and reputation?

- **Grey economy**
  - How much of the economic activity in a non–domestic market is illegal?
  - How much of this grey area activity is controlled by OCGs rather than petty criminals?
  - Whose interests do these activities benefit and who suffers as a consequence?
  - How are the proceeds from these activities laundered?
  - How does this impact on legitimate businesses?

- **Law enforcement effectiveness**
  - Is there a credible government and law enforcement strategy for dealing with organized crime?
  - Do law enforcement agencies have the will, funding, manpower and training to carry it out?
  - To what extent are government agencies and political organizations, including law enforcement bodies, complicit in organized criminal activity?
  - What proportion of organized crime originates in the private sector and how much involves the public sector?

- **Equipment**
  - What sort of weaponry, surveillance and communications equipment is accessible to private buyers?
  - Has there been an armed conflict or cutbacks in military spending recently?
  - Are personnel with military experience hiring their expertise to private employers or OCGs?
  - What does this indicate about the level of violence that OCGs are prepared to use?

- What precautions are necessary to minimize the risk of physical damage to assets and personnel and through information leakage?

● **OCG structure and cohesion**
  - What sorts of OCGs are operating in the non-domestic market?
  - How rationalized is organized criminal activity within the markets?
  - What trends of rationalization or fragmentation of OCGs are evident?
  - Which players dominate?
  - How are they organized (eg by blood relations, ethnic origin, political allegiance)?
  - What are their origins?
  - How do they manage their internal operations and hierarchy?
  - What rivalries and conflicts exist?

● **Scope of operations**
  - In what sectors do OCGs operate?
  - How does OCG presence vary by sector and region?
  - What international links do OCGs have?
  - How are these links exploited?
  - Which methods are favoured by particular OCGs?
  - How do OCGs launder their money?
  - Is OCG-linked funding or personnel a feature of local companies?

● **Competitors**
  - Are competitors involved with OCGs either deliberately or inadvertently?
  - What is the nature of contacts and relationships between them?
  - What are the specifics of their joint business?
  - How does this affect your own situation?

Counterfeiting and fraud

Counterfeiting and fraud rely on people accepting appearances as reality. The main difference between them is that most people seem happy to buy counterfeit goods, but not to be a fraud victim. Most goods can be counterfeited if sufficient skill and demand exist. The key to success is to attach a higher value to items that are actually less valuable than the goods they imitate and then to sell them or use them as substitutes for the real thing. Any sophisticated counterfeiting will involve organized crime and, in some non-domestic markets, up to 90 per cent of goods on offer can be counterfeit. In the past, genuine manufacturers have steadily lost market share to counterfeit products before being pushed out completely.

Counterfeiting damages legitimate business because, by undercutting prices for genuine products and copying styles and brands, it reduces sales of the genuine article. Secondly, when the flaws of counterfeit goods become evident, they bring the reputation of the brand into disrepute. Thirdly, counterfeit goods cheapen the value of the real brand in the minds of consumers. A large confectionery manufacturer's European subsidiary took delivery of sub-standard wrappers for a product, decided that it did not want them and paid a local distributor to take them away and destroy them. The local distributor sold them to an Indonesian manufacturer, who used them to package sub-standard counterfeit confectionery that was used to flood the Indian market. The original confectionery manufacturer had to deal with thousands of complaints afterwards.

The best counterfeit goods require proprietary information from the legitimate company. If high-quality fakes appear on the market, it is likely that there is a leak from within the company itself or at the point of manufacture. If security has been breached, then it is possible that there is collusion between key individuals within the company and the counterfeiters.

Fraud covers a wider range of activities than counterfeiting – in fact, too numerous to list here. Fraud can range from small-scale actions committed by low-level employees to collusion between senior management and suppliers worth millions. Business partners and customers can disappear with goods on credit or money, and banks can lose millions from hacking and illegal transfers. Sometimes, the fraudsters are prepared to engage in legitimate business to build up confidence, until a very large order is placed or goods are received on credit. Then the customer or supplier disappears without trace.

Full fraud risk audits are necessary to provide both internal and external security from fraud. Part of this involves verification of the *bona fide* of employees, partners, suppliers and customers. Relationships, processes and checks also need to be scrutinized to prevent opportunities for criminals. All the above should be monitored for changes, suspicious activity or behaviour that might indicate that fraud is occurring, is about to occur or has already occurred. Some useful points to consider with regard to counterfeiting and fraud are:

- **Intellectual property protection**
  - What is the legal situation with regard to intellectual property ownership and intellectual property violation?
  - What defences do branding and licensing laws offer brand owners from counterfeiters?
  - How effective is information security (see asset security, Chapter 9)?

- **Knowledge of business relationships**
  - What procedures are in place to vet personnel, suppliers and partners?
  - Have thorough and independent background checks confirmed the location, principals, company finances and operations of the company's suppliers, customers and partners?

- **Legislative structure and enforcement measures**
  - Is there a clear legal framework to protect companies against counterfeiting and fraud?
  - To what extent does the legal framework rely on self-protection and self-reporting by companies rather than law enforcement agencies?
  - What is the history of legal enforcement of laws against counterfeiting and fraud?

- **Prevalence of counterfeiting and fraud**
  - To what extent do counterfeiting and fraud affect operations in a particular market?
  - What are the crime statistics and clear-up rates for crime in these categories?
  - What are the favoured techniques for counterfeiting and fraud?
  - What are local levels of demand for the genuine products and their counterfeit equivalents?
  - How vulnerable is your business?

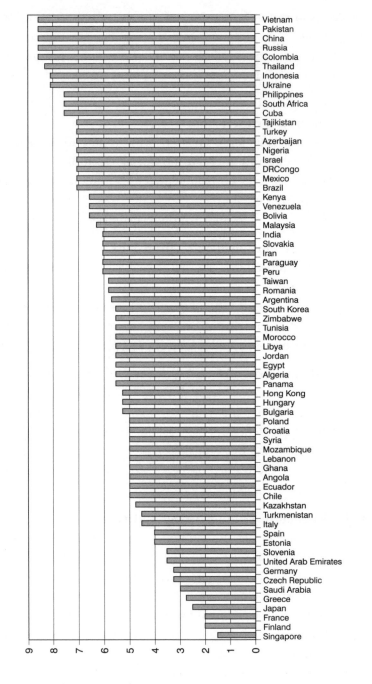

Source: MIG

Figure 7.2 Counterfeiting and fraud GADs 2001

- What countermeasures can be employed to minimize risks and costs?

- **Technological sophistication**
  - How easy would it be for local counterfeiters to manufacture copies of special goods and brands?
  - To what extent is counterfeiting of goods an indigenous activity relative to importing pirated goods from neighbouring markets?
  - What measures could be introduced to distinguish genuine products from illegal copies?

- **OCGs**
  - Which groups might be involved in counterfeiting and fraud?
  - How do they operate?
  - Are there any recent cases of their activity in a particular market?
  - What are their *modus operandi*, structure, contacts? See OCGs, page 79.

Case study: parallel trading and product diversion

Parallel trading and product diversion are the sale of goods in markets for which they were not intended and may or may not involve illegality, depending on where these activities take place. The goods most commonly affected are branded consumer goods of the type likely to be counterfeited.

One company in Canada, Technessen Ltd, actually advertises its expertise in the parallel or 'grey' international car market. Not surprisingly, it has upset the major US car manufacturers. Parallel trading is, essentially, the sale of products destined for one market in a different one, where the retail price is higher. Parallel trading is a form of dumping and is illegal in some countries but legal in others. The problem for domestic producers or traders who do not engage in parallel trade is that they become uncompetitive when the market is flooded with cheaper products from parallel markets. It is possible that a product manufacturer could have its own business undercut, by having its own brands parallel traded against it by a manufacturer or distributor in a nearby market that has a licence to produce or sell the goods. Parallel trading issues can seriously impact on a company's partnership and contractual relationships in this way.

Product diversion more often involves a breach of contract. An example would be where a company agrees with a manufacturer/distributor to provide goods for a particular market but the goods are then diverted elsewhere and sold for a higher profit. Another method is where a manufacturer/distributor deliberately over-produces an agreed quantity of product and sells the over-produced product volume for itself. In extreme cases, the distributor may just refuse to make any payment at all. In both cases, the company licensing the manufacture/distribution of its branded product is unaware of the diversion. This often happens to the largest and most popular brands, where they are targeted for both counterfeiting and parallel trading or diversion.

The company concerned loses out on the additional profits and is unaware of the volume of its goods reaching certain markets, so disrupting sales and marketing strategies. There may also be problems with issues of customer aftercare and guarantees. Many diverted products are smuggled into different markets and the company may face problems from the relevant customs authorities in the states concerned, if this is discovered.

A subsidiary business in a non-domestic market may be tempted to hide what is going on from the parent company with regard to parallel trading and product diversion, because these activities are leading to under-performance. This means that the parent is 'in the dark' about the situation and will not be able to initiate a successful counter-strategy to deal with the problems. Some points to consider are:

- **The problem**
  - Does the company understand how product diversion and parallel trading can affect or are affecting business operations?
  - What is the nature of the threat?

- **Border controls**
  - How tightly is the flow of goods into and out of a market controlled?
  - How easy or difficult is it to smuggle goods?
  - Are customs corruptible?

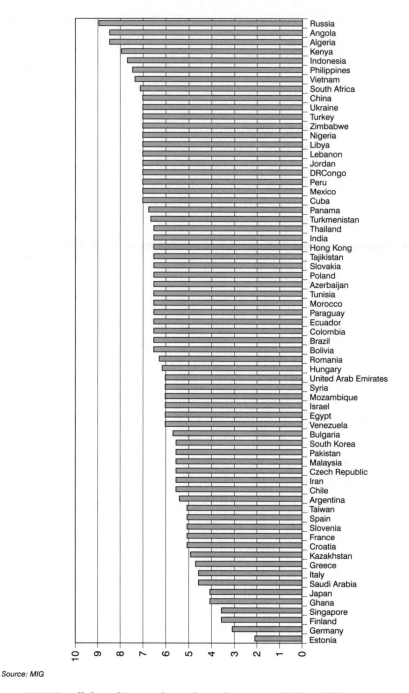

Source: MIG

Figure 7.3 Parallel trading and product diversion GADs 2001

- What proportion of imports and exports is parallel traded or diverted goods?
- Which are the main ports and border crossings for the shipment of goods into and out of the market?
- How effective is the supervision of these areas?

- **Customs, excise and contracts**
  - What is the legal status of parallel traded goods in a particular market?
  - What levels of tax are there on imports?
  - How much protection do contracts provide against parallel trading and diversion of goods?
- **Manufacturing and distribution network integrity**
  - At which points in a company's manufacturing and distribution chain are goods vulnerable to diversion?
  - Are all goods produced and shipped properly accounted for?
  - Does the company have methods of monitoring activity along the chain?
  - How effective are monitoring policies in providing a picture of what is really happening?
  - How are goods parallel traded and diverted?
  - Who is party to these activities?
  - OCGs?

- **Parallel markets**
  - Where might goods be diverted and parallel traded to and from?
  - What price differentials encourage or discourage such activity?
  - Where is there demand for parallel traded and diverted goods?
  - Why does this demand exist?
  - What drives pricing and consumer access to the products?
  - What damage does parallel trading and product diversion inflict on a business?

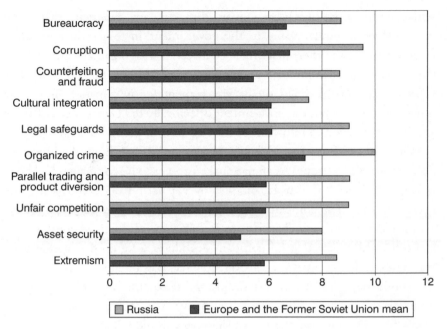

Source: MIG

Figure 7.4 Russia vs Europe and the Former Soviet Union GADs 2000

Case study: Russia

Principal GADs

● Organized crime
● Parallel trading and product diversion
● Fraud
● Asset security
● Absence or effectiveness of legal safeguards

The same corporation that had the problems trying to acquire the South Korean company, described in Chapter 4, ran into problems in Russia. Part of the responsibility lay with the company's home government, which did not give adequate advice on the threat to foreign businesses posed by organized crime. The government ministry responsible for trade, together

with the rest of the bureaucracy, avoided making any statements that could be construed as embarrassing to the government, in respect of companies keen to work with others that might be involved with organized crime. Even the ambassador and embassy in Moscow played down the problem. The company concerned relied on its government for information about the situation in Russia but the government (specifically the Department of Trade and Industry) failed to inform it of the real risks of doing business there.

When the company first looked at Russia, it did so through the introduction of some of its trusted Asian national customers. The companies had been buying goods for the Russian market over a period of several years. The reality was that these companies were major diverters of product. The diverters invited the company chairman to Russia. When he arrived, local adverts and other indications that his company's products were on the market were very visible. He was totally won over by what was, in effect, a highly effective confidence trick. It was very simply and inexpensively put together. The trick was also successful because the chairman was an autocratic leader and so, by winning him over, the rest of the board would follow.

His company then invested millions of US dollars in plants that were to be the biggest of their type in the world. It was intended to produce record tonnage. They will, however, never ever reach production capacity. Without knowing it, the company had become involved with organized crime and was being cheated out of its Russian operations. They then faced the problem of having to buy them out. They had no idea of the size of Russia, of the lack of infrastructure or of the people with whom they were involved. They also had no idea how they were going to get the money back from the customers, with around $50 million owed to them. They approached one of the Russian customers at his warehouse for payment and were met by his bodyguards carrying machine guns. Their perception of what Russia was like was totally at odds with reality. Additionally, the cost of security for the plant alone is $2.5 million a year, something for which there had never been a budget.

Case study: European Union

Principal GADs

- Parallel trading and product diversion
- Counterfeiting and fraud

The very fact that the EU allows what it calls free trade inspires wrongdoing. EU legislation actually encourages parallel trading, product diversion and counterfeiting. In the EU, company A buying a product from B and selling it to C is not a problem, even if A is not the distributor. As long as A can trade effectively and the goods are not stolen, then there is no law against it. It is clear to the distributors, however, that this is damaging their business.

If the diverters cannot get the real product and they are offered counterfeit alternatives, they will take them – and the counterfeiting trade in the region has boomed as a result. This also harms consumers because it is very difficult for some people to know the difference between the real product and a counterfeit product. It isn't until the product goes wrong (computer software is a prime example) and you try to get it fixed that you realize that it is a counterfeit product. This rebounds on the genuine manufacturer, because they receive the complaints and their product is devalued in the eyes of the consumer. Some manufacturers have actually used diverters to dump stock, so they themselves add to the problem. They are cheating both the consumer and the distributor who has paid money for a franchise, only to be made uncompetitive by parallel trading and diversion.

8
The good, the bad and the unethical

The seven social sins:
Politics without principle,
wealth without work,
commerce without morality,
pleasure without conscience,
education without character,
science without humanity,
worship without sacrifice.

Mahatma Gandhi

The question of corporate ethics has become prominent only over the last two decades, with increasing pressure group activity, more intense media scrutiny and the perception by senior executives that bad ethics are bad business. One of the early examples of corporate wrongdoing was the alleged role played by the ITT Corporation in Chile's military coup in 1973. The company was accused of collaboration with the CIA to overthrow the Allende government because the company feared nationalization of its assets. Most people assume that the large corporation is only in it for the money. The difference between now and thirty years ago is that companies can't get away with unethical behaviour quite so easily. Public concern for human rights and environmental issues has grown and Western governments now find themselves at the forefront of the fight to improve global social, ethical and environmental conditions.

The public perception is that, privately, there is no hand–wringing or consternation among senior management about degrading the environment, infringing indigenous peoples' rights or selling arms to dictators. Many believe that most Western companies end up paying bribes as a matter of course in non-domestic markets and that there is no moral trade-off between revenue and wrongdoing. Large companies all claim their ethical credentials and many have environmental and ethical policy advisors but a common perception is that the real concern is over profit margins.

The costs of falling foul of the ethical issue, however, are threats to asset security, reputational risk, litigation risk and loss of revenue and investor confidence. Once this happens or is about to happen, the board realizes that there is a new area of concern on the agenda – and they respond by acting the 'good guy' and being seen to do so. If dirty tricks are under way, such as bribery and corruption, corporate espionage, destroying the environment, using mercenaries and government death squads against indigenous peoples or needlessly torturing animals for profit, then no one must find out. In the Internet age, this is harder and harder to achieve – and a company's unethical behaviour, or even untrue insinuations of it, can move around the world in seconds.

Why should any corporation consider ethics in directing its activities above the legal, financial or security implications? Short-term advantage from ethical conduct does not clearly translate into measurable financial advantage and probably means the opposite, because ethical conduct is more expensive than traditional behaviour. Investments above and beyond that required by law in environmental or social areas may bring reputational benefit, but an improved reputation is very hard to measure financially compared with increased costs and falling sales.

There is mid-to-long-term benefit to be had, however, because there are numerous cases where unethical behaviour (or perceived unethical behaviour) has cost the corporation dearly, for comparatively little financial benefit. Figure 8.1 demonstrates the correlation between decreasing choice for the corporate and increasing cost, relative to the time an issue is in existence (Regester & Larkin, 1997: 61).

The modern Western corporation needs to build up an image of social, ethical and environmental responsibility because, if it does not, then the consumer will not buy its products. Its workers will be de-motivated (some may even whistle-blow to pressure groups or the press) and they will, in the long term, lose competitive advantage. Corporate ethics can be seen as contributing to future business success, because those corporations that ignore them will not be the preferred choice of increasingly well-informed consumers and will be the target of well-motivated and equipped 'ethical'

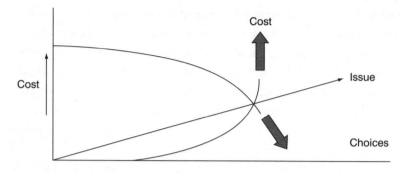

Source: Regester/Larkin, 1997

Figure 8.1 Unethical issues: costs and choices

forces. It is not hard to foresee a future where the eco-warrior becomes a warrior in more than name. Animal rights activists have shown their 'warrior' instincts in the UK in recent years.

The executive leadership has to be aware and responsible for what its company is involved in around the world. There is no denial of the use of child labour or pollution, at least, not when it is in the papers or on TV. Business cultures and ethics differ wildly around the world, but the Western corporation always has to measure up to what is perceived as 'right' and 'wrong' in its native country and, certainly, in its major Western markets. With rapid turnover in management and an ever-expanding geographical spread of operations, coupled with an increasingly intrusive press, it becomes difficult for any board to be in control of events everywhere at once. There is no refuge behind the words: 'I did not know'.

In the UK, consumer advocacy groups have virtually driven genetically modified foods off supermarket shelves. Groups in Europe and the USA forced scrutiny of the way in which child labour was used in Asian manufacturing industries. The dynamics of how ethical issues affect companies are not always obvious however. An American campaign by the Benetton fashion group backfired when the company used imagery of US death row inmates in an advertising campaign. Sears, Benetton's principal foothold in the US market, cancelled a lucrative marketing agreement involving 400 of its outlets, after relatives of the condemned prisoners picketed stores in American cities.

The active management of ethical performance is becoming an important determinant of long-term business success. The Body Shop, in alliance with consultants KPMG, is an example of industry best practice in this regard. As legislation tightens and public concern grows, ethical issues are becoming an area of significant potential expenditure as well as risk. The time is not far off when ethical, social and environmental reporting practices will be on a par with financial reporting.

Case study: Burma

Principal GADs

- Ethics
- Public/media hostility
- Pressure groups
- Bureaucracy, local government and red tape

Chronology of events:

1992: Levi-Strauss pulls out of Burma.

1994: The Coalition for Corporate Withdrawal from Burma files a proposal requesting a shareholder vote at Amoco on operations in Burma. Reebok International states that it will no longer manufacture its products there.

1995: Liz Claiborne Inc. announces that it will stop buying apparel from Burma amid shareholder pressure. Eddie Bauer, a subsidiary of Spiegel Inc., starts buying from Liz Claiborne Inc.'s former Burmese supplier and itself becomes the target of nationwide demonstrations in the US. Bauer then stops sourcing from Burma.

1995: Texaco comes under fire from shareholders and their supporters for its treatment of the environment worldwide and for doing business with oppressive governments such as Burma's.

1996: Student protests result in some universities banning the sale of products by US companies operating in or buying from Burma.

Municipalities and state governments consider boycotts and legislation against companies doing business in Burma. Massachusetts enacts legislation banning state agencies purchasing goods and services from companies operating in Burma. Franchises of Pizza Hut, Kentucky Fried Chicken and Taco-Bell are forced off campus for links to PepsiCo. Legislation is also pending in the US Congress. PepsiCo, Texaco and Arco are among those targeted. Meanwhile, Singapore, Thailand, Japan and Malaysia step up investment in Burma.

1996: PepsiCo, which invested US $1 million building a bottling plant in Burma in 1991 for yearly returns of $8 million, sells its 40 per cent stake in its joint venture, bowing to domestic US pressure. A global competitor of PepsiCo is offered the plant PepsiCo left behind, for $1 by the Burmese government. The board of the company declines the offer after consultation with corporate intelligence consultants MIG, because their products might then suffer the same problems in the US as PepsiCo's, with boycotts by consumers and bans by state governments. The boycott on PepsiCo continues because, even after withdrawal, it has a franchise agreement with its former Burmese JV partner.

1996: Heineken's $30 million Burmese venture is attacked by trade union activists in Europe, as is Unocal, Burma's largest foreign investor ($1.2 billion). Total is also under fire. Lawsuits are filed in the US against Unocal, Total and the Burmese military government together.

1997: San Francisco authorities state: 'We've shown local action can cost global companies not only dismay, but money as well', on awarding a $40 million radio system contract to Motorola (which pulled out of Burma) over Ericsson (which stuck with its Burmese investments).

April 1997: President Clinton bans all new investment in Burma due to human rights abuses and the heroin trade. From February to April, US companies rush to invest before the ban comes into effect, putting in $339 million, more than the previous two years combined. The EU protests to the WTO about Massachusetts's law on behalf of European companies against extra-territorial legislation by US states.

1998: Ericsson suspends business with Burma.

1999: US Federal Court of Appeal rules the Massachusetts law unconstitutional, together with similar laws by 20 other state and local governments. The winning argument is that states cannot legislate US foreign policy.

2000: US Supreme Court rejects appeal by State of Massachusetts to reinstate the 'Burma' Law. Meanwhile, the Japanese government continues infrastructure assistance to Burma, as part of a long-term investment strategy.

Case study: Royal Dutch/Shell

Principal GADs

- Ethics
- Public/media hostility
- Pressure groups
- Environmental hazards
- Threats to physical assets
- Kidnapping
- Civil unrest

Royal Dutch/Shell's stance on the Brent Spar issue, though backed by the British government and most scientific opinion, was completely undermined in 1996 by the heavy-handed treatment of Greenpeace protestors who had occupied the platform. Media and pressure group attention turned the spectacle into a circus and the company eventually 'U-turned', opting for a more expensive and risky onshore disposal rather than sinking the spar at sea. The company also saw 200 fuel outlets attacked in Germany, with two firebombed and one assaulted with firearms. Further to this, the company lost credibility in the eyes of the media, governments and public, and there was disunity within the sector ranks of Shell itself. This occurred in two markets familiar to the company, which it considered 'domestic'.

One might have thought that Shell had learned its lesson but, due to the work of human rights activists, it was already associated with human rights

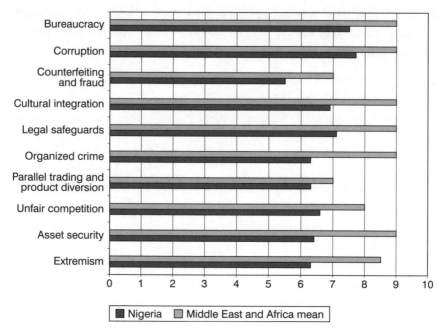

Source: MIG

Figure 8.2 Nigeria vs Africa and the Middle East GADs 2001

abuses and environmental degradation in Nigeria, because of its extraction
of oil in the southern Delta State. Before the execution of rights activist
Ken Saro Wiwa in November 1995, he had accused Shell of destroying the
environment and colluding with the representative military regime (who
guarded Shell facilities) to oppress the local people. As a consequence, Shell
has suffered continual sabotage to its physical assets resulting in repeated
loss of production and its workforce has continually faced the threat of
hostage taking and attack.

Shell has also faced calls for boycotts of its products. Nevertheless, investment continues because, for the board, the perceived benefits of operating
in Nigeria outweigh the risks to its physical and human assets, as well as to
its reputation. Shell's position is not uncommon. Other major companies
have allegedly used private armies or colluded with local dictatorships, and
the perception is that they will deal with whoever has a preponderance of
military force in country (Human Rights Watch, 1999).

Points to consider:

- **Impact**: ethical issues transcend national boundaries and, where large corporations are concerned, are rarely localized. The greatest repercussions may not impact in the non-domestic market at all, but at home.
- **Security intelligence**: know who you are up against in terms of in-country security threats, such as armed groups or activists, as well as domestic opinion, the media, pressure groups and any political/official support they may have or be likely to gain. Try to think in terms of their campaign effectiveness, organization, intentions and locations. Build profiles and gather intelligence that can be used in planning counter-strategies. Are any company employees likely to be sympathetic to outside influences, to the extent that they divulge sensitive information or act against the interests of the company?
- **Information security**: control information flows and restrict unauthorized dissemination of information that would be harmful to company interests.
- **Physical security**: make sure physical assets and key personnel are adequately protected. Hire professionals from outside, if necessary, because lax long-term security can be very costly in terms of lives and property.
- **Manage official responses with care**: manage ethical issues with a systematic and united approach to dealing with the media, pressure groups etc. Assign roles, responsibilities and resources. Prior preparation and planning prevent poor performance.
- **Listen to others**: be ready to shape, respond and harness public emotion. Sometimes, it may be necessary to seek 'approval'. Do not appear as a monolithic organization unwilling to listen, with moral superiority or unethical values.
- **Simplicity**: make the case clear and simple and work with the media and pressure groups where possible. It is much better to co-opt them than to antagonize them.

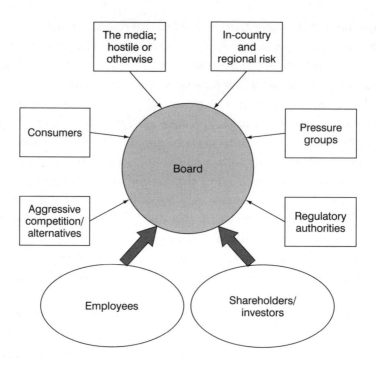

There are many facets to these key headings within Grey Area Dynamic™ risk assessment.

Source: F Milburn/MIG

Figure 8.3 Threats and weaknesses posed by unethical issues

9
Other headaches

Better to be despised for too anxious apprehensions,
than be ruined by too confident security.

Edmund Burke

Asset security is 'The condition achieved when designated information, material, personnel, activities, installations and other assets are protected against espionage, sabotage, subversion, extremism, terrorism and crime, as well as against loss or unauthorized disclosure' (covert intelligence sources).

Asset security is a sound business principle to achieve for non-domestic and home markets alike, as it allows senior management to plan and execute business strategies without interference from competitors or scrutiny by the press, pressure groups or other interested parties. By maintaining security, the corporation safeguards its employees and material assets and is better able to surprise competitors and other actors. The threats to asset security are generally higher in non-domestic markets. Kidnapping, for example, is a widespread 'commercial' activity in countries like Mexico. Businesses are often associated with their government's actions and targeted because their assets are generally poorly protected.

The costs of safeguarding against asset security threats are likely to be high, but not as high as the cost of disruption to business, destruction of property, loss of reputation or even loss of life. Foreign businesses are highly visible because of brand names and associations, and because employees are likely to be considerably more affluent than local people, so making tempting targets for robbery and kidnapping. Extremists in the form of organized groups or anarchic mobs may target foreign businesses for political, nationalist or religious reasons. In the UK, Huntingdon Life Sciences, a British company that ran laboratories involved in animal experiments, which were perceived as cruel, saw its share price plummet, as a fund manager sold an 11 per cent stake in the company in response to bomb threats by animal rights activists. The mainstream British Union Against Vivisection Reform Group also threatened to picket the homes of 1,700 shareholders. Extremism is examined in more detail later. Asset security also impacts on human resources management, because more personnel will not wish to work in a dangerous environment and wages may go up as a result. Theft is another issue, as it provides a ready means to supplement income. It is easy for products to become 'lost' in transit or stolen from warehouses. Piracy is still a big problem in South East Asia. Clearly, a condition of perfect security is unlikely ever to be achieved, but it does represent a goal towards which constant progress needs to be made. The term 'asset security' describes not only the ultimate condition but also all the protective measures designed to achieve it.

Corporate counter-intelligence (CCI) is a collective term that can be used to describe all the measures taken to discover, assess and defeat the threats from other corporations, foreign intelligence services, pressure groups, the media, terrorists, extremists, criminals and others. CCI is broken down into two elements, one offensive and one defensive.

Security intelligence (Sy Int) is derived from the careful study of attempts to break through corporate security controls, combined with knowledge of hostile organizations. One of the principal sources will be the CCI team (if one exists), while other sources may provide Sy Int from which both assessments and reappraisals of the threat to asset security can be made.

The corporation needs to be able to produce Sy Int independently, because home governments rarely provide valuable risk assessments for fear of causing diplomatic offence. Non-domestic governments do not like to reveal their internal problems with law and order or territorial control.

Some corporations may be lucky, in that their close relations with the intelligence agencies of their home country mean that they will receive intelligence and security advice. Other companies will be the espionage

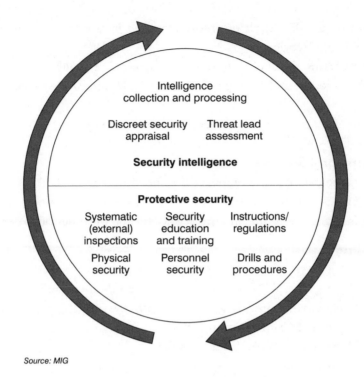

Source: MIG

Figure 9.1 Proactive development and intelligence (PDI)

targets of foreign intelligence services. Risk assessments from banks or other commercial organizations should not be taken at face value either. They may have investments in the country, which will colour their advice or they may be totally ignorant of the real risks that affect the protective measures taken.

Protective security (PS) consists of carefully planned controls that form an independent and interlocking series of defences in depth. These controls are designed to protect information (including IT), material and personnel. PS measures are driven by the threat, which, in turn, is constantly reassessed by the Sy Int acquired. Depending on the security environment, key personnel may require Close Protection (CP) as part of the PS measures.

Methods of attack may be overt or covert. An example of overt activity would be the Greenpeace occupation of the Shell platform Brent Spar or the kidnapping of Shell employees in Nigeria by indigenous rights activists. Covert activity poses a greater threat because it is difficult to detect and because it is often intangible and difficult to neutralize.

The covert threat consists of:

- **Espionage**: the attack on information, eg by a competitor or hostile intelligence service;
- **Subversion**: the attack on loyalty, eg by pressure groups;
- **Sabotage**: the attack on physical assets, eg by disgruntled employees.

Security issues that may require consideration include:

- **Arms proliferation**
  - Is there access to weaponry in a non-domestic market?
  - How often are firearms used in the course of committing crimes?
  - Is it possible to obtain arms legally for the purposes of protection?

- **Crime**
  - What levels of petty and serious crime exist in the market?
  - What geographical and demographic trends are there in crime?
  - How much crime is associated with the illegal drugs trade and Organized Crime Groups (OCG)s?
  - How much violent crime is there?
  - What precautions are necessary to ensure that assets and personnel are adequately protected?

- **Internal conflict**
  - Are there high levels of instability in the country (eg an internal armed conflict or high levels of civil disorder)?
  - How serious is the situation?
  - Are the problems urban or rurally based?
  - How much does it affect business, especially foreign business?
  - How is the situation developing – is stability being restored, is the situation remaining static or is it worsening?
  - Can local armed groups be co-opted?

- **Law enforcement effectiveness**
  - How competent and trustworthy are local law enforcement agencies?
  - Are they sufficiently trained and funded?
  - Can they be relied upon to provide protection for businesses or are additional security measures necessary?
  - Are they corruptible?

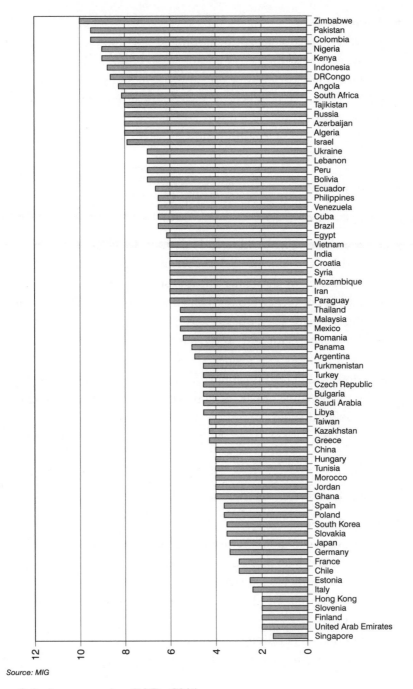

Source: MIG

Figure 9.2 Asset security GADs 2001

- **Social factors**
  - What levels of social inclusion and exclusion are there among the local population?
  - How high are levels of unemployment and poverty?
  - To what extent are they a factor in crime, disorder and internal conflict?
  - Are economic trends causing social conditions to improve or worsen?

- **Xenophobia**
  - How hostile is the local population to foreign business and foreign nationals?
  - Are there heated ethnic and religious divisions in the society?
  - Is there a history of mob action and communal violence?
  - Are there any particular antagonisms that may impact on a specific business or its personnel (such as hostility arising from nationality or the company's activities)?
  - What nationalist and ethnic tensions exist?
  - How are they expressed?
  - How widespread is support for extreme political parties?
  - Is the presence or perceived power of foreigners and foreign business a political issue?
  - To what extent does the political mainstream support extremist platforms?
  - How much support could the company expect from the government if extremist groups target it?

- **Terrorism**
  - Do terrorist and extremist groups operate in the country?
  - What are their strengths and composition?
  - What are their agendas?
  - To what extent do government countermeasures minimize the threat?
  - Do they target foreign businesses?
  - Are they likely to threaten your business?

Extremism

Since 11 September 2001, the subject of terrorism warrants rather more space than the few lines printed above. Not all of those regarded as terrorists are extremists. Some of those we brand as terrorists are criminally motivated or are mentally unstable 'cranks' with a transient fixation.

The term 'extremism' covers the threat posed by individuals or organizations that hold a narrow set of fanatical beliefs. Modern history is full of examples of extremists who are willing to sacrifice themselves for their cause. Palestinian terror groups like Abu Nidal set the example for contemporary extremists in the early 1970s, and Hizbollah took it to new heights in 1983 with the human bomb attack on the US Marines compound in Beirut. For the Islamic extremist, to die in such a way makes them a Shahid or martyr. The religious or ideological aspect of extremism makes it unpredictable, dangerous, hard to placate and a very difficult GAD to counter.

Furthermore, foreign governments often back extremists, directly or indirectly, as instruments of foreign policy by other means. The US government itself supported Islamic extremists in Afghanistan against the Soviet occupation and, in many ways, the Taliban rulers were part of the monster that Frankenstein created. And then the Americans themselves became the targets of extremists sheltered by the Afghan government. The aftermath has been horrific – and its end could be distant.

Many aspects of Western culture and values have been adopted around the world, while others have been violently rejected. In many non-domestic markets, religious and ethnic loyalties are the basis for individual identity; one only has to think of displaced people like the Palestinians or ethnically divided states such as Bosnia Herzegovina. Anti-Western sentiment can erupt at any time. The collective sense of self means that an attack on one is an attack on the whole group. This type of rationalization leads some Muslims, for example, to believe that they are the targets of a global conspiracy by Western states led by the United States. It is vital to remember that the word 'Islam' means submission – a total denial of self. The Western norms of self-preservation do not apply and any security plans in countries with a history of Islamic fanaticism should be structured accordingly.

In Mogadishu, Somalia, in 1993, previously divided Somali clans and militia groups joined against what they perceived to be arrogant American aggressors. The Americans were involved in active operations to capture or eliminate the Somali warlord, Mohammed Farah Aideed. Elite soldiers suffered a humiliating defeat at the hands of low-tech militiamen and mobs of unarmed but enraged local inhabitants (Bowden, 1995).

Western businesses, often associated with the actions of their governments, encourage extremists through their expansion overseas. The penetration of Western practices is perceived by many to foster an unwelcome dependency on the West in economic and power-political terms. This breeds hostility. This hostility can then be directed against the far-flung interests of Western multinational corporations throughout the world. Extremists have targets as well as the rationale.

For many years, companies that had interests in Israel have not been successful in doing business with Arab or Muslim countries, because of the policies of the governments concerned, and because of the threat of extremist action. Thus, a company's own origins may determine whether it is targeted for attack. The more unstable the host government in a non-domestic market, the greater the likelihood of extremist attack and the less likely the host government will be able to protect the foreign company. Such attacks may be symptomatic of the instability or an opportunistic response to it. If their aim is to pressure their own government, then they may want to scare away foreign investors from allied or investing states, as happened in Algeria from 1993.

It is a vital element of due diligence that corporate strategists – not to mention Western governments – should understand and measure accurately the risks arising from extremism. On 15 March 2001, Merchant International Group published one of its fortnightly Risk Updates. It said this:

Political Islam and its Impact on Business

Islam is the world's fastest growing religion and, arguably, the most alien to Western businessmen. It has come to be linked to 'extremism', itself a dangerous development that can set Muslim and non-Muslim apart. The ideological aspect of extremism makes it highly unpredictable and its close association with violence makes it highly dangerous. As a result, extremism of any kind is one of the most difficult Grey Area Dynamics™ to counter. One-fifth of the world's religion is now following the Islamic faith.

The proliferation of the global village, dominated by the Western media, technology, ideas and companies, has caused ethnic, religious and nationalist tensions to intensify in many places. In many non-domestic markets, religious and communal allegiances are central to an individual's sense of identity. The collective basis of loyalty means that to act in any way against that identity is also perceived as an attack on the group. This is a basis for all sorts of religious and nationalist extremism, such as the suspicion among some Muslims that they are the victims of a globally-orchestrated campaign of persecution.

The global nature of business has resulted in many companies branching out from their domestic markets to develop worldwide competitive capability, capital and customer access. Western business in particular has reaped the benefits and continues to seek opportunities voraciously.

The development of an extremist tendency within a section of the Muslim population has come to see Western business interests as legitimate targets. Even actions taken in good faith by Western companies can spark an extremist backlash or bring the mobs on the streets. More importantly, perhaps, many extremist organizations are shrewd enough to recognize that governments can be pressured most effectively by threatening their ability to attract foreign investment.

Some multinational companies consider that the political climate of a market has little effect upon their business. This is profoundly unwise.

The company's own origins may determine whether or not it is targeted for extremist attack. How much protection the authorities are prepared to give it will also depend on how much power and popular legitimacy extremists wield. The more unstable a government, the greater the likelihood that extremist acts will take place, whether they are a symptom of this instability or an opportunistic response to it. Political instability increases the probability of the government failing to protect the targets of extremists, either through lack of ability or lack of will.

There are broadly five issues that need to be assessed in order to determine the extent to which extremism should be judged a threat to a particular business:

- *Integration issues: how stable is the country?*
- *Religious tensions;*
- *Pressure groups;*
- *Terrorist activity;*
- *Xenophobia: what nationalist and ethnic tensions exist?*

Activity undertaken in the name of Islam, or perceived to have an Islamic dimension, has been making headlines on a regular basis for some two decades now. There are global networks, thought to target Western interests, that have moved to the forefront of the collective consciousness. Thus, the recent arrest of more than a dozen Islamic radicals in the UK and Germany was part of an intensified effort to crack down on a group with ties to Osama bin Laden, the wealthy Saudi, who has been accused of masterminding the bombing of two US embassies in 1998.

> *According to an analyst, 'Britain is increasingly becoming aware of the threats that are posed by terrorist support networks and is taking action... Britain's taking action will mean that many other countries in the European Union and the Commonwealth will follow along'.*
>
> *Half a world away, the bloody war in the disputed state of Kashmir has become the gateway for a motley group of young guerrillas, fighting for Islam against 'the Hindus' of India. One such, recently in the news, was a British Asian who acknowledged having 'trained with the Majahedin in Pakistan where there is assistance from some elements of the army... I have got a wife. But this is not a time when I can go picnicking with my wife. It's a time of crisis for Muslims'. (As quoted in The Guardian, Dec 29, 2000.)*
>
> *There is fear and mistrust on both sides: sections of the Islamic community feel threatened by the West, and are keen to participate in the wars of their co-religionists; while the non-Muslim world feels equally threatened by the fastest-growing religious grouping with a powerful ideological underpinning.*
>
> *Religion has once again been firmly signposted on the road map of the new century. It is not a question of whether one is a believer or not. Rather, it is the political and economic ramifications of the development of religious bloc(s) that will surely impinge on all aspects of life. The business world included.*

Six months later, trained Islamic suicide squads struck at New York's World Trade Center and Washington's Pentagon. The world – or most of it – was appalled at the horrific loss of life. Appalled, yes – but the world should not have been surprised. Osama bin Laden has created a cadre of henchmen capable of masterminding similar atrocities – and they are spread across an increasingly volatile world in centres of high Islamic population and extremist Islamic belief.

- **Integration issues**
  - How stable is the country?
  - What are its main divisions?
  - What roles do ethnicity, nationalism and religion play?
  - How intense are internal conflicts in military terms?
  - Does the political system empower different interest groups?
  - How well does the company fit, by cultural and political background, into the marketplace?
  - What can be done to improve how the company is perceived?

- **Religious tensions**
  - How much influence does religion have in society?

- Are there religion-based political parties?
- How much backing do religious groups receive from elites?
- What is the legal status and treatment of religious parties and groups?
- Do they feel persecuted or threatened?
- How do they deal with opponents?
- How likely are they to target foreign businesses, and towards which ones are they most hostile?

- **Pressure groups**
  - Which pressure groups are active in the market?
  - How much popular support do they have?
  - How radical are their protests or demands?
  - Who are they hostile towards?
  - Have they used force?
  - Which groups are hostile towards which businesses?
  - To what degree do the authorities control pressure group activities?

- **Terrorist activity**
  - How common is terrorist violence in the market?
  - Which organizations are pursuing a violent strategy?
  - Do they have links with particular governments or political factions?
  - What motivates them?
  - Do they target foreign businesses; if so, which ones?

Unfair competition

A recurring problem in non-domestic markets is that established players often resort to unethical and illegal means to obstruct the activities of potential competitors, especially recent market entrants. A common method is the use of links with political elites and bureaucracy. Unfair competition is another GAD that can be mitigated against with adequate intelligence, but the secrecy surrounding activities aimed at securing unfair advantage hinders the acquisition of such intelligence.

The danger is to assume that, because there is transparency at home or because the corporate follows ethical rules of its own, then it will face a

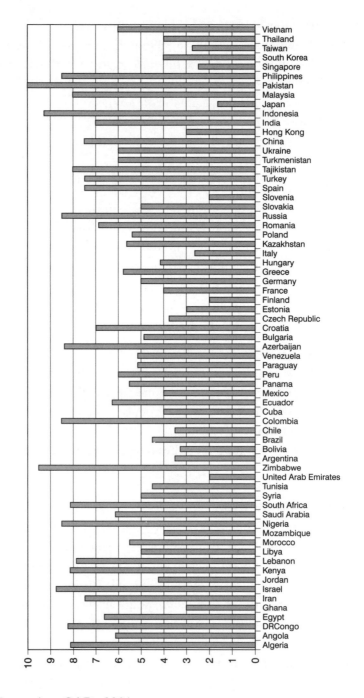

Source: MIG

Figure 9.3 Extremism GADs 2001

level playing field overseas. If unfair or illegal practices are uncovered, many companies do not know how to react or, more importantly, how to exploit the situation. This is where intelligence is vital, because of the detailed insight that can be achieved on competitor activities and the invisible risks present.

The two key questions regarding competitors or other hostile entities are:

- Is senior management open to engaging in unfair, unethical or illegal activity?
- What methods would they use?

If companies in recent history are not above backing military coups, bribing presidents and hiring mercenaries, then it is a safe bet to assume that unfair competition is the minimum that one can expect in certain markets.

Bureaucrats and political figures can be induced to hinder a company's entry into a market or its progress within it. This could come in the form of delays in granting permissions and licences prior to market entry or, post-entry, pending an official investigation into company activities. Privatization and award of public sector contracts are critical areas where unfair competition hinders companies from exploiting their potential, because a competitor's ability to influence key political and bureaucratic figures will affect the outcome. This influence will almost certainly involve money. A competitor with officials or politicians 'in his pocket' will have access to sensitive information about the bidding process, government preferences and rival bids. Competitors may also have financial relationships with the tendering companies.

Foreign and domestic banks advising governments in a privatization may share the same principals as the bidding companies, when they are supposed to operate under conditions of confidentiality and impartiality. In some recent cases, members of the bank's privatization team have had direct financial holdings in, or directorships with, bidders. Such conflicts of interest make for unfair competition.

Some companies with access to bureaucracy and government will use 'whispering' campaigns against competitors, while others have hired organized crime groups to intimidate competitor personnel, sabotage equipment or disrupt supply and distribution. Another method is espionage that could be conducted by one company against another, either using its own agents or professional corporate spies of whom there are plenty on the market. Espionage is used for finding out about competitor R&D breakthroughs, potential bids for deals, customer lists or general strategies. It should be pointed out that the systematic exploitation of open sources can yield significant gains in an ethical manner, without the financial and reputational costs of espionage. Government intelligence agencies are also involved in these activities. Methods include technical and non-technical surveillance (including lip-reading), physical theft and communications intercept. Hacking into IT systems is common and becoming increasingly sophisticated and dangerous but it is far more useful to recruit people inside a target company who have real or potential access to useful information.

Espionage professionals will also be on the lookout for 'unconscious' sources who provide information without knowing its destination. 'Talent spotting' involves the espionage professional cultivating potential agents socially, in such a way that they are unaware that they are becoming entangled in espionage. These potential agents may be vulnerable to pressure such as blackmail or may be prepared to spy for ideological, philosophical or mercenary motives. A stratagem is then employed to ensure that they will work for their controller. This is termed putting the potential agent 'on the hook'.

Most of the world's principal intelligence agencies are engaged in espionage directed against the commercial and industrial world. They do so to gain intelligence for their country's military and technological progression and to support the efforts of their national businesses. It is safe to say that everyone spies on everyone and so-called 'allies' are no exception.

Espionage against foreign companies in former countries of the Soviet Union, like Russia and Ukraine, is standard, as it is in China, where the country's rulers are keen to improve their military and technological edge for their own uses and for re-sale. Their intelligence services are more active than ever and are often employed against tempting and usually poorly protected Western business targets. It is always best to err on the side of caution and assume the worst case scenario about anybody employed by the company in a non-domestic market, or about 'middlemen' offering

Source: MIG

Figure 9.4 Unfair competition GADs 2001

their services, because they could well be foreign intelligence agents. Intelligence agents will go to the trouble of setting elaborate traps – including 'honey traps', the use of attractive women to extract information from the unwary – and will use front companies to glean secrets and to disguise the true nature of their involvement. If one works on the premise that intelligence agencies have years of experience in nefarious activities directed against each other, then the security of the average business is not going to present much of a hurdle for them to overcome.

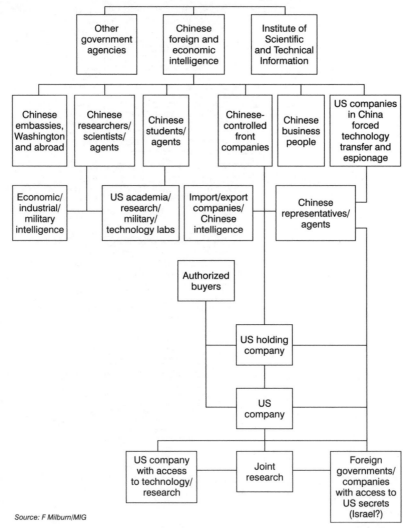

Source: F Milburn/MIG

Figure 9.5 Chinese targeting of US commercial and technological secrets

Points to consider:

- **Market**
  - Is there a history of unfair competition in a market/sector?
  - How has this manifested itself?

- **Competitor behaviour**
  - How have competitors reacted to threats to their position in the past?
  - What, if any, unethical measures have they used or are they reputed to have employed?
  - Which techniques have been favoured?
  - How vulnerable is your company to them?
  - How vulnerable are competitors?
  - Can this be exploited?
  - Are there any invisible competitors not previously identified or assessed?

- **Competitor links**
  - What relationships do competitors have with the political elite and bureaucracy in the non-domestic market?
  - How have both sides exploited these relationships in the past?
  - How have the links been used to obstruct others?
  - In what ways might they be a source of advantage to competitors in the future?
  - How can they be turned against the competitor?

- **Information security**
  - Are you aware of the threat?
  - What proprietary information would be most valuable to competitors or foreign intelligence agencies?
  - How secure is it and what measures are in place to protect it?
  - How could defensive measures be improved?
  - What can be done to encourage employee loyalty and prevent leaks?

- **Political involvement in the sector**
  - How close are the ties between politics and business in the non-domestic market?
  - Which parts of the political elite have interests in your sector?

- What degree of access do you and your competitors have to them?
- What steps do they take to defend their interests?
- How susceptible is the political and bureaucratic elite to bribery?

● **Transparency**
- How clear is the decision-making process involving the award of public sector contracts?
- What efforts are made to ensure that unfair competition is kept to a minimum?
- Is government business awarded impartially by competitive tender or through personal contacts?
- To what extent are personal contacts based on cronyism and nepotism?
- How harshly is corruption treated in law and in practice?
- Are conflicts of interest declared or disguised?

Case study: Russia

Principal GADs

● Asset security
● Organized crime

Company personnel travelling overseas often suffer from 'inhibition loss, a propensity to do things they would not otherwise do'. Adultery and sexual antics, gambling and other activities not only distract their attention from business but provide excellent opportunities for influence attempts to be made against them. One such method is the 'honey trap' and, in places like Russia, there are plenty of 'women of the night' willing, for various reasons, to work for organizations/agencies who have objectives harmful to the company.

In Russia, a certain OCG attempted to do 'business' with a global accountancy firm. It had set up a number of front companies and was attempting to get the firm's senior partner to sign off on certain accounts, so that it could borrow money it had no intention to repay. The partner refused. One night he went to a casino where two women picked him up. Then he took them back to his flat. While he was in bed with one of them, the other one opened the door and let in two men. The women then left and the men ransacked his flat, stating that unless he did sign off and work for them, then this was what his life would be like. It got worse. Rather than keep quiet and listen, he tried to fight back. The base details need no repeating here – suffice to say he is no longer with the accounting firm in Russia.

Lessons that could be learnt from this are:

- Don't believe in your own invincibility.
- Don't go to places where one is in harm's way, if it can be avoided.
- If one is going to be exposed, let as many people as possible know about it before it becomes serious.
- The corporation should devise and implement security procedures and instructions for dissemination to personnel operating in medium- to high-risk environments.

Case study: industrial espionage

Principal GADs

- Asset security
- Unfair competition
- Ethics
- Espionage

There are numerous recent cases of industrial espionage committed by companies – state intelligence services employ better operational security and so detection is more difficult.

1993: in Germany, General Motors' (GM) Opel subsidiary accused Volkswagen (VW) of espionage, after a senior GM executive allegedly took company secrets with him to VW. A US Federal judge ruled that GM/Opel could bring charges under the Racketeer Influenced and Corrupt Organizations Act. Gerhard Schroeder, then premier of Lower Saxony and member of VW's supervisory board, accused GM/Opel of waging war against the German car industry. This case led to the Economic Espionage Act.

1996: The Economic Espionage Act was enacted in the US, making industrial espionage an offence. Eastman Kodak filed an industrial espionage lawsuit against former employees accused of selling information to competitors. UK Department of Trade & Industry warned businesses of the threat of espionage.

1997: VAI was ordered to pay Kvaerner Metals US $1.6 million by London High Court, after espionage activities lost Kvaerner a $1 billion Saudi Arabia deal. The espionage was directed by VAI's CEO, who was previously ousted as CEO from a Kvaerner subsidiary in the UK.

1998: Reuters were accused of industrial espionage for stealing computer coding from rival Bloomberg. Reuters, which listed the 'goodwill' attached to its name as a non-quantifiable asset in company annual reports and accounts, suffered unquantifiable damage to its reputation. In South Korea, 19 engineers were indicted for stealing memory chip technology from Samsung and GL and selling it to Nan Ya Technology Corp of Taiwan. The two South Korean firms estimated their losses at $833 million. The South Korean government began to consider industrial espionage laws of its own.

2000: The EU Parliament set up a special enquiry into allegations that the US uses the 'Echelon' electronic surveillance system for industrial espionage. The US and UK governments deny using the system for this purpose, although it is generally assumed that they get around domestic privacy and espionage laws by spying for each other in the other's territory. The European Airbus consortium allegedly lost a Saudi deal to rival US company McDonnell Douglas because the US government discovered, through communications intercept, that French nationals were offering bribes. The French Justice Minister claimed that Echelon was directed against commercial targets. Meanwhile, the French were developing their own intercept capability dubbed the 'Frenchelon', partly financed by EU partner, Germany.

10
A little light relief

It has probably occurred to the reader that we do not regard an overseas market as an entirely safe haven. Our cynical views are conditioned by the mass of information received daily at MIG's London offices from worldwide sources – some of which are within the very organizations we regard as threats to international commerce. The absorption, corroboration and analysis of this information results in MIG's frequent publications and regular reports to corporate clients with interests – either current or potential – in one overseas market or another. But, sometimes, the written word is not enough. Some corporate clients want more – much more – even to the extent of asking MIG to solve a pressing problem.

Instructions of this kind can involve operatives in some tricky situations. Rudyard Kipling would have described such activity as 'the great game' – and the game invariably includes pretext, deceit, some physical danger and, usually, some humour. Identities – both corporate and individual – have been disguised for the sake of confidentiality.

Needless to say these case studies have been 'doctored' to protect individuals and prevent embarrassment. There are obviously many more cases – some light, others much more serious – covering the globe. What they have in common is a range of Grey Area Dynamics™ – intangibles that have seemingly caught all the managers by surprise. In many cases, a number suffered from that common commercial disease: that of arrogance, ignorance and naivety.

Case 1:

Principal GADs

- Nepotism
- Fraud
- OCG
- Arrogance

A major European accountancy company had carried out an audit for a major multinational in the UK in the purchase of an aviation business supplying, among other things, aluminium heads and equipment to the aerospace industry. In the acquisition, the assets were quoted at one figure but the reality was another. For several reasons, this didn't become clear until much later when the new owners carried out their own audit. The accountants were naturally quite worried that they would face a substantial legal action.

We were asked to identify the reason for the shortfall, who was responsible for it, point to the culprits and bring them to book – and, generally, to find out exactly what had happened. Was it simply human error or something rather more serious? Using a rather elaborate pretext, we contrived to interview all of those on the board of the vendor company and some of the senior management. We fastened on one board member whom we felt was the weakest but not without ambition – and who gave the impression that he had something to hide. Oddly enough, he happened to be both a choirmaster and lay preacher.

A meeting was arranged at the Ritz Hotel in London. We claimed to represent a substantial international organization (a fictional one, of course) seeking a president for a multi-billion dollar plant being set up in the US.

He would be paid many times his present salary and he and his wife would live somewhere rather nice. The reports and papers were professionally prepared and would have stood the test of the most discerning eye.

We then invited him and his wife to Paris where he would meet one or two of the representatives of the fictitious client company. This he fell for and, subsequently, turned up for a meeting in Lucerne. While in Lucerne, we brought in a 'representative' of that same fictitious company whom our target perceived to be with a 'criminal organization'. This went particularly well as our 'representative' turned up with a 6ft 4 inch giant who scared the pants off him. As we left the main restaurant, he said in a rather loud nervous voice, *'Oh my God, am I getting in bed with the mafia?'*. We didn't persuade him otherwise.

The terms of our offer were generous – but we still did not know if or how the asset shortfall had been created or whether this was our man. We strung him along for two more meetings in even more exotic locations with all the luxury trimmings – increasing our terms each time to a level beyond his wildest dreams. By this time, he had become convinced that our client was a Mr Big in the criminal sense – but the offer was so attractive that he felt he had to accept. Quite apart from that, we had been 'honest' about our fictitious client and his business methods as we were trying to induce a little fear into the man.

Finally, and some time later, we met him to conclude the contract at an associate's office in New York – where we went through the contract that he would be taking up and the date when he'd be starting. We briefed him on the situation and then asked him, before he signed the contract, if there was anything we should be made aware of so that our Mr Big would not find out afterwards whether he had any 'skeletons in his closet' – otherwise he would never be trusted. It was at this point that he admitted that he and four others had, in fact, done what is called a 'top hat' exercise over a period of 18 months.

The material (which made up the financial shortfall) had been smuggled out under scrap waste destined for disposal – all over a much longer period than the accountants had realized. He and his cronies had sold them on the black market and put the money into banks in Canada and the US. In fact, he disclosed the bank details to his wife by phone from his room earlier.

We then went into another room and left him in the associate's board-room. We arranged for a confederate to rush in and say that our Mr Big was on the way – he had found out and we were all in trouble. He went white and ran out of the office. We never saw him again. Back in England, much later when the information was passed over to the client, legal action was taken.

To this day, even the new owners – our real client – were unaware of the methodology employed. All they knew was that, at the end of the two-and-a-half month assignment, eight of their staff upped and left.

Case 2:

Principal GADs

- Nationalism
- OCG
- Parallel trading
- Fraud
- Arrogance
- Naivety

Two very large US and European companies are actively involved in manufacturing and retailing sports gear. They manufacture large numbers of sport shoes at varying prices, some in excess of £100 a pair. The American and European managements do whatever they need to do to achieve their targets. They appoint distributors in Germany, Italy and France and other parts of the world. Most of the manufacturing, however, is done in the Asian Pacific region – in places like Taiwan, Korea, Malaysia and the Philippines. Unfortunately, in the Asian Pacific region, the manufacturers frequently and, quite cleverly, engineer overruns and counterfeits.

This case relates to a major Algerian distributor, part of a major gang, who represented these companies for the west coast of Africa. He began by ordering just a few thousand pairs of shoes, which were shipped to Monte

Carlo courtesy of the main distributor for France into bond and free of tax. They would then be shipped to the Ivory Coast and sold. Although some small quantities were exported, the bulk of the product was diverted back through Marseilles and Antwerp into Belgium, France, Germany and Italy. The main French distributor made increased sales (at least to begin with) while the Algerian evaded the duty by 'smuggling' the sports gear back into Europe and then sold the stock at some 60 per cent below the retail selling price. Costs went back to the French company and the profits stayed with the Algerian gentlemen based in Monte Carlo. They even evaded the IVA by selling through 'back street' outlets.

However, the Algerian distributor, not content with the money being made, began to order thousands upon tens of thousands of pairs of shoes. Neither the French company nor the owners cottoned on to the fact that there weren't that many people in the Ivory Coast. But that didn't really matter. They were both making sales but, of course, the Algerian distributor was now diverting shoes to other parts of the world – from the Soviet Union to Italy. Nevertheless, the Europeans and the American owners were happy because they were making sales. When the Algerian started to divert stock into the French and German markets, the legally licensed distributor realized that they had a problem. So, after much wrangling, they bought the Algerian distributor's company – they really had no choice but no one told the American and European owners that the Algerian had not been paying the duty on the shoes either. So we had the task of proving to the Americans and the Europeans that this was the situation and trying to identify which of these shoes were counterfeit and which were diverted stock.

We spent time in Bari, Milan, Frankfurt and Paris and along the south coast of France going through all the various traders – both Arab and local nationals – in the back streets to identify who was doing what to whom. The most difficult was operating in the ports of Antwerp and Marseilles. In one instance, this culminated in an operative being chased through the back streets by three or four toughs with knives – after 'gathering' evidence. One Saturday morning, running down the back streets trying to avoid these nasty people with flick knives, he ran into a Citreon coming the opposite way around a corner (luckily, slowly). The disturbance – attracting everybody from the local peasants to the Gendarmerie – scared the Arabs away.

Although a little bruised, the operative managed to slip away unharmed. We proved to the clients what was happening – but the joke really was on the main French company in that they had acquired the Algerian company but he had continued to trade illegally; diverting stock and avoiding tax and duty. They also paid the customs duties and the Americans achieved the sales they sought. It was the European company who actually suffered most at the end of the day. Nobody was prosecuted.

Case 3:

Principal GADs

- Corruption
- Fraud
- OCG
- Theft
- Company policies (cultural variances)
- Vested interest

We were asked to carry out a physical security audit on a plant in Wales. Although appointed by the board of the US parent, the UK general manager had the impression that we simply had to carry out a covert night-time security review – followed by a general review of the plant itself later. There was no reason given as to why we should be looking at it other than that the owners were improving quality and tightening up security generally.

That night, we found a few major gaps in the fence, a few wandering and drunken workers, several ladies of the night and some petty theft – but nothing serious. We met the general manager the following day – only to be told in an unguarded moment that they had lost a few tons of carbon-less paper over a two-month period. We took it for granted that this stuff had been cut and packed and was sitting on the backs of lorries or in the boots of cars. The reality was that, when we went down to the main plant, we saw rolls of paper 8 to 10 ft long and upwards of 6 ft tall – in fact, the weight of each of these rolls was one and a half tons.

This paper was being produced for a variety of administrative uses and was going out in huge rolls. For example, a lorry would take five or six one-and-a-half ton rolls – not the sort of thing you can stick in a briefcase and walk out of the front gate. Apparently, the firm had increased the quality of the product to become more competitive and was recycling much of the paper that fell below their new quality standards. One of the senior key staff had other things in mind and was diverting more than the odd roll meant for recycling to a side warehouse. When we began our investigations – based on pretexts as work study consultants and trades union representatives – we reached the conclusion that a divisional board member (who was changing his car every six months, having holidays in Barbados and Bermuda two or three times a year with his wife, had three houses and had cleared the mortgages on them all) was doing much more with his salary than most people would do with five times the amount. So we put a tag on him. He was found to be working with a Dutchman out of Rotterdam who, in turn, was reporting to someone in Amsterdam.

Numerous discreet 'reviews' over seven markets in which this US Group manufactured and distributed its products through 100 per cent-owned companies highlighted major inefficiencies, losses and vested interest issues.

Following a number of leads, we were able to identify the people with whom the divisional board member and one or two junior plant managers were working. They were a small branch of an organized crime group – operating out of Amsterdam with a network through Belgium to Germany. They were getting quite rattled by the fact that we had begun to slow down their supply. They were putting pressure on their contact to perform. So we put pressure on him too and, very wisely, he resigned. We began to close down the conduit of the supply to the Dutch.

A footnote to all of this was that, with a close protection officer in attendance, we went to Amsterdam to meet the leader of this little gang and his bodyguards in a hotel. We debated the merits of getting them to walk away without criminal action – and were told that some of this 'wonderful' paper was being chopped up into small rolls and a proportion sold as toilet paper to the Germans.

We left after securing a suitable agreement to their withdrawing peacefully – but with the thought of all those German bottoms turning blue. The paper had all been impregnated with microscopic blue ink capsules. The case actually took the best part of five and a half months and covered seven countries from Europe through to the USA.

Case 4:

Principal GADs

- Arrogance
- Ignorance
- Cultural indifference

An American multi-national group bought a European group of companies that had earlier acquired an industrial process creating tools for use in building and construction. The European group had plants in Belgium, Holland, France and Germany.

Six months after the American group had acquired the plants, it was decided that, by centralizing production and practising economies of scale, turnover and therefore profits could be dramatically improved. So the group appointed an American executive to research and review the situation. As a result, the US parent group, without research or recourse to local senior management, decided to close the existing plants and build a new centralized manufacturing facility in another country, which offered very serious tax advantages and benefits.

The managers and employees of the closed plants were none too pleased. In one case, virtually a whole village had lost the livelihoods on which its residents had relied – and they decided to do something about it. As mad as it might seem, they simply opened their own plant a mile or so from the closed American-owned plant. They had the experience and the skills – and they went further by enlisting the help of the local police, the local banks and the judiciary and began the process of systematically defrauding the American owners to recover what they regarded as their birthright. They also encouraged the management and employees of the other plants planned for closure to do the same. They might have got away with it but the American owners had approved the closures and expenditure of millions of dollars for their new plant to secure tax breaks – and were actually losing twice that sum each month in market-share because of the newly-created competition. The old management knew their customers and even used virtually the same livery on their products, promotional material and packaging.

Our role was to produce a case against the management – at worst, get them to withdraw or, at best, get the plant to close down. Lawyers from New York had charged nearly US$1.5 million in legal fees but had been unsuccessful thus far in creating a case against the management.

We set up a company in Jeddah, placed an agent in Antwerp and began to order equipment from the upstart company for the Saudi market, having it routed through Antwerp. Over four days per month for three months, MIG had personnel skulking about in Antwerp docks to save a client from itself. On one of those occasions, we had to withstand temperatures of −20° to −22°. Even the sea had frozen. On a lighter note, the contact we had in the Communist-led dockers' union took pity on us and, every half hour, would come out to the open dock front with extra strong schnapps. By midday, we could barely stand. At one stage, we both slid, laughing hysterically, onto the ice and had to be rescued by our contact.

When in Antwerp, our pretext allowed us to buy the equipment for Saudi Arabia, take it into the docks at Antwerp, divert it by changing all the numbers and the details as if it was still going to Jeddah and then re-route it all the way back to our client's new plant's customers. The Americans would then not lose market share and still actually make some money from the deal.

We ultimately forced closure of the Belgian factory because of market erosion, without the client actually having to revert to legal recourse. The forecast as to how long before a suitable legal result could normally have been achieved was between two and three years – whereas we took five months. The old plant management never understood how it was done. Two months afterwards, we took a call at a sterile number in Antwerp. It was one of the last calls we took prior to closing down our operation. It was from a German who said 'Mein Herr, I don't know how the f**k you did it. It was a very clever job. But, if ever we see you, we will kill you'.

Case 5:

Principal GADs

- Corruption
- Espionage
- Extortion
- Blackmail

The **** Hotel in East Berlin was the showpiece of the GDR (East Germany) and utilized by the fat cat managers of the larger Kombinats – east German commercial conglomerates – the Stasi, the KGB, everyone and his uncle. There they would meet local politicians, dignitaries from overseas and various other business people for whom they were putting on a show pre-perestroika.

The hotel was little short of a brothel. On the first floor was a crescent-shaped bar with about eight or nine barstools, each of which was the property of a local prostitute who was ultimately controlled by a member of the Stasi. The Stasi themselves worked for the GDR and for many of the Kombinats. One such company had some four Stasi members run by a Lieutenant Colonel of the Stasi who was also KGB. Part of his role was to gather data on key western products for, and under the direction of, the Kombinat management and the KGB, which they could effectively steal and reproduce themselves in East Germany, the German Democratic Republic (as it was then). One such product was made by a large US multi-national. A number of the US company's managers had visited the GDR over a period of time and stayed at the hotel. On one such visit, one of the executives made the mistake of meeting one of the young ladies and taking her to his bedroom not realizing that there were full audio and visual facilities. In fact, that was true of a number of the hotel rooms. But, in this particular instance, some time later, he was invited to another location – the Stasi 'offices' (for want of a better description) – which we later viewed in some detail.

The setting of the Stasi offices was rather like an extract from *The Ipcress File*. Part of Eastern Germany is very much as you would envisage from the books by Len Deighton. He wrote about the rain falling down over cobbled streets and drab brick walls. The 'offices' (living quarters and operating centre) used by the Stasi and the prostitutes were very much the same on the outside – even to the point of having a small brick alcove, with discarded rubbish and builders' materials that stank of urine, the proverbial length of electric lead with a bulb stuck on the end of it and a huge metal door to one side. We gained access through the door – following a carefully planned pretext. Inside, there was another door covered in leather through which we gained access to the inner sanctum.

Inside, we were surprised to find an extraordinarily well-lit succession of rooms with Axminster carpets, huge walk-in fridges with turkeys and bottles of Scotch almost two feet high; an amazing place. It had saunas, plunge pools, rest areas and garages in which there were several antique vehicles. One was an ancient but grand Mercedes (the property, no doubt, of a German officer of the Third Reich), another an SS motorcycle and sidecar complete with machinegun mounted on it, and another a Mercedes complete with its Nazi emblem. These were really collectors' items and this was March 1988, before the wall came down. They also had bedrooms, again with full camera and audio equipment installed.

They could have clearly lasted for some time without going out for supplies. They also had files on companies and dignitaries, all very carefully annotated. They could very quickly pull out the 'who's who' and know which politician was which and which company had which product. This was at a time when brother spied on brother and you trusted no one, not even your wife. The Stasi, of course, thrived in such an oppressive environment.

Our role was to prove the innocence of a number of individuals who had been targeted previously and to identify cross-border movements of individuals under various government projects.

In one case, this related to one individual and was specific to movements of Stasi operating in the West. The finale to this took place in late 1989/ early 1990, with part sale of one of the largest of all the Kombinats – Robotron, under the privatization programme following perestroika – when a major Spanish group made a bid to buy part of Robotron's property assets in East Berlin near the Alexanderplatz. While carrying out discreet due diligence for the Spanish group, a friend called from a Spanish

Government agency in Madrid asking us to look into the situation without realizing that we were already doing just that. He asked whether or not it was appropriate that a US$10 million fee should be paid into a Geneva bank for this particular acquisition. It later transpired that the acquisition was the very one that we had carried out the due diligence on and the $10 million fee was to a member of the legal department of a government body whose position and responsibility were to expose corruption. This department was responsible for bringing to trial any of those who could be charged – while one of their own was actually trying to extract $10 million from the Spanish for the very company we were looking at.

The art of the pretext and the very nature of instructions risk bringing operatives face to face with criminals and unsavoury characters generally. There is not always danger. In fact, some of the storylines have very romantic overtones that it would be wrong to disclose – but that is another story.

Case 6:

Principal GADs

- Arrogance
- Fraud
- Espionage (unfair market competition)

People see the US market as above corruption. However, unfair market competition (to win by whatever means are available or to be one step ahead of the competition) is not unusual and there have been several assignments where we have confronted industrial espionage. One oil company in the north of the US repeatedly came out one step ahead of its competition in Texas. Firstly, it bugged a boardroom in Houston following a visit by two senior executives, one of whom left an electronic device.

Secondly, the same company utilized the capability of one of the law enforcement agencies in the USA to eavesdrop and to monitor movements of a potential acquisition target. One of the individuals was an ex-police officer, while the others moonlighted for a fee.

Armed with a full file of movements gathered discreetly over a number of months, a highly-priced recruitment group then targeted individuals. In one of those cases, a particularly attractive woman had targeted two executives employed by our client to generate useful market intelligence. However, her methods bordered on extortion and blackmail – and she was supported by two heavies. One of the executives, ironically and somewhat belatedly, became suspicious and reacted. Needless to say, the executive (with more than his ego bruised) neglected to report the matter to the police or his wife.

We became involved when the chief executive got wind of the incident and became a little fed up with the continued success of 'the competition' winning bids and deals and decided that 'a little bit of research of our own is necessary'.

Working from 'the outside' to gain access into the European operations, we targeted the movements of two key executives within the competing company whom we identified as being linked with a surveillance team spotted near our client's offices as a consequence of a 'motor accident'.

After tagging the surveillance team and identifying the two executives as go-betweens, we ran a pretext against one of the operatives. Short of money, nervous and under serious pressure from his boss in the States, he panicked and phoned his HQ from the phone we had 'tapped' in his hotel room. This call provided us with the key and therefore access to the competition's office, again under a sophisticated pretext.

In short, over a period of time, we too built up a dossier of evidence on how the oil company had used clandestine methods to obtain valuable information on its competitors' practices and intentions. Our own methods included the use of 'bugs' to ascertain the full extent of the opposition's covert activities. We had to play the same dirty game. Eventually, we confronted the president of the oil company with our dossier of evidence. The 'compensation' paid to our client ran into tens of millions of dollars.

Case 7:

Principal GADs

- Ignorance and pride
- Fraud and theft
- Corruption

The president of a large US conglomerate had taken on two very senior Brits to run his operations in the Middle East. It was a multi-billion dollar organization with investments in over 40 countries. Over a period of two years, margins began to decline. Although there were indicators pointing to fraud or theft, neither the auditors nor the accountants had produced any concrete evidence in a market where fraud and theft against a principal could cause serious loss of face.

The company, despite its size, was facing problems and the president's position was being challenged. Any further negative vibrations would not only have brought the share price down but would also have cost the president his job.

The whole matter had to be handled very discreetly. Intelligence was required to prove the duplicity of the two Brits and make them resign. If at all possible, any money or assets were to be recovered without legal action.

Two separate and totally independent operations were planned and implemented, initially to gather research on the targets and their markets. The first phase of our operations took us covertly through the client's international offices in Chicago and then into Africa and the Middle East – with emphasis on certain activities in one particular Middle Eastern country.

Once the first phase was complete, we researched one or two lowly but well-placed executives and one male secretary who had some unusual perversions which, if declared, would have seen him imprisoned. In addition to acting as a go-between for the two Brits and a contact in the Chicago office, the secretary liaised with a very senior Arab prince who had some unusual connections with a terrorist group. All of this made the assignment more difficult. Quite clearly, some of the money 'leaking' out of the company was going to questionable bodies.

Our pretext had to stand close scrutiny and, if possible, actually work.

After six weeks, we located and obtained access to the senior of the two lowly but well-placed executives. We had taken a convoluted route through a number of commercial parasites and Mr Fixits. Our pretext included our own involvement in a search for a sponsor for a National Guard deal for over $240 million. Our target had, it seemed, engineered a deal for two per cent in cash. The target, however, suggested a payment up front 'to cover the expenses of certain of my sources'.

Subsequent tracing of bank transfers (along with all the other evidence) enabled us to prove the guilt of the two British targets. Concerned that repercussions might impact on the company, a profile of the activities in duplicate was provided to certain individuals within the government of the Middle Eastern country to ensure that the client could continue to trade without interference.

The two executives and their confederates were forced to resign and, in two other cases, individuals were fired without pay after signing a specially prepared letter taking full responsibility and promising to maintain complete confidentiality.

At best, $10 million was returned to the client.

End note: The male secretary was killed four weeks later in a 'car accident'. The connections between those involved and established terrorist groups made this a particularly hazardous exercise – which we have no wish to repeat too frequently, unless the price is right.

There are many, many other cases – diverse and complex – ranging from problems arising from cultural misunderstanding to religious diversities and from simple theft to terrorist involvement in client operations.

The major failings inevitably have, as common factors, the arrogance and ignorance of executives who wanted to cut corners and were not prepared to spend money on research. All of them thought that they knew better but didn't.

Other more complex and more recent cases must remain totally confidential to protect our sources and field operatives.

Part Two

The World's Troublespots

11
Introduction

This section of *Risky Business* points to what carefully collated and assessed intelligence indicates are the *troublespots* of the world. Some are dramatically less troublesome than others – but even those countries that were quick to align themselves to the call by President Bush for an international coalition against terrorism have their problems. Poor economic performance brings poverty and unemployment, perhaps to millions. Poverty breeds resentment and crime.

Some political and religious activists – whatever their ultimate objectives may be – rely heavily on crime to fund the purchase of arms and ammunition. Any surplus keeps the wolves from several doors and it is common knowledge within national security services that some activists enjoy a standard of living some of us less zealous mortals might envy. The discovery in the UK of a cache of £180,000 in the flat of an Islamic activist – also in receipt of benefits and allowances from a benign UK government – makes the point.

It follows that risk assessment by corporate strategists must go beyond standard due diligence. Assessment must extend beyond the well-publicized acts of terrorism by extremists. It must examine governmental economic

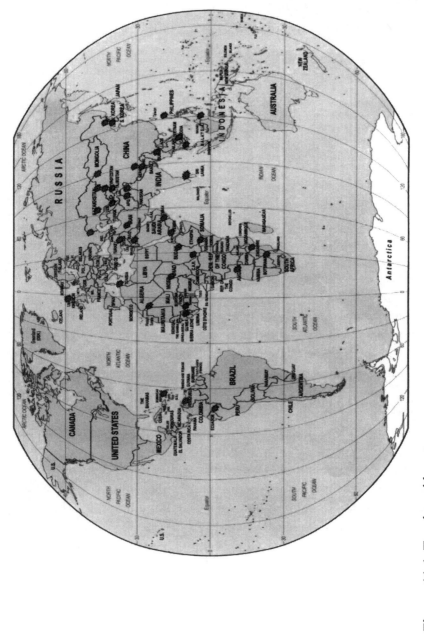

Figure 11.1 Travel troublespots

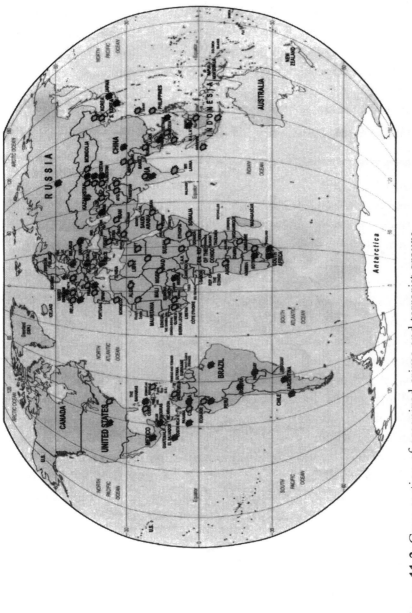

Figure 11.2 Cross-section of organized crime and terrorist groups

White: Terrorists; Black: Organized Crime

Source: Information: MIG; Maps: The University of Texas Library – The Perry-Casteñada Library Map Collection

performance, its direction and likely results. In fact, it must examine all of those things listed as Grey Area Dynamics™ that we identified in Part One.

The world can be a perilous place and the safety of executives is in jeopardy whenever they travel, work away from safe places or pass through, or even close to, areas of concern or risk. It is of little comfort to be reminded that, for every executive or manager harmed in any way, literally thousands remain totally unscathed. In spite of this statistic, the fate of a few individuals is important enough to call for extreme care and vigilance to ensure that neither company executives nor their families are placed in jeopardy while working in hostile environments.

It must be clearly understood that the response of the company and its executives to any of these events could determine whether lives are saved or lost. The threats to organizations posed by criminal (organized crime) and terrorist activity have never been greater than they are today. Organizations in all sectors of business and in all areas of the world are increasingly finding themselves the targets of various types of criminal and terrorist action and, consequently, there is a fundamental need to ensure the protection of assets, both human and material.

However, this book has not been designed as a substitute for a comprehensive company security policy but as a guide to the main issues to be addressed by senior management. It should be used as a basis for the formulation and implementation of such a policy for executives travelling in difficult and dangerous countries.

It may appear that, in certain areas, the book over-emphasizes the extent of the threat and the measures required to reduce the risk. In addition, it may also cause an over-reaction among those who feel that the book is, in itself, an over-reaction. Although it is important that the reader understands that some of these threats may never arise, proactive preparation is not only cheaper, it is a far safer way than having to react to a crisis. It is up to senior management to ascertain the degree of risk and threat relative to their company before implementing these recommendations.

12
Origins of the threat to business

Religious fanaticism and creeping Islam

Terrorism can take many different shapes and forms. Arguably the biggest global threat is that of religious fundamentalism. The last twenty years have seen a dramatic rise in Islamic radicalism, which is transforming not only the Middle East, but also much of the Western world. Impoverished and politically disaffected Muslims in Indonesia, Nigeria, North Africa and the Middle East have been attracted to the appeal of fundamentalism, which blames the 'infidels' and the 'Great Satan' in the West for all their society's problems.

The fundamentalists are seeking, through violence, to replace secular governments with Islamic States that are based on their own rigid interpretations of (the *Sharia*) Koranic law. On occasions, they have even declared a *jihad* (holy war) against those who oppose or merely question their views. Osama bin Laden found his sources of personal wealth in the Middle East and chose to centre his terrorist nucleus in Afghanistan. The Western democracies are unlikely ever to forget his name or his acts of terrorism. Nevertheless, the influence of Islamic fundamentalism is dramatically wider.

The main sponsor of such terrorism is Iran followed by Libya. Many of the terrorist groups in countries such as Lebanon, Algeria, Sudan, South Africa, Nigeria and Egypt are guided and funded from Teheran or from groups like Hamas and Al Qaida. The German Customs Intelligence (ZKA) warned of attempts by Iran to build a pesticide plant capable of producing chemical weapons of mass destruction. Although an Indian consortium had carried out much of the work, it appeared that Western companies were approached for items such as reactor vessels and graphite heat exchangers.

Elsewhere, power in Sudan, the largest country in Africa, is held not by Parliament but by the leader of the Nationalist Islamic Front (FIS). Events in Algeria resulted in the massacre of hundreds of thousands of women and children. These acts were allegedly carried out not by the FIS, which has denounced the violence as 'crimes against humanity', but by a more radical organization known as the Armed Islamic Group (GIA). However, there were rumours that the Algerian government was itself directly responsible for the massacres in order to create instability over the sale of oil, a commodity that Algeria has in abundance.

In Egypt, the activities of terrorist gunmen made travel to parts of the Upper Nile too dangerous for many Westerners. While there was talk of some areas being re-opened for transportation, the situation actually got worse before it improved.

The main reason for the increase in fundamentalist appeal in many cases was the lack of an effective democratic process. Evidence indicates that authoritarian politics breed the economic and political conditions to make the simplistic answers of fundamentalism attractive. The best course of action for Western governments would be to encourage and support moderate, democratic Muslims, rather than to support repressive govern-ments or to court fundamentalists.

International organized crime syndicates

The most infamous international crime syndicate, the Mafia, is very much alive. It continues to exert its influence in most areas of Europe and America with protection rackets, gambling, prostitution and drug syndi-cates as its main areas of activity. They are currently operating in the US,

Italy, Spain and Monaco. Their authority has now been undermined to some extent by the emergence of other syndicates in their markets. The Russian Mafia, originally content with organized crime in their own country, have expanded their interests to wealthier areas such as Israel, Austria, Germany, France, England, Canada, Poland and the US. They began with street kiosks in Moscow and St Petersburg and moved swiftly into the highest echelons of business and government. Their threats are to be considered extremely real. The murders of leading businessmen, politicians and bankers in Russia are just a few of the publicized cases.

In January 1998, Eduard Rossel, one of Russia's most powerful regional leaders, was the target of an assassination attempt when a bomb exploded close to his passing car. Mr Rossel, Governor of the Sverdlosk region in the Urals, had stated earlier that week that his overriding concern was to get his industrial region moving again. However, Yekaterinburg, the region's capital, has gained the infamous reputation of being the centre of organized crime and Russia's criminal bosses are becoming increasingly prepared to challenge local administrations. In August 1999, for example, Mikhail Manerich, deputy governor of St Petersburg, was shot dead by a sniper. When doing business in Russia, consideration must be given to the actions of organized crime against personnel and fixed assets, as well as against a business's 'brand'.

In Japan, the Yakuza are well organized; and strictly regulated. The Japanese police have a working relationship with the Yakuza that allows them to control prostitution, gambling and drug syndicates under agreed rules. The main rule is do not resort to violence. However, their agreement is now being tested by the entry of Triads (Chinese Mafia) in Japan. The tremendous socio-economic changes taking place in China have given rise to a new generation of Triads that are benefiting from the reduction in central control. They, too, have expanded into other markets over the last decade and are now operating in the Philippines, South Korea, New Zealand, Austria, Italy, Colombia, America and the UK. The Triads are dominant in the areas of drug- and people-smuggling, arranging the shipment of Chinese who are willing to pay for the chance to become illegal immigrants in the West. Many of these people arrive in the countries of Western Europe, where Chinese communities currently thrive.

The Turkish Mafia is also expanding the markets in which they operate. These now include Burma, Thailand, Laos, Bulgaria, Germany, Spain and England. The Mexican Cartel operates mainly in Mexico and America but has also moved into Germany and is continuing to expand.

13
Political terrorist groups

Though not the threat of twelve years ago, it would be extremely unwise to overlook the potential threat posed by such groups as the IRA splinter groups and loyalist groups such as the UFF, the Red October Group and November 17.

The main targets for this category of terrorist have historically been the military, political bodies and individuals. Many of their victims have been high-profile business executives of large companies. Recently, victims have included any business traveller associated with high-profile companies. Consequently, a company with a high profile should, of necessity, be vigilant at all times, especially when operating in high-risk, non-domestic markets. Also in this category are rebel groups seeking political power in countries like the Philippines, Malaysia, Indonesia and Colombia. As an illustration, in Sierra Leone, a military coup led by Johnny Koroma was reversed by force of Nigerian arms. However, such occurrences are commonplace in African countries. Indeed, Nigeria still has significant difficulties in the North.

In Russia, following Vladimir Putin's election to power, there has been a surge in regional power. Local bosses have now found that they also have substantial political clout; for example, in 1996, without the help of these local bosses, Boris Yeltsin would not have won re-election. However, under Putin, there is now very little that local bosses cannot get away with. This point was proved in 1997, when Yeltsin attempted to rid himself of Yevgeny Nazdratenko, an extremely incompetent elected governor of the Primorsky (Maritime) territory. The other provincial bosses supported Nazdratenko by persuading Yeltsin that it would be unwise to sack one of their own. Yeltsin was forced to back down.

Northern Ireland still suffers from extremist violence. In May 2000, there were several punishment beatings. In London, a bomb was planted under Hammersmith Bridge and the MI6 headquarters was targeted. High-profile companies must take this into account when reviewing their security measures in the UK and elsewhere. Even with the peace accord, there are still many factions involved that do not take their orders from those affected by it. They may very well continue to refuse to accept the conditions laid down, choosing to protest in typical terrorist fashion, but for profit.

It does not matter where you operate, organized crime, terrorists or extremists seeking either to make political capital or profit can still reach you. The need to be attentive, alert and aware when outside one's home base is critical. More importantly, one needs to know what and where the threat is and how it can affect the executive abroad. Only then is it possible to know the dangers.

14
Global scenario update

The world has changed. This, for many businesses, is an unpalatable fact. After 11 September 2001, the world at large stopped in shock at the breach in the wall that was Fortress USA and wondered just where the next atrocity might occur. Countries around the globe are feeling, and will continue to feel, the ripples.

An unholy trinity has been formed against the various *terrorist groups* that make up the Muslim Brotherhood with Russia, the USA and China all taking advantage of the opportunity to settle scores and address situations that the civil rights groups would have raged over. In the Xinjiong Province of China, the authorities have imprisoned and killed a number of *religious zealots*. In Russia, the security services are cracking down and have killed a number of alleged *terrorists*. Around the world, Muslim militants from the Philippines to Algeria and from Indonesia to Pakistan are heeding the call for al-Jihad affecting the economic stability and physical security of us all.

The economy in Argentina, a few months after an US$8 billion bailout, is in chaos. The deepening political crisis, in advance of the elections, rising unemployment and the worsening economic situation, threatens to engulf

Brazil and, for that matter, Latin America with it as a whole region. This, in turn, will add to the already deepening economic crisis in the US.

Pakistan has done a deal with the US over *support and bases* in exchange for debt relief and assistance and pressure on India over Kashmir. Saudi Arabia is on the brink – as it, too, is challenged by the Wahabbis. Even the Royal Family has had a *fatwa* issued against it *for supporting the infidel*. In Saudi Arabia, Osama bin Laden is portrayed as a hero.

In short, whether we look north, south, east or west, very few countries are exempt from the ripples of change sweeping the world. The 11 September 2001 terrorist attacks, combined with the effects of the recession that had already started to spread across the world, have led some economists to revise their forecasts for growth substantially downward. The worst hit will be East Asia, Latin America and countries with strong trading ties with the US. On 6 November 2001, the US Federal Reserve cut its interest rate to 2 per cent, the lowest level in nearly 40 years in an attempt to revive its economy. Japan shows no signs of emerging from a decade of recession. In fact, it may be entering another recession. One positive factor for the industrialized world is the low price of crude oil, just under US$20 per barrel. However, the Middle Eastern countries will shortly begin to suffer and may face payment problems. The recent OPEC decision to reduce output and increase the price of oil points the way.

In the meantime, what will the terrorists do next? Where next will they strike? It is in the light of these momentous changes that this section of the book seeks to answer just such a range of questions, and examines the possible effect on business and investment. Since 11 September 2001, business has had to rethink its strategy to address the fast changing dynamics being felt across the world's markets. No one was prepared for 11 September, although with the benefit of hindsight, the signs were there for all to see. Thirty days on, we learned that members of the CIA had heard rumours of an attack on the US mainland. Three years ago in Baku, Azerbaijan, when Ahmed Salama Mabruk was arrested, no one believed the story he told the authorities (Mabruk was the personal assistant to Ayman Zawahiri, Osama bin Laden's lieutenant). Months later, bombings and shootings in Azerbaijan, Uzebekistan and Dagestan, in fact throughout the region, increased markedly, including terrorist activity in the Philippines, Indonesia, Nigeria and in the Middle East. Indeed, terrorism across the board has increased.

Even the less fanatical groups, working purely for profit, got in on the act, increasing the claims for kidnap with insurers. There has been an 80 per cent increase, year on year, resulting in payouts (ransom) of over £350 million per annum. Ultimately, it is the insurers that will take the impact as the world prepares for what 2002 and the years ahead will bring.

In an attempt to ease understanding of the problem, each area has been given a risk rating. In each case, we have broken down the regions to help provide a wider perspective of the overall threat to investment and business generally.

15
Risk ratings

This part of the book attempts to predict the likelihood of worst-case scenarios occurring. We provide threat level indicators that may be used to decide whether or not the scenarios are indeed unfolding. In addition, it provides background information on the current crises and the roles and objectives of key players.

It is important to note that, while all of the scenarios described could come to pass, there is no certainty that all or even one of them will do so. They are all, however, highly plausible and, given certain circumstances in which they were able to develop, their consequences could make the business losses resulting from the 11 September 2001 attacks look insignificant by comparison.

The likelihood of scenario occurrence has been graded as follows:

- *Very high;*
- *High;*
- *Very possible;*
- *Possible;*
- *Low;*
- *Very low.*

Each of these has a numeric threat level as follows:

Threat Level 1	Very low	Unlikely to occur.
Threat Level 2	Low	Little chance of it occurring.
Threat Level 3	Possible	This has a 50:50 chance of occurring.
Threat Level 4	Very possible	There is a likelihood of this happening.
Threat Level 5	High	This could very well occur in the short term.
Threat Level 6	Very high	It will happen.

The scenarios depicted are not a definitive guide to the future. There is no crystal ball that enables analysts to predict future aspects of international relations with certainty. They are also not simply an extrapolation of past history into the future. They are, however, an objective assessment of the current situation and how it might develop in the future, subject to certain dynamics.

The purpose of this scenario analysis is to challenge the mental maps that managers use to think about the world. How does their business fit into it? What influences their decisions; how do they identify trends that may be unclear today; how to understand predictability and uncertainty; and how to provide a background against which business strategies may be formulated and tested. The aim of scenario analysis is not to be occasionally right about the future but to avoid being wrong. MIG has had a great degree of success in the past and, in this instance, has sought to be as objective as possible, seeking intelligence and information from its wide resources.

Discussions over scenarios should uncover the following factors: driving forces that determine the outcome of scenarios; given elements that can be taken as fact and that are unlikely to change; predetermined events that have already occurred, but the consequences of which have not yet developed fully, or which will almost certainly occur. In addition, discussions should take into account factors that are happening today but which are untenable (impossible events that the analysis shows cannot occur), such as uncertainties, the conditions and events that no amount of study can ascertain. The information and opinions expressed in the assessments are drawn in part from leading academics, senior military and intelligence officials, former diplomats and regional specialists within the MIG network.

16
Middle East – the Saudi domino effect

This section for the Middle East threat presents five broad scenarios broken down as follows:

1. Instability in Saudi Arabia
2. Expanded US operations against Iraq
3. Re-radicalization in Iran
4. Higher intensity in the Israeli–Palestinian conflict
5. Instability in Turkey

Instability in Saudi Arabia

Assessed likelihood of occurrence: very possible, giving a Threat Level of 4. Saudi Arabia's interior minister, Prince Nayef, has warned security forces against sympathizing with Muslims opposed to the regime.

Assessment: *such unusually public remarks suggest that Riyadh doubts the loyalty of elements in the security forces.*

The government has just cause for concern. Dissatisfaction with the royal family's extravagant spending has simmered below the surface of Saudi society for years. In the south-west of the country, several seemingly unrelated incidents suggest growing dissatisfaction with the government and its relationship with the US. Funds are still available in support of Osama bin Laden.

Assessment: *although a popular uprising in Saudi Arabia is unlikely, a rebellion from within the security forces of organized Islamic militants from the south-west is possible.*

The government's strict control over all aspects of society has, so far, kept organized political opposition in check but growing animosity towards Riyadh's relationship with Washington, as shown by recent protests, has prompted the royal family to reconsider the basing of US troops on Saudi soil.

Splits within the royal family pose a political problem for the US.

Assessment: *The emergence of a radical Islamic opposition could force Riyadh's hand, resulting in the expulsion of US troops and a reduction of ties with Washington.*

Western Saudi Arabia is home to the holy cities of Mecca and Medina, the spiritual centre of Islam, the guardianship of which gives the royal family its legitimacy, internally and externally. Once an independent state, the region is even more staunchly conservative and deeply religious than the capital, Riyadh. The area is a bastion of support for Osama bin Laden and is home to a large Yemeni immigrant population. It is renowned for its religious significance but has not enjoyed the affluence and economic development of eastern Saudi Arabia.

Inequality is a key problem. High unemployment and government spending on defence rather than internal infrastructure projects for the benefit of all Saudis has highlighted differences between the haves and have-nots in the kingdom. Despite its oil wealth, national debt stands at around $300 billion. It is no coincidence that Osama bin Laden, who the Saudi government supported in Afghanistan during the war with the

USSR, is revered by many as an *icon of Islamic self sacrifice, a man who puts his religion and life before worldly wealth.*

The southern provinces of Asir, Jizan and Najran are even more isolated, making them a transit point for drug traffickers and a hotbed of radical Islam. During the 1990s, the south–west became a haven for Afghan Arabs – Muslim volunteers who fought the Soviets in Afghanistan. Investigations into the bombing of USS Cole in Aden have centred on the region and 12 of the 19 suspected hijackers involved in the 11 September attacks are believed to have come from the area.

In January 2000, the Saudis captured frontier territory from the Yemen and, in April, cracked down on Shiites (many of whom are based in Yemen), in Najran.

Assessment: *any uprising involving radical Islamic elements in the south-west could be supported by Saudi Arabia's rival, Yemen, and possibly Iraq.*

Hints of political unrest in the south-west have surfaced and there have been reports that an arms depot in the region was raided and weapons stolen. There have also been reports of sporadic and quickly dispersed demonstrations, denied by Riyadh. There have been further reports of *members of the security forces from the south-east being involved in radical opposition to the royal family.*

Assessment: *the geographical and political isolation of the south-west provinces make them ideal locations for radical Muslims, and the availability of weapons and recruits makes the region difficult to control. Riyadh's growing concern with unrest suggests that discontented members of the military, National Guard and police could be merging with radicals and opposition groups. An isolated military revolt may not be enough to oust the royal family but could have dire consequences for a continued US presence in the kingdom. Terrorist attacks such as the November 1995 bombing of a US military centre in Riyadh, the June 1996 attack on the US military complex in Alkhobar and the petrol bombing of two German businessmen in Riyadh in October 2001 will become more commonplace.*

Added to these problems is the on-going uncertainty about the succession to the Saudi throne because of King Fahd's long-failing health. This, in turn, will trigger more intrigue within the royal family and generate doubt in the population at large, already divided by inequality, tribal ties and fundamentalism.

Assessment: in the current situation, competition within the royal family could be exploited by Islamic fundamentalists who claim that the family is not dedicated to curing the country's ills.

The over-riding concern of Western states, led by the US, is the security of the eastern side of the Arabian Peninsula with the eastern Saudi oilfields, Kuwaiti oilfields and those along the eastern Arabian coastline. Any unrest in Saudi Arabia would have a domino effect in the Gulf States along the eastern seaboard.

During the first Gulf war between Iran and Iraq (1980–88), Western powers supported Iraq to prevent Iranian dominance of the Gulf region and the oil. During the second Gulf war (1990–91), the US and its allies neutralized an overt Iraqi threat to the oilfields.

If bin Laden and his followers, assisted by members of the ISI (Pakistan Secret Service) reach Yemen, they will be temporally secure. In time, Osama bin Laden and his followers will wait until the Hajj pilgrimage and move through into Mecca. Once there, any move, *any move*, by the US or its allies to extract Osama bin Laden from Mecca will unite the Arab World and set light to the tinder box that is the Middle East.

Assessment: *in the event of any unrest in Saudi Arabia threatening the kingdom and other Gulf States, the US would move directly to protect all the oilfields so threatened. This could take the form of supporting a new regime in (a potentially partitioned) Saudi that was more pliable to US interests or it would take the form of a physical occupation. There is no way that the US can allow any power hostile to US vital interests to control the oilfields; the cost to Western economies and to the US military's mobility would be strategically unacceptable. Occupation would be an operation of last resort, but would definitely be carried out if the oilfields were threatened.*

If an occupation were to occur, war would be sparked throughout the region drawing in most, if not all, the Arab states and Israel and, possibly, Iran and Turkey too. Such a conflict could last for years and throw the entire world into chaos. With war widespread geographically, there would be massive destruction to infrastructure, huge disruption to trade, and stock markets could be frequently closed because of erratic price movements and terrorist threats. America's leadership would be increasingly challenged by other states, leading to the deterioration or even break-up of the international system.

Expanded US operations against Iraq

Assessed likelihood of occurrence: possible to very possible, giving a Threat Level of 3.

Even before the crisis, in which Iraqi intelligence support to the 11 September hijackers may or may not have been provided, the US had, for some months, been considering an increased tempo of air strikes against Iraq on the pretext that it had tried to shoot down a US U-2 spy plane and fired upon an E2C surveillance aircraft in Kuwaiti airspace.

Real US concerns focus on signs that Iraq is regaining its military strength following the end of the second Gulf war. Alleged facilities for production of weapons of mass destruction (WMD) were heavily bombed in December 1998. With the recent Anthrax attacks in the US, this issue has moved to the top of the agenda. Iraq has, in recent months, significantly escalated its defiance of the no-fly zones with more surface-to-air missiles fired than last year.

Assessment: *any strike would aim to cripple air defences and further damage Iraq's infrastructure in order to disrupt renewed efforts to develop/hide WMD, or to dissuade Iraq from taking advantage of any potential crisis in Saudi Arabia. Any hunt for WMD could involve limited use of special forces but a major ground campaign is unlikely. The problem would be that Saddam Hussein could then proclaim that the US was engaged in a war against Islam and the Arab world.*

During the second Gulf war, Iraq's army of occupation in Kuwait was largely degraded but enough of Saddam's best divisions (the Republican guard) and his substantial attack helicopter force were left intact by the US military campaign to deal with internal security problems. In 1991, in the aftermath of the war, Iraq was faced with a Shia uprising in the South, a Kurdish rebellion in the North, extensive Turkish military operations on Iraqi territory, and Iranian units infiltrating the border in the South.

Assessment: *the US may seek to degrade Iraq's ability to threaten its neighbours but will be wary about leaving Iraq open to fragmentation as was quite possible in 1991. Alternative means to overt force would include covert actions or increased support for the Iraqi opposition, but neither of these options has been successful in* *the past. Also the Iraqi opposition is a fractious coalition of various groups and has little credibility. No one seriously believes that they are a credible opposition.*

Saddam Hussein has been keeping his head down thus far, wary of the possibility that America's full attentions could still fall upon him and that, this time round, the Americans would seek to remove him from power if any connection with the 11 September attacks were proven or implied.

Assessment: Iraq's ability to threaten its immediate neighbours remains, but there are undoubtedly other factors that will pre-occupy its leadership. Even if a direct Iraqi link to the attacks on the US were proven, it is extremely doubtful that a ground campaign would be launched against Iraq. For one thing, the Saudis and other Gulf Arabs would be opposed to such a campaign and would not allow their bases to be used; for another, such an action would spark wider conflict.

The most likely US course of action is the intensified bombing of Iraq but even this carries risks of further inflaming Arab passions, especially at a time when Israel is occupying Palestinian Authority (PA) territory. One possibility is that Iraq could manipulate the price of oil either through increased production or through sponsorship of attacks on Gulf shipping with fast attack boats, as the Iranians did during the latter part of the first Gulf war. In the event of increased tensions with Iraq leading to expanded operations, the price of oil could be expected to rise significantly. Iraqi or terrorist use of WMD in the region or Western states remains a possibility.

Re-radicalization in Iran

Assessed likelihood of occurrence: very possible, giving a Threat Level of 3.5.

Iran is a key player, in relation to both Afghanistan and the Gulf region. This was why the US supported it in the 1970s, why the US opposed revolutionary Iran in the 1980s and why there has recently been an attempt by the US to find some common ground with Tehran.

Some common ground does exist: the Iranians supported the Northern Alliance forces in Afghanistan and were happy to see the removal of the Taliban regime. A new Iran-friendly regime in Kabul is definitely one of Tehran's aims. The more moderate Iranian regime of recent years under President Khatami has toned down Iran's anti-Western rhetoric; it is keen to have Iran removed from America's list of states that sponsor terrorism, to have Iranian assets unfrozen and to attract foreign investment to improve the economy.

Khatami, now in his second term, walks a fine line between hard-liners, the reform movement and the masses. This state of affairs, since his first term began in 1997, marks the collapse of the Islamic regime's popular support and reveals Iran's inherent instability. Iran's Islamic revolution is on the verge of collapse. After more than 20 years in power, the clerical regime is threatened by a popular reform movement that challenges its legitimacy. Prior to the June presidential election, conservative factions within the regime intensified their crackdown on political dissent.

Khatami is a moderate reformist cleric caught between the two camps. He has used his position to push through a reform agenda. His first term was won on a platform of economic and social reforms to diversify Iran's stagnant economy.

Iran's instability is partly due to an identity crisis. While moderate and conservative clerics are united in their desire to retain power, they are divided over how to deal with the problematic economy and relations with the outside world. The hard-liners oppose Khatami's moderation, arguing that the regime must remain radical and Islamic in order to justify and maintain its existence.

Other clerics argue that Iran's economic isolation is a social and political time bomb and, if the regime is to retain power, it must moderate its policies enough to encourage economic growth and investment. Although high oil prices have given Iran some room to manoeuvre, unemployment remains between 15 per cent and 25 per cent and more than 50 million of the 65 million population live below the poverty line, according to one source. This is dangerous in a country where 65 per cent of the population are 25 or younger.

Even the reformist movement is divided. It enjoys widespread support among the country's youth but has also become a vehicle for revolutionaries. Many of the groups that helped topple the Shah from power in 1979 were later pushed from power by the clerics. They are now exploiting the current situation.

In a strategy aimed at encouraging foreign investment and diversifying the economy away from oil (oil accounts for 50 per cent of the budget and

80 per cent of foreign currency earnings), Khatami has increased press freedoms and revamped laws to give foreigners greater control over their investments. Like Gorbachev in the Soviet Union, Khatami's reforms have effectively opened the floodgates of change. Opening the economy to the outside has also exposed the regime to criticism and opposition.

Assessment: *the hard-liners could continue their crackdown and return Iran to economic and political isolation but this would undercut economic reform and spark a social uprising that could lead to the overthrow of the regime. Alternatively, the regime can allow further reforms and run the risk of a steady erosion of power. Khatami appears to be trying to determine how to continue his policy reforms without causing the regime to fall. Sooner or later, however, the real test will come and the regime will have to decide if it is to remain in power by force, indefinitely.*

The current crisis over terrorism is merely exacerbating these tensions. Khatami sees co-operation with the US as an opportunity for rapprochement and economic development, as well as a favourable new government in Kabul. The hard-liners, led by supreme leader Ayatollah Ali Khameni, oppose any co-operation with the *Great Satan America*, regardless of the cost.

Assessment: *Tehran will tread very carefully. The current crisis goes to the heart of internal power divisions within the regime. While there are doubtless benefits to be derived from rapprochement with the West, the prospect of a wider American war against Islam, whether real or imagined, could greatly influence the political situation inside Iran. Iran underwent an extremely violent transfer of power in 1979, and there is no guarantee against this happening in the future. Faced with the downfall of the regime, there are those prepared to use any means to stay in power. This is not to say that the medium- to long-term prognosis is negative, just that most observers believe the process of reform will be two steps forward and one step back.*

The hard-liners will use any opportunities arising out of the current crisis to rally themselves. Any major disturbances in Iran, a key oil producer, would send a shock wave to the oil price, have global economic effects and would threaten the stability of the entire region.

Higher intensity Israeli–Palestinian conflict

Assessed likelihood of occurrence: high to very high, giving a Threat Level of 5.

One could argue that the Israeli–Palestinian conflict was already increasing in tempo before the assassination of hard-line Israeli tourism minister, Rehavam Zeevi. His death put the Israeli government in a difficult position. Prime Minister Ariel Sharon is under enormous domestic pressure to clamp down on Palestinian militants, but the US will continue to press him to ease tensions with the Palestinians in order to maintain the anti-terrorism coalition.

The Israeli army was pulled back from Palestinian Authority (PA) areas that had been occupied in the aftermath of the assassination. The occupation caused uproar in Arab states, and the more this went on, the weaker their support became for the US – but subsequent events have intensified Israeli–PA hostilities.

Assessment: *the PA under Yassir Arafat will be under pressure to step up arrests of PFLP members who carried out the attack and other radicals, but this really shows the weakness of Israel's position. They are relying on Arafat to arrest those groups that he himself allows to operate in order to pressure the Israelis. To occupy PA territory totally and do the job themselves would merely replace Arafat with something worse. It would cause uproar in the Arab world and further strain US-Israeli relations.*

The current situation is causing a sea change in US-Israeli relations and this is causing instability for Israel's security position, as the US backs away from its unwavering half-century of support for the Israelis. The Jewish lobby in Washington is challenged by growing US Muslim political leverage. Several Arab states are under enormous domestic pressure from fundamentalists and Washington must reduce support for Israel to induce stability.

Two factors guaranteed US support for Israel for the last half-century. The first was the Jewish lobby in Washington; the second was Israel's strategic importance as a counterweight to the USSR's Arab allies, in case a move was made to deny Western access to the oilfields and to safeguard the Suez Canal zone and access to the Arabian Sea. Israel was also a natural ally for America's other key regional ally, Turkey.

The passing of the Soviet threat negated much of Israel's utility to the US and there were already signs in the late 1980s that Washington was backing away from the relationship. The process was interrupted by the second Gulf war, but it is significant that the US did everything possible to keep Israel out of the war for fear that the anti-Iraqi coalition would unravel. The powerful military force in the Middle East, which the US had so assiduously built up over decades, was thus useless in the context of US strategic considerations.

In 1997, Muslim groups in the US organized themselves into a Muslim voting bloc. While they may not match US Jews in funding or organization, they comprise around three per cent of the population, similar to the Jews. At the last Presidential election, they voted as a bloc, giving George Bush around 70 per cent of their vote.

Assessment: *the US will not abandon Israel completely, as it needs access to Israeli human resources and intelligence and will also require military support if the current crisis gets out of hand and region-wide conflict develops.*

However, the US is already putting significant pressure on Israel, especially over talks with the PA chairman, Yassir Arafat. Washington is also threatening Israel financially. US officials are reportedly reviewing part of the aid package to Israel (US$900 million), which accounts for one per cent of Israeli GDP. Military aid at almost US$2 billion appears untouched.

Assessment: *Israel may be pushed into a corner over concern for its security, but without being able to rely on the US for unwavering support. In addition, the more the US cuts its means of leverage, the more the notoriously intransigent Israelis are likely to go their own way. This could lend itself to more extreme actions on the part of the Israeli leadership, including total occupation of the PA territories if attacks in Israeli territory reach crisis proportions or WMD are used in Israel. It is likely that the recent Israeli incursions into PA territory were partly to gather tactical intelligence and entry routes for an occupation proper. A war with the Palestinians would come at a high price – fighting in built-up areas is notoriously intensive in terms of loss of life and the Israeli armour advantage would be blunted.*

The Israelis would become bogged down in a bloody occupation of a hostile population. An assault would spark large-scale refugee flows to Egypt, Jordan and Syria, causing instability and fomenting fundamentalism. Such internal pressure could push Israel's neighbours into war with her.

Occupation of PA territory and war with the Palestinian people would be seen by surrounding Arab states as a big escalation of an already unjust and aggressive Israeli policy of colonization, occupation and repression. Egypt and Syria might consider this a prelude to war with them. At the very least, Syria would facilitate more vigorous PFLP, Hizbollah and Islamic Jihad attacks on Israeli targets.

The Syrian military is weak and the Egyptians have readiness problems, but the Israelis still suffer the problem of lack of strategic depth for their armoured units to manoeuvre to meet any thrusts into their territory and would need to safeguard the security of their airfields to maintain air superiority.

Assessment: *Israel has done it before and would doubtless use pre-emptive strikes again to achieve surprise and ensure that any ground campaign was not fought on its territory; that enemy formations were destroyed and disrupted; and enemy aircraft put out of action early on. The Israeli Defence Forces' nuclear free-fall bombs, surface-to-surface missiles and submarine-launched cruise missiles would all be at high readiness.*

In the event of a conventional military disaster for Israel (unlikely) or use of WMD by Egypt or Syria, Israel would not hesitate to retaliate with her own WMD. In such a situation, all civil flights and shipping would be expected to avoid the eastern Mediterranean and Red Seas, and the Suez Canal zone would be effectively closed.

Instability in Turkey

Assessed likelihood of occurrence: very possible to high, giving a Threat Level of 5.

Turkey is already going through a difficult period. This stems from two quarters: the military's stifling of the continued attempts of banned Islamic parties to form new organizations to appeal to an ever-broader coalition of voters and a financial crisis that has seen 600,000 layoffs and 50 per cent devaluation of the Turkish lira against the US $.

The Turkish government has been secular since 1923, when Kemal Attaturk took over the remains of the Ottoman Empire and created a modern state with the military at its core. Since 1923, the military has taken over government three times to maintain internal stability, to keep itself in power and to keep Muslim activists out of politics.

The military is also under pressure from the civilian government for a reform package of amendments to the military–dictated constitution, demanded by the EU as a precondition for Turkish accession. The package includes a reduction of the military's role in politics (making it more difficult for the military to shut down political parties it doesn't like), abolition of the death penalty, removing legal barriers to rallies and expanded rights for trade unions and associations.

Some observers have put the Turkish economy as close to collapse. Turkey is also linked to the crisis–ridden Argentinian economy through emerging market debt.

Assessment: *a crisis in one would quickly affect the other since both states' debts are pegged to US $ currency. Each has approximately one quarter of total emerging market debt issued. Such interconnected debt relationships helped export the 1997 Asian financial crisis from Thailand to Russia and then on to Brazil. A deeper US or EU downturn could also tip Turkey into recession. Turkey relies heavily on US and German financial assistance.*

Turkey is also the second largest purchaser of Russian natural gas, and past episodes have affected the Russian stock market.

Assessment: *Turkey's troubles will have a wider impact.*

A crisis could also originate in Turkey or close to Turkey's borders.

Assessment: *A new Kurdish uprising and consequent military clampdown would deter investors. Turkey's military has historically shown no qualms about deploying forces beyond its borders and routinely operates in northern Iraq to destroy Kurdish military camps.*

Any crisis in Iran or Iraq would result in Turkish military operations either to stem the flow of refugees or to counter Kurdish militants. Turkish bases could also be used for expanded US/UK operations against Iraq. In the event of a new Arab-Israeli war, Turkey would, at a minimum, remain neutral, but would very possibly mass troops on the Syrian frontier to tie down Syrian forces there, allow Israeli flights over its territory and possibly allow use of its bases.

17
Latin America

Regional recession

Assessed likelihood of occurrence: high, giving a Threat Level of 5.

Speculation that Argentina would default on its debt has now turned into certainty – listed as the biggest default in history. Argentina has been negotiating a domestic debt swap with local banks and pension funds. Argentina's latest debt restructuring constitutes a default according to Standard & Poors and Fitch.

Assessment: *the default has already pulled down the fragile Brazilian economy and is likely to throw Latin America into regional recession, but a severe global contagion may be averted. It is unlikely that a full-scale global contagion will spread to emerging markets in Asia and Eastern Europe, as they are in a better position to weather the storm than in past financial crises, but this is without factoring in the possibility of war in the Middle East or other regions.*

The situation in the more mature emerging markets is different to what it was in 1998 in several respects. Unlike the Thai and Brazilian defaults that caught most of the world off guard, global markets are already prepared for an Argentine default. Brazil's currency has already devalued 30 per cent this year in anticipation of more negative sentiment and rating agencies have issued a string of warnings for Brazil, Turkey and Argentina.

Assessment: *Argentine default is a significant but regional event, without the sort of sharp shock that followed the Thai and Brazilian devaluations or the Russian debt default of 1998, so long as oil prices remain stable and confidence in the global economy is maintained.*

With 1998 still fresh in investors' memories, many have lessened exposure to emerging markets. There is therefore less money tied up in emerging markets and less money in speculative hedge funds. The reduction in capital inflows means that there is less outflow when a shock comes.

The various regions are also in much better shape to stand a shock than they were in the late 1990s. Most South-East Asian economies (Malaysia is an exception) have floating exchange rate mechanisms that allow for market feedback. This helps mitigate the selling pressure which, combined with the regional devaluations, led to capital flight in 1997 and 1998. The other exception is Indonesia, with high political instability and inability to attract long-term foreign investment. But again, this is subject to regional political confidence and stability. The fragile Turkish economy could be prone to a Latin American shock.

The concern for Latin America is that a default by Argentina would throw the whole region into doubt and the greatest impact will be upon Brazil, Argentina's closest trading partner. Brazil has its own debt problems and will struggle to meet external financing requirements estimated at US $80 billion next year, or more than 300 per cent of foreign reserves. Efforts to meet its debt obligations come on top of severe economic contraction, resulting partly from an energy shortage.

Assessment: *these pressures and the global perception of Brazilian instability will rise as Argentina goes under. Any sharp rise in oil prices as a result of conflict in the Middle East will greatly compound the problem. The rest of Latin America would likely be dragged down by the collapse of two of its three largest economies.*

One hope is Mexico that has maintained a stable currency and, until recently, looked a strong contender for mid-term growth.

Assessment: *as the US economy slips into recession, so will Mexico, with 80 per cent of its exports going north across the US border. Mexico will not rebound until the US does. The net effect will be a regional recession encompassing most, if not all, of Latin America, characterized by sinking consumer confidence, limited availability of foreign and domestic credit, falling commodity prices, slowing business investment and weaker trade. Investors may sit tight as Argentina defaults but the consequences of Middle East instability cannot be overstated. Western economies, as well as emerging economies, are vulnerable to oil price shocks, disruption of trade and economic dislocation. Thus, the effects could be global rather than regional.*

18
Asia Pacific

This section for Asia Pacific presents seven broad threat scenarios broken down into the following:

1. An Indo–Pakistani war over Kashmir
2. US operations extended into Pakistan
3. A Sino–Indian war as a result of Indo–Pakistani war
4. A widened Sino–Indian war to include Vietnam and certain other South-East Asian states and Japan
5. A new Taiwan crisis
6. A Korean crisis
7. Islamic revolution in Indonesia

Indo–Pakistani conflict over Kashmir

Assessed likelihood of occurrence: high, giving a Threat Level of 5.

Pakistan is the key to America's war on terrorism in Afghanistan and has been among the first regimes in the region to be negatively affected by the on-going US military operations. The extent of the Pakistani government's stability or instability has direct and immediate implications not just for the war against terrorism in Afghanistan but for the stability of the region and further afield as well.

Tensions in Afghanistan and Pakistan are spilling over into Kashmir, disputed by both India and Pakistan. As Islamic extremists come under fire in Afghanistan and Pakistan, they are likely to increase activities in Kashmir. On 1 October, suspected Pakistan-based Islamic militants detonated a car bomb in (Indian-controlled) Jammu-Kashmir the day before Indian Foreign Minister, Jaswant Singh, was due in Washington.

The disputed territory is a veritable hotspot and the reason for two out of three Indo-Pakistani wars (1947 and 1965), heavy fighting in 1971 (during East Pakistan's secession), and the summer 1999 Kargil crisis. Kashmir is a prize for Pakistan's extremist Muslim population that wants to see the territory fully independent from India. Pakistani president and military ruler, Pervez Musharraf, has been accused of using Kashmir as a safety valve, encouraging Pakistani militants to fight there against the Indians instead of focusing their anger on his government.

Assessment: *as the conflict in Afghanistan spreads, it is likely that Musharraf will do so again, to preserve his government and boost his standing with extremist Pakistanis angered by his co-operation with the US. However, the coming winter will tie down Islamic insurgent forces in Kashmir.*

The US recently dropped sanctions against Pakistan, imposed following its 1998 nuclear tests, and is in deep negotiations on economic aid, debt restructuring and military co-operation as a reward for its current position as a frontline state. A key US aim is to prevent the Pakistani government falling under the influence of, or being overthrown by, fundamentalists.

Assessment: *it is unlikely that the US will do anything to push the Pakistani government to curb the radicals and will instead continue supporting Pakistan to the detriment of its nascent courting of India, in exchange for continued Pakistani support. Today, however, we can expect US and India to have joint defence meetings and the US to sell arms to India, as clearly it will also need India in the future.*

It is not surprising therefore that tensions continue to escalate along the Line of Control (LOC) separating Indian- and Pakistani-controlled

Kashmir. Attacks by Pakistani-trained and -based militants against Indian forces have brought Indian and Pakistani troops along the entire border to high alert and the heaviest fighting so far this year is threatening what passes for stability.

Assessment: *there is a distinct possibility that, if the situation gets out of hand and Indian forces fail to exercise self-restraint in the hot pursuit of Pakistani militants across the border, a general war could ensue.*

In recent years, both sides have restricted themselves to mortar and artillery strikes, with the odd aircraft shot down. But, as soon as both sides bring up heavy artillery and reserves, as they are currently doing, then the situation becomes more tenuous and the possibility of a general war along the Indo-Pakistani border increases. Both sides are nuclear powers. On 20 October, India called on Pakistan to control militants in Kashmir and warned that India would take appropriate measures suggesting it might strike across the border at terrorist camps in Pakistan. Pakistan warned India against *being adventurist.*

General Musharraf is faced with a number of dilemmas. He desperately needs US support to legitimize his regime, to bring the economy back on track and to legitimize Pakistan's nuclear status. At the same time, he faces a multitude of problems at home. His country is home to 25 million ethnic Pashtuns, the same tribe that most of the Taliban leadership came from and which many radicals in Pakistan support. Opposition to support for the US has already led to the Pakistani security forces firing on their people. There are extremist Islamic elements in Pakistan dedicated to the overthrow of the current regime and the establishment of an Islamic theocracy along the lines of the Taliban (or Iran in 1979).

Musharraf cannot necessarily rely on his own military. He has already replaced several senior officers including the head of the powerful InterServices Intelligence (ISI). For years, the ISI was the conduit for American, Saudi and Chinese aid to the anti-Soviet forces in Afghanistan and, up until the present crisis, the Pakistanis were actively on the Taliban side. Musharraf also faces manpower problems. He has had to deploy his troops along the Afghan frontier against continuing Taliban infiltration and refugees, in the major cities and towns against civil unrest and terrorism, around bases used by the Americans and along the Indo-Pakistani border.

For their part, the Indians have reinstated former Defence Minister George Fernandez, a staunch believer in a broader geopolitical role for India in the Indian Ocean and East Asia, including the South China Sea, and who considers Pakistan a mere obstacle to achieving this goal.

Assessment: faced with growing extremist unrest and possible terrorist acts against the government, or moves by senior army officers against him, Musharraf could well manufacture a crisis with India over Kashmir to maintain his rule and regain state unity. (It is widely accepted that the 1965 war began with the infiltration of Pakistani guerrillas into Indian Kashmir.) Such a crisis could then develop first into limited incursions by Indian forces along the Line of Control and then into a general war along the entire Indo-Pakistani border with the scope of military operations extending to the skies above the region and the Arabian Sea. Normal commercial activities, transport and shipping would all be affected.

A new border war would have grave implications for the internal security of India, with its own large Muslim population (around 12 per cent of the total) as well as many other minorities such as the Sikhs. Radicals among India's ethnic minorities could be expected to take advantage of any such crisis for their own ends and, together with the war, severe disruption to normal economic activity could be expected in the Indian states of Gujarat, Rajasthan, Punjab, Himachal Pradesh, and Jammu and Kashmir.

India would have the advantage in a war with Pakistan, as Indian forces outnumber the Pakistani's by three to one. This is offset, however, by Pakistan's strategic relationship with China, which is examined in the section on Sino-Indian war.

US operations extended into Pakistan

Assessed likelihood of occurrence: very possible to high, giving a Threat Level of 5.

There is another possible scenario that could be played out. As the war in Afghanistan moves beyond the initial air-bombardment phase towards more involved ground operations, the Pakistani border region (with Afghanistan) becomes ever more crucial to US operations. This is where the war will be decided because, if the area cannot be sealed off, then the remnants of the Taliban regime will continue to enjoy sanctuary and supplies, and could continue military operations at a tempo to cause mounting casualties to US and allied forces in a protracted guerrilla war.

The future of Pakistan in this war is very much in doubt, and recent reports by US agencies within Pakistan may indicate a Taliban-orchestrated or Taliban-sympathetic campaign against US forces there. There have also been reports of Pakistanis crossing the border to join Osama bin Laden. This means that the Pakistani government is either unwilling or unable to control its own frontier. Pakistani territory serves to support both the US operations and the Taliban. General Musharraf has also made clear that US operations from Pakistan must not result in the Northern Alliance dominating a future Afghan government.

In addition, the US is reliant on Pakistani troops to protect its bases in Pakistan. If the Pakistanis could not protect the US forces, or were involved in operations against them, the US forces would be forced to protect themselves. Under this scenario, the US has three options: the first is to accept the situation. The second would be to conduct operations to stem the flow of arms into Pakistan without attempting to clear the border area of pro-Taliban camps. The third would be to extend US operations into Pakistan itself. The logic of the situation would dictate the third option as enough weaponry is already in Pakistan to support anti-Taliban or anti-bin Laden operations.

Assessment: *the third option would require large force deployments and would be opposed by the Pakistani government and the Muslim world at large. This option would be increasingly attractive to the US but would unravel the coalition against terrorism and alienate all Muslim states, and probably push many, if not all, into overt hostility to the US. It would drag the US deeper into a regional quagmire and, very likely, an endless conflict that it could not win. Under such a scenario, one could expect to see widespread terrorist activity against US/Western targets, both in the region and in the home countries.*

If the US conducted operations within Pakistan, possibly against an Islamic regime, there are two options for India. The first is that India could take advantage of any crisis within the Pakistani government, with regard to the LOC in Kashmir or along the Indo-Pakistani border unilaterally. If the Musharraf regime fell to Muslims, this would threaten India's vital interests and would, in India's view, be justification for total war between the two states, not just limited operations along the LOC or artillery duels along the border.

Assessment*: the most likely occurrence under the above scenario would be for India to act in concert with the US, as they would share a mutual interest in seeing an Islamic regime in Pakistan, armed with nuclear weapons, undermined or brought down. Any Indo-US co-operation or joint military operations would cause massive hostility across the Muslim world, as well as a protracted war in Pakistan/ Afghanistan. Under such a scenario, one would expect to see increased terrorist activity against both Indian and US/Western targets, both in the region and in the home countries.*

An Islamic, nuclear-armed, Pakistan would almost certainly upset the nuclear deterrent relationship between Pakistan and India, in the sense that both sets of current decision-makers are rational, the mutual deterrence is credible and both sides perceive this to be the case. Because its policies and foreign policy in particular would result from an extremist interpretation of Islam, Pakistan could not then be perceived as a rational actor in control of its nuclear weapons. If used, these weapons would most likely be directed against either India or concentrations of US forces in the region. Other targets would be a possibility if an Islamic Pakistani government's aim were to create wider conflagration and instability. Under such a scenario, operations to destroy Pakistan's nuclear weapons could be conducted by a number of actors, including India, the US, Russia, China or Israel.

Sino–Indian war as a result of Indo–Pakistani war

Assessed likelihood of occurrence: possible, giving a Threat Level of 3.

The People's Republic of China (PRC) is put in a difficult position by the current situation in Afghanistan and Pakistan. Ostensibly, the US operations against global terrorism serve the interests of the People's Republic, as it has its own large restive Muslim population, which has seen irredentism, sabotage and bombings within China. It could be argued that China, Russia and the US constitute an 'Unholy Alliance' of sorts against radical Islam.

But the PRC is deeply aware of the dangers of US failure in Afghanistan. The Soviets' inability to pacify the country (the Mujaheddin were also supported by China) led, in China's view, not only to the collapse of the Soviet Union but also to the rise of Islamic states in Central Asia that directly challenge Chinese interests. Conflict in Afghanistan could unleash forces that create a dangerous ripple effect in Xingjiang and other Chinese provinces with large Muslim populations. Chinese concerns lie with two of the possible scenarios put forward in the preceding section on Pakistan, India and Kashmir.

China supported Pakistan in its 1965 and 1971 wars with India, both diplomatically and with considerable economic and military assistance. Pakistan is an essential counter-weight to India and friendly relations and military co-operation between China and Pakistan are an important part of PRC foreign policy. China has been helpful in developing Pakistani ballistic missiles and, allegedly, its nuclear programme.

At the same time, the PRC has considered recurring Sino-Indian border clashes as a threat to its security. Negotiations since the Sino-Indian border war in 1962 have failed to resolve the conflicting claims and each side continues to improve military and logistic capabilities in the disputed regions. China has continued occupation of the Aksai Chin area, through which it has built a strategic highway linking Xizang and Xingjiang autonomous regions. China has a vital interest in maintaining control over this region. India's primary interest is in Arunchal Pradesh, its north-eastern state bordering Xizang Autonomous Region. After a brief border clash in 1986, tensions have remained.

Assessment: *the mountainous terrain, high altitude and difficult logistical support situation make it unlikely that a protracted or large-scale conflict would erupt along the Sino-Indian border during periods of low tension. However, in the event that a crisis over Kashmir led to a large-scale Indo-Pakistani war, there is no guarantee that the PRC would not pressure India along the Sino-Indian border, either by massing forces or by overt military action against Indian forces. Overt use of force would become increasingly likely if Pakistan was perceived to be losing to India or was close to collapse, because such an outcome would directly threaten vital PRC interests – although it could be argued that China and India would then have mutual interests.*

If there were problems in the PRC leadership or widespread social and political unrest in the country, an external conflict would also be a useful way to marshal national support behind the Chinese Communist Party.

If the current Pakistani government were to fall to an Islamic regime and the US alone, or in concert with India, were to intervene in domestic Pakistani power struggles, Chinese interests would be threatened both by the possible emergence of an Islamic Pakistan armed with nuclear weapons (and possibly supportive of Muslim separatist aspirations in China) as well as by the loss of a major ally and India's relative increase in regional power and dominance.

Assessment: *in this situation, China could well use military force to protect its interests, both with regard to an Islamic Pakistan and India, dependent upon the situation. The most likely course, however, would be Chinese support for a regime of any hue in Islamabad, so long as it was pro-Chinese. We must not, however, forget China's inherent dislike of Islamic fundamentalism.*

A widened Sino–Indian war

Assessed likelihood of occurrence: possible, giving a Threat Level of 3.

Developing Indian ties with traditional Chinese enemies, Vietnam and Japan, further complicates the Sino–Indian strategic relationship. In recent years, the Indians and Vietnamese have signed agreements on sharing military intelligence, a military exchange programme, naval co-operation and mutual conventional military support in the event that either is threatened directly by the PRC. Vietnam and China still have territorial disputes over the Spratley Islands, over which they fought naval engagements in the early 1970s. They also fought a bloody border war in 1979 and, by proxy, in Cambodia. The US and the Philippines have historical and current interests in South China Sea and Spratley Islands – Taiwan even fears a Chinese invasion.

Assessment: *a Sino-Indian border war would have a direct impact on confidence in the region, especially if the conflict widened in scope to encompass naval operations in the South China Sea and the strategically important Straits of Malacca. In the event of the PRC directly threatening India with force concentrations along the common border, or overt use of force, mobilization could be expected along the Vietnamese side of the Sino-Vietnamese border in support of India. Sino-*

Vietnamese tensions and/or conflict could then ensue. In such an eventuality, an Indian carrier battle group could be expected to operate from a forward base on the Vietnamese coast. There would be the possibility of naval engagements between PRC and Vietnamese and Indian forces, possibly supported by other ASEAN states (Thailand, Singapore, Malaysia and the Philippines), which view China with suspicion. As well as disruption to shipping in the South China Sea, there would be a threat to vessels in the Straits of Malacca and in the Indian Ocean, where PRC fast-attack boats based in Myanmar would aim to intercept Indian shipping in the Bay of Bengal.

There is evidence of an evolving Japanese strategic relationship with India. China also has a maritime dispute with Japan, as well as a long history of occupation and conflict.

Assessment: *in the event of Sino-Indian hostilities widening in scope beyond the Sino-Indian border, once could expect to see Japanese naval forces deployed to protect the strategic shipping lanes in the region, in concert with either the Indians or the US, or both, depending upon the situation and the perceived threat. This could raise the prospects of a conflict in the region or bring a measure of confidence to a crisis situation. If a protracted Sino-Indian war broke out and began to suck in other states in the region, Japan could be expected to fill a regional power role, especially with the US heavily engaged elsewhere. All Asian states with memories of Japan's wartime atrocities would feel threatened by this perceived Japanese re-militarization. Japan could also rapidly develop ballistic missiles and nuclear weapons for protection. This could cause fear, tension and instability throughout the region for decades to come.*

Russia maintains a naval base in Vietnam and has strategic interests in Asia Pacific, best served by stability in the region. The Soviet Union and then Russia have traditionally supported both India and Vietnam against China. In 1979, during the Sino-Vietnamese border war, the Soviet Union staged amphibious landings in Vietnam as a warning to China. Russia sees the PRC as a direct threat because of its regional and world power aspirations.

Russia would keep out of any conflict in the region unless its direct interests were threatened. Russia would be likely to attempt to mediate any potential Sino-Indian or Sino-Vietnamese conflict before it got out of hand.

There is a question as to how much leverage the US has with India now that it is overtly supporting Pakistan as it did during the Cold War, while non-aligned India was supported by the Soviet Union. The Clinton, and now

George W Bush, administrations' courting of India was partly because India is a natural PRC rival, and partly because the US feared a tripartite relationship between the PRC, Russia and India to challenge US dominance in Asia.

The US and India had a long way to go to become strategic partners even before the current crisis and American reorientation towards Pakistan. India's military have long distrusted the US, as do most Indian opposition parties, including the Congress Party and the Communists. The increasingly blue water capabilities of the Indian navy are another source of contention in the shipping lanes dominated by the US. Any meaningful US–Indian cooperation will depend upon how the crisis in Afghanistan develops, and whether Pakistan undergoes the type of turmoil mentioned above. We can expect the US to follow up strongly with the Indian government through Defence Secretary Donald Rumsfeld to mend fences and strengthen the US/India alliance.

Assessment: the United States would be hard pressed to react to a widened Sino-Indian war and instability in South-East Asia and the South China Sea with so many assets tied up in the Middle East and Arabian seas. It would therefore rely on regional allies such as Japan to help maintain stability in the region but, as noted above, this would present problems of its own.

The economic consequences of a wider Sino-Indian war and instability in South-East and East Asia are not hard to grasp. With a US economy already facing recessionary forces and Japan facing a continued crisis in its banking system, potentially catastrophic results could ensue from disruption to shipping lanes and a normal trading environment. The region and the global economy would take years to recover, assuming tensions were reduced.

A new Taiwan crisis

Assessed likelihood of occurrence: very high, giving a Threat Level of 5.

Since its first months in office, the George W Bush administration focused on China as the biggest threat to US interests. Last year, China staged the largest war games in the Taiwan Straits for half a decade. They were larger than in 1996 and 1998, when the US sent carrier battle groups to warn China, and larger than May 2000 during Taiwan's presidential inauguration.

Last year also saw the Chinese downing of an American surveillance aircraft, the US pressing ahead with National Missile Defence (which potentially threatens China's limited nuclear forces), the prospect of Theatre Missile Defence (TMD), Washington's approval of an unusually large arms sale to Taiwan and a strong reaffirmation of US commitment to Taiwanese security. These incidents are all symptomatic of an already existing crisis underlying Sino-US relations. Tensions also exist over human rights and market access for US companies under Chinese accession to WTO, and both states are natural rivals for economic, political and strategic influence in the Pacific region.

Before the present crisis broke, Defence Secretary Rumsfeld issued a review of US military strategy, which concluded that the Pacific basin was the primary area of US concern and that the US should re-orientate its forces away from Europe towards the Pacific and East Asia. This was based on the premise that China was becoming increasingly aggressive. Following the aircraft incident, both sought to defuse tensions, if only because Russia was seen to be exploiting the situation.

Assessment: *any US redefinition of China as a regional partner rather than rival is likely to be temporary, as there are simply too many issues of contention in the relationship under the PRC's current mode of government. Sooner or later, another major (PRC manufactured) crisis is likely to erupt to overcome any areas of mutual concern and this crisis is most likely to be over Taiwan.*

Ostensibly, the current crisis over terrorism creates an opportunity to refocus Sino-US relations away from mutual antagonisms and towards Islamic extremism, a threat to US interests and to the PRC's internal stability. The current crisis and refocused relationship give China time to bolster its economic, political and social stability. Some observers argue that, having recently gained entry to WTO and won the right to host the 2008 Olympics, China is seeking to expand its influence in the Asia Pacific region and the world through economics and culture rather than by force and will attempt to undermine any notion that China is a threat.

China has significantly toned down condemnation of the US and even offered tacit support. This sits in stark contrast to condemnation of the US bombing campaign in Kosovo, especially after the PRC embassy in Belgrade was targeted (deliberately or otherwise).

Assessment: *the US has an interest in a stable China because of mutual and regional economic interdependence. US companies are heavily leveraged in China and any social and political unrest in China would be the final nail in Japan's financial coffin. Any Japanese collapse could bring down the global banking system with it.*

The US views relations with the PRC as fundamentally secure and so periodic crises and tit-for-tat brinkmanship will blow over and the relationship will remain intact. Underpinning this view is the belief that China is too economically interdependent (and dependent) upon the US and too militarily weak to take confrontations with the US beyond a war of words. While this view has been fairly accurate for years, it fails to account for pressures mounting in Beijing that could alter the equation completely. Within the Chinese government, a debate that has been going on for centuries is raging. China's leadership is split over whether the economic benefits of contact and global integration are worth the potential social and political consequences of that integration.

On one side of the debate are those arguing that China must choose between national unity and stability or the inevitable political fragmentation that will come with reform. These hard-liners cite a pattern played out in Chinese history where central authority and national unity are undercut when the country engages in economic contact with the West. While economic prosperity continues to grow in coastal China due to increased trade with the outside, the interior lags behind. This creates regional disparities, raising tensions between the interior and the periphery and weakening the centre.

These concerns are played out today, as demonstrations and protests are growing, fuelled by the unemployed and unpaid victims of Beijing's economic reforms and the privatization and collapse of state-owned enterprises (SOEs). Allowing SOEs to fail, as they must inevitably do under WTO competition, will result in increased unemployment (already around 20 per cent). The World Bank recently estimated that around 70 million workers could lose their jobs, thus contributing to internal security problems. This comes alongside Muslim irredentism and the Falun Gong.

Social and political unrest threatens the very survival of the regime. The Chinese reform process is similar to that which occurred in Eastern Europe and the Former Soviet Union, leading to those regimes' collapse and which were watched with dismay by the Chinese leadership. There must, there-fore, be outlets for popular anger; otherwise the pressure cooker economy could blow up in the faces of the Chinese leadership. The spread of the Internet and concepts of liberalism and free choice mean that the Chinese Communist Party (CCP) may not be able to keep the genie of political change in the bottle for ever as they tried to do at Tiananmen Square.

The Chinese leadership faces a dichotomy, pursuing economic integra-tion and the growth that brings the trade, capital and technology to support the needs and aspirations of 1.2 billion people, and which Western states hope will pull China away from central planning and political oppression. At the same time, allowing the very process of change threatens the viabil-ity and legitimacy of the Party. Either way, it has to deliver benefits for the people unless it is to maintain power through force indefinitely, which may be difficult to achieve. The lack of a clear-cut strategy for reform is, to borrow a Chinese proverb, *like crossing a river by feeling for the stones*. Using this analogy, however, it should be noted that China is prone to flooding.

These concerns are exacerbated by Chinese fears that Washington is using the economic opening presented by WTO to undermine the government and the CCP. Since the time of Mao, China has harboured suspicions that US economic and political contact with China was part of a plan to foster a gradual peaceful evolution away from the communist system. This belief has been strengthened by Beijing's view that Washington deliberately exploited the economic policies of former Soviet leader Gorbachev to bring about the disintegration of the Soviet Union.

With most of China's leadership in agreement about the dangers facing the system and the potential for Washington to exploit them, there is an emerging convergence of views among moderates and hard-liners that Beijing must regain control of China's internal fragmentation and that Beijing must engender more respect from Washington.

Assessment: *Beijing will need more showdowns with the US to re-centre US views on China and to gain internal unity by stirring up Chinese nationalism. Manufacturing a crisis is a classic Chinese tactic and Beijing will continue to use demonstrations of force to strengthen its hold on power.*

The US surveillance aircraft incident was easily exploited by China for the above reasons with minimal response from Washington. The minority hard-line faction in Beijing views this confrontation as the first step in the inevitable degradation of relations with the US. They are confident that, as relations continue to decline, their position will be vindicated. As Washington continues to operate under the belief that relations are ultimately stable, and so continues to use brinkmanship with China, so the hard-line position in Beijing may gain ground.

Assessment: *ultimately, the internal factors underlying China's decision-making process will become increasingly focused on internal stability and security, and Beijing's possible range of actions could move into uncharted territory. The result will be increasing military confrontations with the US and Taiwan. As the US has made Chinese containment one of its most important foreign policy goals, this could see the Chinese risking military confrontation with US forces in the Taiwan Straits.*

In past demonstrations of Chinese force over Taiwan, there were no major deployments of US forces to cover other major crises as there are now. The danger with the current crisis is that, with US attention centred on Afghanistan and the Middle East, China has both motive and opportunity to seek a confrontation with Taiwan. If the Afghan crisis continues and, perhaps, extends to other areas as described in these scenarios, there will be ample opportunity for China to exploit the situation to its advantage. But a future confrontation with Taiwan could involve overt use of force rather than threats. It would not be hard for China to justify force over, for example, alleged US plans for inclusion of Taiwan in Theatre Missile Defence.

The Chinese military simply do not have the capability to stage amphibious and/or airborne landings on Taiwan with the objective of capturing the island. They would find it almost impossible to achieve air parity, let alone air superiority even in the absence of US forces coming quickly to Taiwan's aid. The PRC does, however, have the ability to intercept shipping and severely degrade Taiwan's infrastructure with surface-to-surface missiles.

Assessment: *if the PRC were to use force against Taiwan, this would have a considerable effect on the region, with shipping endangered, and loss of confidence in Taiwan and China — the former a major actor in the regional and global economy, and the latter increasingly so. There is also the possibility that PRC forces could come into contact with US and/or Japanese forces as a direct result of hostilities. South Korean interests would be directly threatened, as would those of the ASEAN states. A major regional and global economic crisis would ensue directly as a result of conflict and it could take years to restore confidence in the region and promote economic recovery.*

A Korean crisis

Assessed likelihood of occurrence: possible, giving a Threat Level of 3.

The threat of a North Korean (DPRK) invasion of South Korea seems to have waned in recent years, although the spectre of an attack as part of a last ditch attempt by the North's leadership to remain in power has remained. The new US administration has taken a much harder line on Pyongyang, while expressing concerns that Seoul and the Clinton administration were moving much too fast in engaging the North.

The CIA has publicly stated that they believe the North to have *a few nuclear weapons* – and observers have pointed to the build-up and improvement in North Korean weapon systems near the Demilitarized Zone (DMZ) and in range of Seoul. There is no doubt that the US has put Korea on the backburner for now and that the inter-Korean momentum towards reconciliation of the past 18 months has stalled.

The fact remains that the DPRK is a heavily-armed Stalinist state with an ageing but numerous military, two thirds of which are directly across the DMZ from South Korean and US forces. In recent years, the North has suffered incredible hardship because of its leadership's flawed economic policies and failure to modernize, resulting in reports of cannibalism.

The DPRK also remains wary of opening up to the world for similar reasons to the Chinese, although China is obviously very much further along this road. There are those in the leadership who are desperately opposed to the *sunshine* policy of reconciliation with South Korea, fearing absorption by the prosperous South. From their point of view, the policy of contact – economic, social and political – is a plot to bring about the downfall of the DPRK hatched by Seoul and Washington. DPRK hardliners may also fear that, once the US is finished with Afghanistan and the Middle East, it may divert its newfound sense of purpose and willingness to take military casualties elsewhere, including the Korean peninsula.

Assessment: *there are clearly elements in the DPRK leadership who would favour war as a means of avoiding the fall of the regime and who are prepared to risk all to prevent this. Like China, with US attention elsewhere, the DPRK has both motive and opportunity for such a move but conflict on the Korean peninsula remains an outside possibility. Nevertheless, it should be factored into decision-making because, if* *it occurred, the ripple effects would engulf the region much as in the preceding scenario and have severe consequences for the world economy. Widespread chaos and economic dislocation could ensue and it would take years to restore confidence and prosperity.*

Islamic revolution in Indonesia

Assessed likelihood of occurrence: low, giving a Threat Level of 2.

Alarmist reports have appeared recently in the international press about Osama bin Laden's terrorist network in Indonesia. It is likely that Al Qaida has secretly recruited some radical Islamic individuals and probable that some radical Indonesian Islamic groups have received funding from Al Qaida. However, evidence is lacking to suggest that such links have decisively influenced their behaviour.

There is speculation that bin Laden's agents may have helped to organize anti-American demonstrations after the US attack on Afghanistan began, but it is hard to believe that Indonesia's radical Muslims needed outside assistance for this or, indeed, to target McDonalds as a suitable target. The capacity of Indonesia's two largest radical Islamic organizations to sweep Americans out of the country is very limited and the activities of these groups are not of the type to suggest that they have fallen under the control of a sophisticated international network like bin Laden's.

Indonesia's radical Muslim population represents only a tiny proportion of the total population of 210 million (Indonesia is the world's most populous Muslim state). Nevertheless, the outrage expressed by the radicals against the US is widely shared by the moderate Muslim majority. This has created a dichotomy for the government of President Megawatti Sukarnoputri. It has pledged to support international action against terrorism but does not want to be seen to be supporting a US attack on a Muslim country with attendant civilian casualties.

The recent demonstrations in the country have rarely involved more than a thousand people and are not, in themselves, a serious threat to the government. But, in the context of Indonesia's democratic transformation being accompanied by a crisis of lawlessness, it is quite possible that anti-foreign sentiment could prejudice prospects of economic recovery. Little could do more harm to the government's efforts to persuade investors to return than attacks on Western property or isolated physical assaults on Westerners.

Several recent bombings, including the September 2000 attack on the Jakarta stock exchange and World Bank offices, were directly attributable to Achenese separatists. One other bombing aimed at the Philippine embassy was most likely the work of Philippine Muslim extremists. No other outside involvement is suspected.

Assessment: *radical Islam in Indonesia is still quite weak and its purported goal of turning Indonesia into an Islamic state is yet to be achieved. Even in the worst-case scenario, there is no likelihood that the present crisis will result in the emergence of a radical Islamic regime in Jakarta. What is more likely is the continued ungovern-ability of many regions, leading to possible disintegration of the Indonesian state in the medium to long term.*

19
The lesser risks – country by country

Asia and the Far East

China

China has a low crime rate but crime is increasing in the major cities. Theft is the most common crime, occurring mostly in crowded public areas, such as hotel lobbies, bars, restaurants and transportation areas. Care should be taken around street markets and at expatriate bar areas. Robbery with knives is common. Avoid large crowds and demonstrations.

Petty crimes and sexual harassment can occur on overnight buses and trains. Beware of smuggling if crossing Chinese borders by bus or train. Keep your baggage with you where possible. On a train, search your compartment before securing the door.

Bombings have occurred on a small scale in recent years, mostly in parts of China inhabited by ethnic minorities. Such activity has not, so far, been directed against foreign visitors but buses and bus stations have been targeted.

The Hong Kong Special Administrative Region has a low crime rate. Petty crime, however, is common and occurs mainly at the airport and in tourist areas. Do not leave personal belongings unattended.

Typhoons are common along the southern and eastern coasts. Flooding is common in central and southern China. The monsoon season occurs from July to October. Severe rainstorms can cause flooding and reduce the provision of essential services. Inclement weather can seriously disrupt travel plans. Visitors should keep themselves informed of weather forecasts when visiting countries in affected regions.

If a passport (together with Chinese visas) is stolen, visitors must immediately obtain a police report regarding the theft. It usually takes at least two working days to obtain a new passport and Chinese exit visa (contact your Consulate for both documents). Valid visas are required to exit China and to travel and register in hotels within China.

The Public Security Bureau (police) rigorously enforces visa validity and residency registration requirements for foreigners. There have been raids and spot-checks of residential areas in Beijing. Violating local regulations can result in fines and/or detention. Ensure that your documentation is kept up to date at all times.

Foreign businesspersons have been detained and their passports confiscated as a result of business disputes with Chinese counterparts. Seek legal advice from professionals in China – as well as at home – before proceeding with business agreements. Ensure that all documents are translated and all conditions, terms and limitations understood. Disputes are costly and prolonged.

India

In popular tourist areas, do not walk in isolated spots on your own, especially after dark. Visitors should respect local codes of dress and behaviour. Theft of valuables – especially passports – is a particular risk at major railway stations and on trains. Visitors should not travel alone in India.

Be careful when travelling anywhere in India, especially in crowded areas and where demonstrations may occur. Political rallies and demonstrations have the potential for violence, especially before and after elections. Particular care should be taken in the vicinity of religious sites and national monuments.

Major civil disturbances pose risks to personal safety and can disrupt transportation systems and city services. Indian authorities may occasionally impose curfews and/or restrict travel. There is a potential for religious and inter-caste violence. Mobs have attacked Christian workers, including foreigners.

Driving on Indian roads can be hazardous, particularly at night and in rural areas. Inadequately lit buses and lorries, poor driving and badly maintained vehicles are all hazards.

Foreigners should avoid Jammu and Kashmir, including Ladakh and Leh and parts of Assam, Manipur, Nagaland, Tripura, Mizoram and Meghalaya, as well as areas along the Indo-Pakistani border. Political violence is common. Bombs have exploded in public places in these areas, including on public transportation. Several foreigners have been kidnapped and killed by militants in Jammu and Kashmir in recent years. The security situation has improved in the Punjab, but visitors should exercise caution at all times.

Indonesia

Indonesia is going through a period of extreme insecurity and visitors should exercise maximum caution. It is inadvisable to travel to some areas.

Jakarta

Jakarta is in a state of unrest and liable to frequent demonstrations which can turn violent. Visitors should monitor the media (eg BBC World Service), carry mobile phones and avoid large crowds. Make a note of embassy/police contact numbers.

If trouble begins, stay indoors. If you get caught in a demonstration, remain calm. Go with the flow. Maintain a friendly attitude and do not respond to provocation. Try to get to a 'safe' place, eg police station/hotel.

There has been a rise in crime. Take special care at banks and cash machines. Beware of pickpockets in crowded areas.

Bengkulu, Southern Sumatra
A strong earthquake hit Bengkulu and Lampung provinces on 4 June 2000, extensively damaging local infrastructure. There have been several after-shocks. Visitors are advised to avoid the area.

Maluku Province
Travel to Maluku Province is inadvisable. Violence between Christians and Moslems makes the situation dangerous.

Central Sulawesi
Christian/Muslim violence has occurred in Poso and Central Sulawesi. An earthquake causing damage to infrastructure recently hit the area of Kabupaten Benggai. Travel in this area should be avoided.

Aceh
Non-essential travel in Aceh should be avoided due to the poor security situation.

West Timor
Foreigners have experienced violence and threats. Avoid non-essential travel.

Bali and Lombok
Bali and Lombok are currently calm. Tourist/visitor services are operating normally.

East Kalimantan
There has been hostility to foreigners. Non-essential travel should be avoided.

Irian Jaya
Caution should be exercised as an independence movement is active. Unrestricted burning in northern Sumatra and in west and central Kalimantan periodically causes unhealthy levels of atmospheric pollution. There is a potential for health-threatening haze to develop, particularly during the dry season.

The Philippines

Following the kidnapping in Spring 2000 of foreigners on the Malaysian island of Sipadan, there is potential for similar action throughout the rest of the Philippines.

There were fatal bombings in Manila in May 2000 and a device exploded at Manila International Airport on 4 June. These bombs were not aimed at foreign nationals but were indiscriminate.

Travel to Mindanao, where armed Islamic groups and other bandits are active, is inadvisable. There have recently been bomb attacks in several cities across Mindanao. In April 2000, 21 people, including foreign tourists, were kidnapped from a resort in Sabah, Malaysia, and taken to Jolo Island where they were held for ransom.

There have been bombings in public places and foreigners have been targeted by kidnap-for-ransom gangs in southern Zamboanga peninsula, (provinces of Zamboanga del Norte, Zamboanga del Sur and Zamboanga City) and islands south west of Mindanao (the provinces of Basilan, Sulu and Tawi Tawi).

Non-essential travel is inadvisable in the other Mindanao provinces of Maguidanao, Lanao del Sur, Lanao del Norte, Sultan Kudaraat and North and South Cotabato. The army has been conducting operations against insurgents in these areas.

Visitors elsewhere in the south Philippines should take all security precautions possible. There have been bus hijackings on principal highways. It is advisable to stay on national highways and paved roads and avoid night travel outside urban and tourist areas. Visitors have been robbed by strangers who have offered drugged food and/or drinks.

The typhoon season occurs between July and December. Earthquakes and volcanic eruptions can occur at any time. Visitors to the region should keep themselves informed of regional weather forecasts and plan accordingly.

South Korea

The crime rate in the Republic of Korea is low but, in city areas such as Seoul and Pusan, there is greater risk of pickpocketing, purse snatching, hotel burglaries and residential crime. Foreigners should take precautions against petty crime, especially in urban areas.

Women should exercise extreme caution when travelling alone in taxis, especially at night. There have been reported incidents involving unwanted attention by taxi drivers towards unaccompanied foreign females. There have also been occasional reports of rape of foreigners.

Korea has one of the highest rates of road traffic deaths in the world. The driver of the car is presumed to be at fault in all accidents involving motor-cycles or pedestrians. Criminal charges and heavy penalties are commonly laid when accidents result in injury, even if guilt is not proven.

The monsoon occurs from the end of June and lasts until August with July usually being the wettest month. Severe rainstorms can cause flooding and reduce the provision of essential services. Inclement weather can seriously disrupt travel plans.

Taiwan

Although there was an increase in the crime rate in 1999–2000, the overall crime rate in Taiwan remains relatively low. Residential burglaries and thefts are the most common crimes affecting foreigners in Taiwan but other more serious crimes do occasionally occur.

Visitors to Taiwan should follow the basic security precautions that would apply in any large city. Female visitors should exercise caution when travelling alone in taxis, especially at night. There have been incidents involving violence against unaccompanied female taxi passengers.

Thailand

Travellers arriving at Bangkok airport should only use airport limousines or licensed taxis with yellow numberplates from the official taxi rank. There is a reliable airport bus service to the centre of Bangkok.

Passport theft is common. Passports should not be given to third parties such as hotel owners, vehicle hire shops etc. Pickpocketing and petty crime are common in tourist areas. Credit card fraud has also been increasing.

Foreigners may wish to protect their credit cards and use them only in known or established businesses.

Be wary of accepting food or drink from strangers as it may be drugged. Visitors should be especially careful when visiting Bangkok's red-light district. Visitors should also be aware of gem scams.

The Thai/Burmese border remains unstable. Travellers wishing to visit remote or border areas should consult local authorities for advice on the current situation and on designated crossing points.

The monsoon season occurs from July to October. Travellers should be aware that severe rainstorms can cause flooding and reduce the provision of essential services, especially in remote locations such as islands in the south of the country. Inclement weather can seriously disrupt travel plans. Keep informed of weather forecasts.

Europe and the Former Soviet Union

Czech Republic

The Czech Republic has a low rate of violent crime but there has been a dramatic increase in street crime. Pickpocketing is extremely common at the main tourist attractions, the main railway station, on trains and on trams, particularly the No. 22 route to and from Prague Castle. Thefts from hotels have also risen.

Visitors should be alert to substantial overcharging by taxis, particularly to and from areas frequented by tourists. Reputable taxi companies should be used.

Beware of bogus plain-clothes policemen asking to see your foreign currency and passport. If approached, decline to show your money but offer to go with them to the nearest police station.

Carry ID at all times and keep a photocopy of your passport.

Hungary

Visitors are advised to take sensible precautions against bag snatching and pickpocketing, which are common in Budapest in particular. Street crime, which occasionally involves violence, has increased, especially at night near major hotels and restaurants and on public transportation.

Theft of passports, currency and credit cards is a frequent problem, especially in youth hostels, at train stations and on public transport. Leave valuables in a hotel safe. Do not carry large amounts of cash. Do not use street moneychangers. Criminals sometimes pose as police officers; always ask for credentials and/or insist on going to a police station.

There are occasional incidents of tourists being overcharged, sometimes accompanied by threats of violence, in certain bars and restaurants in Budapest. Visitors should remain wary of strangers inviting them to unfamiliar places and of establishments that do not properly display prices. Do not order beverages or food without first verifying the cost.

Theft of and from vehicles is common. Be vigilant against staged 'incidents', particularly on the Vienna–Budapest motorway, which are designed to stop motorists for robbery.

Poland

Crime rates in Poland vary. Foreigners have been targeted in some areas of major cities. The cities of Gdynia, Sopot, and Gdansk have seen an increase in muggings. Organized groups of thieves and pickpockets operate in train stations, at major tourist destinations and on trains, trams, and buses in major cities. There is a serious risk of robbery at main rail stations and on all train services.

Thefts have occurred on overnight trains, including thefts from passengers in closed compartments. Keep valuables out of sight. Do not leave the compartment unattended. Most pickpocketing on trains occurs when boarding.

Be vigilant for thieves in busy streets, tourist sites, areas near main hotels, money exchange facilities and trams.

Car theft, car-jacking and theft from cars are common. Drivers should be wary of people indicating that they should pull over or that something is wrong with their vehicle. Beware of cars following in such instances. Cases of vehicles with foreign number plates being stopped by gangs posing as policemen are increasing, especially in rural areas. Driving on Polish roads can be hazardous due to poor conditions. Driving long distances at night out of the main centres is not recommended.

There have been reported cases of racially motivated assaults against foreigners. Poland is a highly racist and anti-Semitic country.

Russia

Because of the security situation, it is inadvisable to travel to the Chechen Republic, Ingushetia, Dagestan, North Ossetia, Kabardino-Balkaria and to eastern and southern parts of Stavropol Krai. There is a terrorist threat in these areas and kidnapping for financial gain is commonplace. The safety of foreigners in these areas cannot be effectively guaranteed. There is also a terrorist threat against the Black Sea resort of Sochi.

Over the past few years, there have been unexplained acts of terrorism, including bombings, in large Russian cities. These bombings have occurred at Russian government buildings, hotels, tourist sites, residential complexes and on public transport. While foreigners have not been singled out for attack, visitors should be alert for unusual behaviour, unattended luggage in public areas and anything out of the ordinary.

Crime against foreigners is a problem, especially in major cities. Pickpocketing, assaults and robberies occur frequently and at any time or place. The most dangerous areas include underground walkways and the subway, overnight trains, train stations, airports, markets, tourist attractions, restaurants, hotel rooms and residences, even when locked or occupied. Be wary in Moscow of women and children who beg and pick pockets around the main railway stations. Groups of children are known to have assaulted and robbed foreigners.

Foreigners who have been drinking alcohol are especially vulnerable to assault and robbery in or near nightclubs and bars or on their way home. Do not drink with casual acquaintances and do not leave drinks unattended in bars/restaurants, as they may be drugged.

There has been an increase in harassment and attacks on foreigners of Asian and African descent by groups of skinheads, individuals and, in a few cases, by local police.

Demonstrations are not uncommon. While they are generally peaceful and controlled, it is best to avoid such gatherings.

Extortion and corruption are common in the business environment. Organized criminal groups target foreign businesses across Russia and have been known to demand protection money under threat of violence. Small businesses are particularly vulnerable. Since the mid-1990s, half a dozen foreign business people have been attacked, kidnapped and even killed.

International aircraft maintenance procedures on some internal flights are sketchy. Where possible, fly directly to your destination on a scheduled international flight.

All foreign visitors should register with their embassies/consulates.

The Middle East

Algeria

Travel to Algeria is inadvisable. Since the beginning of 2000, over 700 deaths have been reported across the country. Over 120 foreigners have been kidnapped and murdered in Algeria since the ultimatum issued by the Armed Islamic Group (GIA) in November 1993, urging foreigners to leave or be killed. The security situation generally worsens during the Muslim holy month of Ramadan.

Visitors should limit their stay to a few days to avoid possible detection and action by terrorists. Visitors should ensure that they seek an appropriate security briefing before their arrival and remain vigilant at all times. Travellers should remain discreet when engaging in telephone conversations and refrain from disclosing information about their travel plans.

Remember, foreigners stand out. Those staying in the country longer should continuously reassess the security situation and avoid routine predictable behaviour.

Travellers should dress conservatively and respect religious and social traditions.

Algiers airport is a potential terrorist target. Visitors should not travel between the airport and the city centre in any form of public transportation, including taxis, especially late at night. Visitors should arrange to be met and accompanied by armed guards upon arrival at and departure from the airport as well as while travelling around the city centre.

In Algiers, visitors should stay in one of the hotels that take security precautions: Sheraton, Sofitel, El-Djazir, International and El-Aurassi. On arrival, visitors should familiarize themselves with hotel security measures and retain their hotel key at all times.

Local security advice should be taken before going to any part of Algiers and secure transport should be used. The Casbah and the western and southern suburbs should be avoided.

Crime is an increasing problem. Armed men pose as police officers, entering homes and robbing them. Armed car-jackings also occur. Pickpocketing and purse snatching are common, as is theft of personal belongings left in hotel rooms and on public transportation. Avoid displays of wealth.

Political demonstrations can turn violent. Avoid them.

Outside Algiers, the situation in the sparsely populated, mountainous coastal areas encircling the capital is dangerous. Bandits, criminals and terrorist groups operate in these areas. Road conditions are poor, and signposting is rare. Travel in these areas should only be undertaken with a full security escort provided by relevant government authorities to fully-protected workplaces.

Outside the mountainous areas around Algiers, the security situation varies considerably. Terrorist groups (in uniform) often put up false roadblocks on major highways and minor roads in order to rob and kill. Along the coast, trains have been frequent targets of terrorist activity.

In the Sahara, there has been bandit/terrorist activity in the northern parts of the desert and along the border with Mali, including the killing of foreigners. The extreme climate and the lack of water and infrastructure mean that travel in this region must be carefully evaluated.

In all of the above situations, visitors should bear in mind that armed protection and other security measures will not guarantee their safety. All foreigners are still vulnerable to random acts of violence.

Algeria is located in an active seismic region. In the event of an earthquake, visitors should contact their families/friends and company/government contacts to update them on their situation. International communications may not be working. Satellite phones may be required for use in an emergency.

Egypt

Visitors to Egypt should monitor developments in the Middle East and Egypt itself as any increase in regional tension will affect the risk level to travellers.

Visitors should dress modestly and respect local customs and sensitivities.

Since 1992, Islamic extremists have been seeking to undermine the Egyptian government through a campaign of violence occasionally involving foreign tourists. Most of the violence has occurred in the Nile Valley provinces of Minya, Assiut, Sohag and Qena, but there have been sporadic attacks in other areas. On November 17, 1997, fifty-eight foreign tourists were killed and many others injured in an attack by Islamic militants in Luxor. The Egyptian authorities have upgraded security measures, particularly at tourist sites. However, the potential for further violence exists.

Such violence is more likely in the Upper Egypt region as this is where most Islamic extremist groups are located. Visitors should be aware that tourist buses have been a particular target. Taxis or rental cars are an alternative and safer form of transportation. Security has increased significantly throughout Egypt, particularly at airports, international hotels, banks and diplomatic missions.

Travel between Cairo and Luxor should be by air only, as there have been tourist attacks on trains and boats. Travel between Luxor and Aswan by boat is safe. Travel to Minya, Assiut and certain other areas in the Upper Nile region should be avoided. Egyptian Police may insist on escorting travellers in some areas.

Those wishing to visit areas near Egypt's frontiers, including oases near the border with Libya and off-road areas in the Sinai, must obtain permission from the Travel Permits Department of the Ministry of the Interior.

Travellers should be aware of the possible dangers of off-road travel. There is a small risk from unexploded mines in some desert and coastal areas. Visitors should exercise caution and follow local advice, especially if travelling off road. As a rule, all travellers should check with local authorities before embarking on off-road travel. Because known minefields are not marked by signs but are usually enclosed by barbed wire, travellers should avoid areas enclosed by barbed wire.

Local driving conditions and poor vehicle maintenance make road travel outside the main cities hazardous, especially at night because vehicles often travel without lights. Due to numerous serious road accidents, it is recommended that foreigners ensure that any hire vehicles used are provided by reputable travel agencies and that the vehicles are in a serviceable condition. Inspect essentials such as fuel, oil, water etc, especially for long road trips.

Medical facilities are adequate for non-emergency matters, particularly in areas that most foreigners visit. Emergency and intensive care facilities are limited, especially outside Cairo. Hospital facilities in Luxor and Aswan are inadequate and are non–existent at most other destinations.

Serious medical problems requiring hospitalization and/or medical evacuation home can cost thousands of dollars. Doctors and hospitals often expect immediate cash payment for health services.

Beaches on the Mediterranean and Red Sea coasts are generally unpolluted. There is a risk of exposure to hepatitis and to the parasite Bilharzia when swimming in the Nile or canals, walking barefoot along the Nile River or drinking untreated river water.

Properly prepared and thoroughly cooked meat in tourist hotels, Nile cruise boats and tourist restaurants is considered safe. Eating uncooked vegetables should be avoided, as should tap water.

The crime rate in Egypt is low. While incidents of violence are rare, purse snatching, pickpocketing and petty theft are not uncommon. Unescorted women are vulnerable to sexual harassment and verbal abuse.

There are restrictions on photographing military personnel and sites, bridges and canals, including the Suez Canal.

Foreigners contemplating onward travel to Lebanon and/or Syria from Egypt should bear in mind that foreigners have been denied entry into these countries, because their passports bear: (a) an Israeli visa; (b) an Israeli border stamp; or (c) an Egyptian or Jordanian border stamp issued by an office bordering Israel (such a stamp would indicate that the traveller entered from Israel).

Iran

Visitors to Iran should monitor developments in the Middle East and Iran closely. Any increase in regional tension will affect the level of risk to the traveller.

Visitors should make sure that travel documentation is in order and check the expiry date of their visa before travelling. Overstaying a visa can result in detention.

Declare all foreign currency taken into the country on a customs declaration form or at the Bank Melli branch at Tehran (Mehrabad) Airport. Failure to do so can result in undeclared foreign currency being confiscated on departure. It is only possible to change traveller's cheques in major cities and only into Rials. Substantial service fees are charged. Visa travellers cheques (and Visa cards) do not seem to be accepted, while MasterCard travellers cheques may be. ATMs are not available. Visitors should bring sufficient hard currency (US dollars) to cover the unexpected; these should be crisp bills, as well-worn banknotes may not be accepted.

Iran is an Islamic state. Laws and customs relating to dress, behaviour and sex and the prohibition of drugs and alcohol must be respected. Women, especially, should cover their heads and follow dress and behavioural codes. Behaviour regarded as innocuous in other countries can lead to serious trouble in Iran. A German businessman was detained for over two years for having intimate relations with a Muslim woman.

Iranian security may place foreigners under surveillance. Hotel rooms, telephones and fax machines may be monitored and personal possessions in hotel rooms may be searched.

Photography of government and military installations, such as ports, airports and their surroundings, is strictly prohibited. Such areas are not always identifiable. Foreigners should refrain from taking pictures, except at recognized tourist sites. Taking photographs of anything that could be perceived as being of military or security interest may result in problems with authorities.

A number of kidnappings involving foreign tourists have occurred recently in the cities of Kerman and Bem and the Sistan-Baluchistan provinces in south-eastern Iran. Avoid travel to these areas.

Security forces and anti-government groups in Kurdish and Baluchi-majority areas periodically clash, particularly in the north-west and south-east of the country. Travel is safe in most other areas, although road and traffic conditions can create problems.

Foreigners travelling in sensitive border areas (Azerbaijan, Khuzestan, Kurdestan and Baluchistan) attract the attention of security forces. This can result in short detentions. The borders with Azerbaijan and Turkmenistan are open only to nationals of those countries.

It is probably unnecessary to say to the reader to avoid travel to Afghanistan. Increased Iranian security prevents access to areas along the Afghan border. Avoid travel to the Iraqi border.

Avoid overland trips to Pakistan. Anyone travelling this way should exercise extreme caution, travelling only on main roads in official parties. Avoid travelling at night.

Although urban crime is not a serious problem, travellers have occasionally been victims of petty theft. Travellers are advised to take normal precautions, such as keeping their valuables in a safe place.

There have recently been a number of cases in the major cities of foreigners being asked for identification by bogus policemen, who have then made off with the visitor's wallet and currency. If approached, decline to show money and documents but offer to go with them instead to the nearest police station. Keep passports separate from other valuables.

Road conditions are good in cities and the highway system is relatively developed. Local drivers routinely ignore traffic lights, traffic signs and lane markers and almost never yield to pedestrians at crosswalks. Driving is dangerous on poorly-lit city streets as some motorists drive without their headlights on. Although there are pavements/sidewalks on main roads in urban areas, they are often obstructed by cars. Sidewalks are rare in residential areas.

Four-wheel drive vehicles are particularly liable to theft.

Many visitors to Tehran have been robbed by young men in unmarked cars posing as taxi drivers. Visitors should only use taxis ordered through legitimate agencies. Tourists have also had bags/handbags snatched by young men riding on motorcycles. Visitors are advised not to carry large amounts of money (especially hard currency).

Iran is located in an active seismic region. In the event of an earthquake, visitors should contact their families/friends and company contacts, as well as local consulates/embassies, to update them on their situation. International communications may not be working.

Libya

On 5 April 1999, the UN sanctions against Libya, including severance of air links, were suspended. Some, but not all, of the airline connections to Libya in place prior to 1992 have been re-established, but the results of the ban may affect the safety and reliability of internal flights.

Visitor/tourist facilities are not widely available and there is limited hotel capacity even in the cities. Confirmed hotel reservations may not be honoured if there is a sudden need to accommodate an important official or business delegation. Westerners must have their travel arrangements and itineraries approved. Visitors must obtain their Libyan visas through approved travel agencies.

Libyan customs authorities strictly enforce regulations concerning the introduction or removal from Libya of firearms, religious materials, antiquities, medications and currency.

Visitors should adhere to Islamic practices and be sensitive to the country's customs, laws and regulations. Visitors should dress appropriately. Stern penalties are imposed for the possession/use of alcohol or drugs and for criticizing the country, its leadership or religion.

Libyan security personnel may place foreign visitors under surveillance. Hotel rooms, telephones and fax machines may be monitored and personal possessions may be searched covertly.

Do not take photographs of anything that could be perceived as being of military or security interest. It is unwise to use or carry cameras except under the supervision of official guides.

Libya's economy operates on a 'cash only' basis for most transactions; credit cards are not accepted. Hard currency cash should be declared on arrival at the airport. Libyan dinars are not convertible and cannot be imported or exported. Only purchase dinars at official exchange counters at hotels or banks in Libya. Severe penalties can be incurred for using unauthorized currency dealers. Be aware, this is a common method used by foreign intelligence services to entrap the unwary.

Crime is a growing problem in Libya. The most common types of crime are auto theft and theft of items left in vehicles. Muggings and purse-snatchings occur on beaches and in desert regions. Travel to such areas is best done in groups.

Traffic is heavy on the main east-west coastal highway, especially close to the main cities of Tripoli and Benghazi. Public transport is limited to taxis. In the desert regions to the south, it is essential to travel by a four-wheel drive vehicle and have a competent guide. Many 'roads' are just tracks.

Avoid the area east of Benghazi where violent disturbances have occurred in the past. The border with Egypt is subject to closures.

Ferry services between Valletta (Malta) and Tripoli are often over-booked.

Morocco

The political situation in Morocco is stable. Only two regions pose possible risks: (a) the desert area between Morocco and Mauritania (anti-personnel mines); and (b) the mountainous Rif region (northern coast) where narcotics are produced. The penalties for possession of drugs are severe. Visitors travelling through the Rif mountains should be aware of the drug factor.

Visitors should respect all Moroccan laws and customs regulations, especially with regard to religion.

Morocco has a moderately high crime rate in urban areas. Criminals have targeted tourists for assaults, muggings, thefts, pickpocketing and scams of all types. Commonly reported crimes include falsifying credit-card vouchers, and shipping inferior goods as a substitute for the goods purchased by the visitor. Be especially vigilant when using ATM machines.

Harassment of tourists by unemployed Moroccans posing as 'guides' is common. Only hire guides from hotels or travel agencies and ensure that they display the official badge.

All visitors should avoid streets late at night, if unaccompanied. Women should dress conservatively throughout Morocco, especially outside urban areas. Unescorted women in any area of Morocco may experience verbal abuse and/or harassment.

Beware of persons of any nationality offering food, drink or cigarettes that may be drugged.

Visitors should avoid large gatherings, not be provocative and keep a low profile. Incidents should be reported to the nearest police station.

Roads are in generally good condition, but standards may vary according to the weather and/or location. The roads in rural and mountainous areas are poorly lit and maintained. The rainy season lasts from November until February and flash flooding is frequent and sometimes severe. Advice should be sought before travelling to the mountains or any remote region of Morocco.

Traffic accidents are a significant hazard. Driving standards are poor, often resulting in serious injuries and fatalities. Driving on highways is dangerous and pedestrians often run across the road. Public buses and taxis are dangerous due to poor driving habits and buses are often overcrowded.

Be aware that criminals sometimes bump cars from behind and rob their victims when they get out of the car to inspect the damage. Moroccan police routinely stop drivers in cities and on highways. In the event of a traffic accident, the parties should not move their vehicles and must wait for the arrival of the police.

Adequate medical care in Morocco is available, although not all facilities meet high-quality standards. Specialized care may not be available. Medical facilities are adequate for non-emergency matters, particularly in the urban areas, but medical staff will most likely not speak English. Doctors and hospitals often expect immediate cash payment for health care services.

Travellers planning to drive in the mountains and other remote areas should carry a medical kit and a Moroccan phone card for emergencies. In the event of car accidents involving injuries, immediate ambulance service is unlikely.

The beaches as well as the ocean in the immediate vicinity of urban areas are polluted and considered unsafe for swimming.

Saudi Arabia

There is a terrorist threat to British/American interests in Saudi Arabia. Any increase in regional political tensions will affect the level of the threat. It is advisable to keep a low profile, reduce travel within the kingdom and vary travel routes and times.

Saudi Arabia is a Muslim country where Islamic codes of dress and behaviour are rigorously enforced. Visitors should respect them. Transgressors have been harassed and even assaulted by locals. The importation and use of narcotics, alcohol, pork products and religious books and material are forbidden. Penalties for importing drugs include the death penalty.

. It is illegal to hold two passports in Saudi Arabia. Immigration authorities will confiscate second passports.

Anyone involved in a commercial dispute with a Saudi company or individual may be prevented from leaving the country pending resolution of the dispute.

Crime is not a big problem but normal precautions should be taken.

There have been recent fatal cases of cerebral malaria; medical advice should be sought before travel.

UAE, Bahrain, Qatar and Oman

There is a terrorist threat against British interests in the UAE, Bahrain and Qatar. Individuals should maintain a high level of security awareness. Any increase in regional tension will affect the security situation.

Bahrain has experienced occasional acts of politically related arson and vandalism over the past several years. There have been demonstrations in and around the capital Manama, in which foreign-owned property has been damaged.

Visitors to Bahrain should avoid village areas, especially after dark. Taking photographs of anything that could be perceived as being of military or security interest may result in problems with authorities in Bahrain.

In the UAE, videos are subject to scrutiny and may be censored. Penalties for importing and consuming illegal drugs can include the death penalty. Visitors are warned not to consume illegal drugs before travelling to the UAE.

The possession/consumption of alcohol in the UAE can lead to arrest and imprisonment. Visitors should dress modestly, behave courteously and respect local customs and sensitivities.

Street crime is low in Oman and violent crimes are rare. Travellers to Oman should take normal precautions such as avoiding travel in deserted areas or alone after dark. Valuables and currency should not be left unsecured in hotel rooms.

Religious and social sensitivities should be observed and respected in all the above countries. Western women should, at the very least, have their elbows and knees covered in deference to local dress customs, especially outside Western expatriate compounds and facilities.

Latin America

Argentina

Violent crime is rare in Argentina's cities, but petty crime such as bag-snatching and pickpocketing on trains and in public places is common-place, especially in the suburbs of Buenos Aires Province.

Pickpockets often work in pairs and employ a variety of ruses to trick the unwary. Con men have frequently robbed tourists while an accomplice pretends to help remove ketchup or mustard that has been 'accidentally' spilt on them. Handbags are often slit in crowded places while attention is distracted.

There are frequent instances of passengers being robbed in taxicabs, as well as armed robbery at restaurants, shops and residences in the more fashionable suburbs. Caution should be exercised when travelling in the city.

Be alert at all times: passports should be left in a hotel safe/security box unless absolutely necessary and a photocopy used for identification. Avoid carrying too much cash or wearing ostentatious jewellery.

Reports of corruption in the police force are fairly common. Officials may use a foreigner's ignorance of national laws to extort money as fines for imaginary breaches of the law. If in doubt, contact your embassy.

Demonstrations and protests are not uncommon though they are usually non-violent. Nevertheless, avoid large gatherings and demonstrations.

Brazil

At the international airports in Rio de Janeiro and Sao Paulo, only use registered airport taxis. Tickets for these are purchased from taxi offices in the airport arrival halls. Beware of being distracted from property while checking in/loading and unloading and going through security checks.

Taxis and the metro are much safer than buses and trams, but it is always better to use a reputable taxi company known to hotel security.

Crime against foreigners is highest in areas surrounding hotels, bars, discos and other establishments that cater to foreigners, especially after sunset. Be aware of your surroundings and play it safe.

Avoid poorly lit and deserted areas. In both Rio and Sao Paulo, avoid the old central areas after dark. Avoid poor slum areas.

Never take valuables to the beach and remain vigilant in areas adjacent to beaches.

Drug trafficking is a growing problem with severe penalties in Brazil.

Chile

Following the return of Pinochet to Chile, British nationals should continue to keep a low profile.

Street crime is a problem in Santiago, specifically in the city centre. Special caution should be taken after dark and in quiet areas. In Santiago and other large cities, thieves are active during the rush hour and aboard crowded public transport. Crime is high at tourist locations, at Metro (subway) stations, on trains and buses and some taxis. Special care should also be taken in restaurants and outdoor cafes.

Outside Santiago, robberies and assaults occur frequently in the Vina del Mar and Valparaiso areas, which become increasingly crowded during the height of the summer season (December–February).

Between 11 and 18 September is traditionally an active period for public demonstrations. Violent political, labour or student protests can occur at other times, near government buildings in Santiago and Valparaiso or in the vicinity of major universities. Visitors should take common-sense precautions and avoid large demonstrations or protests.

There are reports that land mines pose a danger in remote sections of several national reserves and parks near northern border areas, including Lauca and Llullaillaco National Parks, Salar de Surire National Monument and Los Flamencos National Reserve. Visitors should check with park authorities before entering less-travelled areas and heed warning signs.

Chile is earthquake prone. Warning reports should be checked before travelling outside the city.

Colombia

Colombia had an estimated 23,000 homicides in 1999, maintaining its position as one of the world's most dangerous places. Non-essential travel should be avoided.

Travellers at airports should be met by company transport with a reliable and known driver. Radio-despatch taxis can be used, but all fares should be negotiated beforehand and identification badges checked. Do not hail cabs in the street and avoid buses and all forms of public transport.

In Bogotá and other cities, company transport operated by suitably trained drivers (with offensive/evasive skills) should be used. Close-quarter attacks at traffic lights and in slow traffic may necessitate use of amour-protected vehicles. Attacks will involve firearms. Street crime is endemic, especially in business districts and around major hotels, by day and night.

Medellín has the highest homicide rate of all urban areas in the region. Exercise extreme caution. Walking unescorted anywhere is dangerous by day and night. Visitors should remain in or close to hotels at night, and use only radio-despatch or taxis where company transport is unavailable. Guerrilla and paramilitary groups are active just outside the city.

Cali is equally dangerous. Armed assaults on pedestrians and vehicles are commonplace, as is petty crime, drugs-related violence and paramilitary activity (death squads). The coastal town of Barranquilla suffers from frequent violent crime.

In Cartagena, beware of fake tour guides or people offering their services as such. Extreme vigilance and security measures should be exercised in all parts of the country.

The borders with Panama and the Uraba region of Antioquia are especially high risk, as are other areas outside the government's control, such as the guerrilla-controlled zones declared in Meta and Caqueta Departments, and those parts of the country where there is extensive culti-vation of illegal crops and processing of illegal drugs.

Drugging is a common form of attack as a prelude to robbery (or worse). Victims should be taken to hospital immediately. Drugging attacks may involve liquid sprayed into the face or administered into food/drink or by cigarettes. Visitors to bars/night clubs etc should order only unopened drinks and keep a close watch on them.

For residency, apartments should be selected above the third floor, in buildings with 24-hour armed guards and in districts regularly patrolled by police/security. Residences should include extensive electronic and physical deterrents to break-in. A reinforced 'secure room' is an ideal feature of a secure residence, together with telephone and/or radio for emergency communication. Power generators are useful in a country of frequent power shortages.

Kidnapping is one of the greatest security threats in Colombia, with one of the highest kidnapping rates in the world. Foreign business people face a high risk of being kidnapped. Foreigners undertaking inter-city road travel face a high risk of being kidnapped at rebel roadblocks set up specifically for the purpose. Foreigners in rural areas are particularly vulnerable. There is virtually no place in the country that is kidnap-risk free.

Training in anti-kidnap techniques is essential for foreigners. Acquaintance with prominent Colombians is a risk in itself. Kidnap risk may be part of extortion attempts against foreign companies.

Visitors should not stray from major urban areas. Travel by air is strongly recommended to all parts of the interior.

The roads between Bogotá and Medellín and between Bogotá and Villavicencio are particularly high risk, as is the entire Magdalena Medio region (near Bucaramanga and Barrancabermeja).

Bombings do occur and are on the rise in urban centres. Favoured targets are military and police vehicles and installations, banks, gas stations and highway tollbooths throughout Colombia.

Mexico

Extreme caution should be exercised at all times while travelling throughout Mexico. Crime rates remain high in Mexico City, Tijuana, Ciudad Juarez and in many other towns. Several random shootings involving foreigners have occurred over the past few months. Other violent crimes (including armed robberies, rapes and assaults) as well as street crimes have increased dramatically.

Be careful using ATMs and use them only during the day at large protected facilities, eg inside commercial establishments. Avoid highly visible ATMs on streets where criminals can observe transactions.

Visitors should be careful when accepting food or drink from strangers, as there is a risk of drugging followed by robbery/assault. Kidnapping for profit is a growth industry in Mexico. Be vigilant at all times. Not only the wealthy are targeted. There has been an increase in attacks, rape and sexual assault against foreigners. Women should exercise caution in dealing with strangers or recent acquaintances. Visitors should not hike alone in backcountry areas nor walk alone on remote beaches, ruins or trails.

Be aware of the possibility of police harassment, abuse and extortion. Policemen have been arrested for crimes against foreigners including murder; those in uniform do not necessarily represent protection and safety.

Be careful when crossing the road. In some towns, vehicles do not obey speed limits and do not stop at traffic lights.

There have been many incidents, particularly in Mexico City, of passengers being robbed/shot/sexually assaulted/beaten and/or car-jacked by thieves working in co-operation with, or posing as, taxi drivers.

The area behind the US Embassy and the Zona Rosa, a restaurant/ shopping area near the Embassy, are frequent sites of street crime against foreigners. Avoid driving alone at night anywhere in Mexico City. Care should be taken on the Mexico City Metro where there is a high incidence of pickpocketing.

There has been guerrilla activity in the states of Chiapas, Michoacán, Guerrero and Oaxaca. Other dangerous areas include the mountain highlands north of San Cristobal de las Cases, the municipality of Ocosingo, Ciudad Juarez, Cancun and Campeche. Some locals in remote areas are openly hostile to foreigners.

Peru

Peru has some high-risk areas, including Peruvian government-designated 'emergency zones' where armed insurgency/terrorism occurs. Visitors should seek specific advice before travelling outside Lima. Visitors can find 'Tourist Police' offices in most destinations where officers speak English.

Guard against thefts of luggage and other belongings, particularly passports, at Lima's international airport. Visitors are strongly advised to carry identification with them at all times and remain vigilant.

Political demonstrations in Lima and in other major cities have occurred recently. Demonstrations can become violent. Monitor news broadcasts and avoid all large gatherings. If in doubt, consult local police or hotel staff.

Use private taxis if travelling alone within major towns and cities. Do not hail taxis on the street. Taxis should be reserved through reputable hotels or by calling reputable taxi companies.

Photography at airports, railway stations, naval bases, air bases, military installations, public water and energy plants, police stations, harbours, mines and bridges is prohibited.

Violent crime has increased in urban centres. This includes mugging and car-jackings. Violent attacks by armed gangs are common. Kidnappers forcibly enter vehicles and force occupants to withdraw funds from various ATMs. Other victims are picked up from the street. Armed kidnappings around ATMs have increased dramatically, especially along the route to Lima's airport.

There has been a growing number of violent attacks on foreigners outside bars and nightclubs late at night.

Robberies have increased in and around Arequipa (including the Colca valley), Juliaca and Puno. In Cuzco, violent crimes such as car hijacking and mugging are common. Do not travel alone to areas outside Cuzco. Avoid travelling through remote Peruvian jungle areas.

Travelling in groups is recommended, using only air, rail or reputable bus companies. Avoid travelling by road outside the major cities after dark.

Do not accept offers of transportation or guide services from individuals seeking clients on the streets.

Drug-related crimes incur stiff penalties. Prison conditions are harsh. Pack your suitcase yourself and keep it with you at all times. Do not carry anything through customs for someone else. Maintain vigilance. Some drugs and other products readily available over-the-counter or by prescription in Peru are illegal in other countries. An example is coca-leaf tea.

Terrorist activity continues to occur in the Central Highlands and in remote areas. Try to avoid these areas. Insurgent activity includes village raids, roadblocks and ambushes on government forces.

Landmines are a problem in the isolated Cordillera del Condor region along the Ecuadorian border. The border area with Colombia along the Putumayo River should be avoided. Exercise discretion in all border areas and avoid taking photographs.

Travellers to all remote areas should check with local authorities about geographic, climatic and security conditions. Be aware that rescue capabilities are limited, especially for hikers. Most rescues are carried out on foot because helicopters cannot fly to high-altitude areas. Travellers who participate in mountain climbing, river rafting or other travel in remote areas should leave detailed written plans and a timetable with appropriate company contacts or local authorities in the region and should carry waterproof identification and emergency contact information.

There is a risk of flooding during the Peruvian summer months of November–April. Altitudes of over 9,000 feet can have a debilitating effect. Visitors to Cuzco and other high-altitude areas are advised to rest for a few hours after arrival.

Malaria is a serious problem in jungle areas east of the Andes. Cholera, yellow fever, hepatitis and other contagious diseases are also present. Medical care is generally good in Lima and usually adequate in major cities, but less so elsewhere. Urban private health care facilities are often better staffed and equipped than public or rural ones. Serious medical problems requiring hospitalization and/or medical evacuation are expensive. Doctors and hospitals normally expect immediate cash payment for health services. Some accept credit cards.

Safety of public transportation in Peru is poor, along with urban and rural road conditions. Road travel at night is dangerous due to poor road markings and frequent unmarked road hazards. Drivers should not travel alone on rural roads, even in daylight. Convoy travel is preferable. Check spare tyres, parts, fuel, oil etc, when travelling long distances. Fog is common on coastal and mountain highways and the resulting poor visibility frequently causes accidents.

Inter-city bus travel is dangerous. Fatal bus accidents are common, frequently caused by excessive speed, poor maintenance and driver fatigue.

Africa

Angola

All non-essential travel to Angola should be avoided because of widespread civil conflict. Many areas of the countryside, including many secondary roads, are heavily mined and often unmarked.

Scams have been perpetrated by Luanda airport personnel. Immigration and customs officials sometimes detain foreigners without cause, demanding gratuities before allowing them to enter or depart Angola. Airport health officials sometimes threaten arriving passengers with 'vaccinations' with unsterilized instruments if bribes are not paid. Any question about documentation or identification, including vaccination cards, can lead to delays or rejected entry.

Pickpockets are active outside the arrivals gate of the airport. Travellers should avoid arriving at the airport after dark and travelling to the airport at night. Before arrival, ensure that you have arranged for reliable transportation from the airport. Only unregulated taxis are available at the airport and in Luanda. They are unsafe and should not be used.

The least affected part of the country is the capital, Luanda. There is a substantial security apparatus in the oil industry ports of Cabinda, Soya and Lobito/Benguela. The southern coastal province of Namibe is also relatively safe.

Crime levels, including armed hold-ups, are high. Violent crime occurs regularly in Angola. In Luanda and other cities, visitors should be alert at all times, especially after dark. Large crowds and demonstrations should be avoided. Foreigners have been the targets of violent robberies in their homes and hotel rooms.

Armed soldiers and police officers patrol the streets. Their behaviour can be unpredictable and their authority should not be challenged. All motorists should stop at night-time police checkpoints if so ordered. Uniformed police officers frequently participate in elicitation of bribes, muggings, car-jackings and murders.

There have been police operations against private companies that have resulted in the deportation of foreign nationals and the loss of personal and company property. Some foreign business people have been forced to sign statements renouncing property claims in Angola before being deported. Carry all relevant immigration and business documents at all times.

There are severe shortages of food, lodging, medicine, transportation, utilities and water in Luanda and other cities. Poor sanitary conditions can develop as a result of these shortages.

Visitors should avoid travelling by road beyond city limits because of guerrilla activity. Diamond mining areas are particularly dangerous. Travel outside Luanda is normally by air and should only take place under the auspices of organizations that can provide security. This does not include humanitarian organizations. Armed groups have shown no respect for road vehicles clearly identified as humanitarian and UN planes have been shot down. Destinations in the interior are accessible safely only by private or chartered aircraft. Overland routes to neighbouring countries are generally not open.

Angolan civil aircraft are often dangerous due to poor maintenance. Landing strips in some provincial towns are sometimes dangerous.

Adequate medical facilities are virtually non-existent throughout Angola, and most medicines are not available. Chloroquine-resistant and cerebral malaria are endemic to the region.

Nigeria

Violent crime occurs regularly in Lagos and other major urban centres, although the government has been increasing the number of roadblocks. These have had some deterrent effect but add to traffic congestion and may be intimidating. Burglaries, particularly in the expatriate areas of Lagos, are reported regularly.

Violent crime, committed by ordinary criminals as well as by persons in police and military uniforms, occurs throughout the country.

Travel between cities by vehicle, particularly at night, is dangerous as robberies and car-jackings with physical violence are common. Exercise utmost caution and prudence when travelling on the road to the Lagos airport, where traffic congestion may put passengers at risk. Inter-city travel by road involves risk, due to the frequency of armed robbery. Streets are poorly lit and many vehicles are missing headlights.

There are frequent incidents of attempted armed robbery on the Warri/Port Harcourt roads, Jos Bauchi road, the Maiduguri/Gombe road and, less often, on the road from Lagos to the border with the Benin Republic, and on the Lagos/Benin City and Lagos/Ibadan expressways.

Use of public transportation throughout Nigeria is dangerous and should be avoided. Public transportation vehicles are unsafe and often over-crowded. Passengers in taxis have been driven to secluded areas where they have been attacked and robbed.

Although there are some modern, well-maintained road arteries in Nigeria, roads are generally in poor condition, causing damage to vehicles and contributing to hazardous traffic conditions. Excessive speed, unpre-dictable driving habits and the lack of basic maintenance and safety equip-ment on many vehicles are additional hazards. There are few traffic lights or stop signs and, even where these may exist, they are not always heeded. Motorists seldom yield the right-of-way and give little consideration to pedestrians and cyclists. Gridlock is common in urban areas.

Unauthorized vehicle checkpoints occur throughout Nigeria. These may be operated by armed bands of police, soldiers or bandits. Many incidents, including highway banditry and murder, have occurred.

Non-essential travel to the Niger Delta region of Nigeria is inadvisable. Hostage taking for ransom, involving foreign nationals, has increased. There is a separate risk of being caught up in local disturbances in the same region. Military operations and curfews operate in many areas. Northern Nigeria is also dangerous following religious conflict. There has been extensive rioting and fatal violence.

In the light of rebel attacks on the UN peacekeeping forces in Sierra Leone, Westerners could become targets of RUF sympathizers in Nigeria and other West African countries.

Avoid large crowds and demonstrations and remain vigilant at all times. Care should be taken not to offend local sensibilities (photography is often unwelcome).

Violent street crime and armed robberies are prevalent throughout the country, as is harassment by the police. Do not travel outside cities after dark. Visitors should arrange to be met on arrival to ensure safe transport to their destination.

Fraud against foreign businessmen, charities and others is commonplace. Credentials of Nigerian business contacts should be checked thoroughly.

Some Nigerian-registered aircraft operating flights within Nigeria are unsafe. There have been attacks of piracy/armed robbery against ships at anchor in Nigerian waters and at many of the harbours in the Niger-Delta area.

Those conducting business in Nigeria or with Nigerians should be aware of the high rate of commercial fraud.

Permission is required to take photographs of government buildings, airports, bridges or official-looking buildings. Avoid taking photographs of anything of a non-tourist nature.

Cholera, dengue fever, hepatitis A, malaria, meningitis, tuberculosis, typhoid fever and yellow fever (regional) can occur in Nigeria. Medical facilities in Nigeria are not up to US/European standards. Diagnostic and treatment equipment is most often poorly maintained and many medicines are unavailable. Counterfeit pharmaceuticals are a common problem and may be difficult to distinguish from genuine medications. Hospitals often expect immediate cash payment for health services.

South Africa

The violent crime rate remains high throughout South Africa. Visitors should take all possible precautions. Daylight robbery is common.

The crime rate in and around railway stations and on trains is high. Avoid travelling on trains where possible, especially between Johannesburg and Pretoria. Theft is endemic in the baggage and immigration areas of international airports.

South Africa has the highest number of recorded rapes in the world. As with other crimes, most incidents occur in the townships but can happen in affluent areas as well. Women should never travel alone, especially after dark.

There is a high risk of vehicle hijacking and armed robbery in many areas. Drivers should park in well-lit areas and not pick up strangers. Avoid driving in rural areas at night or to townships and surrounding areas. Take care at traffic lights or when the vehicle is stationary.

Some public gatherings have provoked violent clashes between political factions, resulting in casualties. The highest incidence of such violence occurs in the province of Kwazulu-Natal. Some foreigners have been caught up in such disturbances. Townships in the vicinity of major cities such as Durban, Johannesburg and Cape Town have been scenes of violent conflict. These areas should be avoided.

In August 1998 and January 1999, American franchise restaurants in Cape Town were bombed. The possibility of future bombings exists. Visitors to Cape Town should be aware of street crime in the town centre especially after dark.

Visitors to Johannesburg should avoid the Hillbrow and Berea areas. Care should be taken in the Central Business District (CBD), in particular the Rotunda bus station, where muggings often occur. The CBD and surrounding areas should be avoided after dark.

Caution should be exercised at all times in Durban's city centre and beachfront area, especially after dark. There have been hijackings and robberies in northern KwaZulu-Natal and Zululand. In some of these incidents, tourists have been raped. Visitors should keep to the main roads in the area and avoid driving at night. Avoid isolated beaches. Take care when driving on the N2 highway between East London in the Eastern Cape and Port Shepstone in KwaZulu-Natal. Avoid detours off this road.

Zambia

Visitors to the Kafue National Park should be aware that a series of attacks were perpetrated in early 1998 by armed gunmen on cars travelling the Lusaka-Mongu Road in the immediate vicinity of the park.

Armed gunmen occasionally launch attacks on cars near the northern border with the Democratic Republic of the Congo (formerly Zaire) and near the western border with Angola. There are confirmed reports of combat in Angola near the Zambian boarder with periodic incursions into Zambian territory. There have been instances of air attacks in and adjacent to Zambian territory.

Land mines in the Gwembe Valley near Sinazongwe (along the south-west end of Lake Kariba on the road from Livingstone to Siavonga) make travel to that area potentially hazardous. Visitors should not travel on that road nor drive off established roads in that area.

Avoid political rallies and street demonstrations and maintain security awareness at all times.

Crime is widespread in Zambia. Armed car-jackings, muggings and petty theft are commonplace in Lusaka, other major cities and the Copperbelt, especially in commercial districts and housing compounds. There are increasing numbers of armed robberies with violence. Mugging and bag snatching are prevalent. Do not display valuables and important documents such as passports and always keep a copy of important documents in a safe place.

Car thieves often target four-wheel drive vehicles. Thieves have stolen possessions from private and public transport vehicles stopped in traffic. Vehicle hijackings (sometimes using firearms) are common and may be accompanied by violence if resistance is attempted. Car doors should be locked and windows rolled up at all times. Travel at night is particularly risky both in Lusaka and on roads outside the city.

Outside Lusaka, there are regular police roadblocks and identity checks. Travel on Zambian roads can be hazardous, especially at night, due to poorly maintained vehicles and roads. During the rainy season (October to March), travellers not driving in a four-wheel drive car will encounter problems on rural roads. Public buses and taxis are generally unreliable and unsafe. Road travel should be limited to main roads, with stops planned to avoid night travel. Drivers should be extra cautious in rural areas to avoid hitting pedestrians, cyclists and animals.

Travel to military areas and photographing military facilities are prohibited.

Government hospitals and clinics are understaffed and lack supplies. While private medical clinics in major cities can provide reasonable care, they are not equipped to cope with major medical emergencies, which usually require medical evacuation abroad. Basic medical care outside major cities is extremely limited. Doctors and hospitals often expect immediate cash payment for health services. Visitors are strongly advised to carry a first-aid kit and have comprehensive medical insurance, including cover for medical evacuation by air.

Outbreaks of cholera and dysentery occur regularly. Drinking water should be filtered and boiled or bought in brand bottles. Visitors should avoid eating food purchased from local street vendors. Malaria is endemic.

Visitors should take malaria prophylactics and consult a doctor about relevant vaccines, including rabies. There is a very high prevalence of AIDS/HIV and tuberculosis.

Zimbabwe

President Mugabe's hard-line approach to 'white' farmers and opposition parties, journalists and other critics of his policies spell an uncertain future for his country. The presidential election in March 2002 – the continuance of Mugabe's term of office – was, perhaps, a foregone conclusion but the conduct of it could result in the imposition of EU sanctions. These will be aimed at freezing the assets of senior Zanu–PF Party members. Mugabe himself and 19 other named individuals could be refused entry to all EU countries. All of this points to continuing political unrest – although Mugabe has some support among other African leaders. Illegal farm occupations continue and visitors should not travel to commercial farm areas or communal lands.

Visitors should be alert to signs of disturbances and avoid any political rallies or other meetings. Travellers should maintain a very high level of personal security awareness.

Fuel supplies in Zimbabwe are erratic although public transport is largely unaffected. Visitors driving their own vehicles should keep their tanks topped up as much as possible and carefully plan long journeys.

Crime levels in Zimbabwe are on the increase. Muggings, rape, purse snatching, car thefts and credit card fraud are on the increase due to high rates of unemployment and inflation. Mugging and pickpocketing are prevalent in city centres especially in Harare. Foreigners are perceived to be wealthy and are therefore frequently targeted. Visitors should exercise caution when leaving banks and ATM machines. Visitors to Victoria Falls and other tourist centres should be wary.

Visitors should be watchful of their luggage at airports, railway and bus stations and when making calls from public phones. Visitors may take the preventive measure of leaving all valuables such as passports, money, jewellery and credit cards in the hotel safe when they are not being used. Travellers should not carry large sums of money or multiple credit cards while shopping.

Thefts from vehicles are fairly common. Drivers should keep their vehicle doors locked and be cautious when travelling by car from Harare airport and at filling stations. Anyone offering to help to change tyres, which are sometimes deliberately punctured, should be regarded with great caution. In the event of a flat tyre, travellers should drive to a service station or a residential area. Travellers who suspect that their vehicle is being followed should drive to the nearest police station.

If possible, vehicles should not be left unattended in isolated scenic spots in the Nyanga and Vumba areas of the Eastern Highlands. There has been an increase in the incidence of car-jacking. Do not leave valuables unattended in vehicles. Car doors should be kept locked and windows shut at all times.

Traffic drives on the left. Inter-city bus travel, except by luxury coaches, can be dangerous due to overcrowding, inadequate maintenance and careless drivers. Driving out of main towns at night should be avoided as vehicles are poorly lit and roads badly marked. Abandoned unlit trailers and heavy vehicles are a particularly dangerous hazard. Pedestrians and stray livestock are additional dangers. Emergency services can provide only limited help in the event of an accident.

The incidence of opportunistic theft, especially of handbags etc, is high. Passports are at particular risk so care should be taken at railway and bus stations, and particularly when using public phones. Visitors should carry photocopies of their passports, although banks will not accept photocopies for monetary transactions.

Photography of government offices, airports, military establishments, official residences and embassies, in addition to other sensitive facilities, is prohibited unless permission is granted from the Ministry of Information. Special permits may be needed for other photography. Laws are strictly enforced.

Land mines along the Mozambique border make travel to that border area potentially hazardous.

Zimbabwean medical providers usually insist on verifying insurance coverage prior to treatment. Hepatitis A and B, malaria, schistosomiasis and tuberculosis occur in Zimbabwe. HIV/AIDS are also highly prevalent. Medical facilities outside Harare are limited. Some medicine is in short supply. Doctors and hospitals often expect immediate cash payment for health services.

Part Three

Threat and Defence

20
Introduction

Part Two concentrated on global risk in the world's most sensitive regions – analysed in political and economic terms. There are, of course, other risks that corporate strategists must face – risks to their investment, buildings, stock and personnel.

Threats take different forms – and their severity varies according to location and political and economic factors. But here we examine the risks faced by personnel employed in non-domestic markets – and their families because they, too, are vulnerable, certainly in relation to crime. In some areas, there are health hazards. There are risks of the kind we face in the UK and USA – mugging, theft and assault. But others – which we regard as remote in our everyday lives – may be all too frequent in other locations.

Extortion/blackmail

Possibly the most well-known example of this particular brand of terrorism is the Tylenol crisis that faced Johnson & Johnson in the early 1980s and the subsequent Eau Perrier case. In both cases, companies were faced with external tampering with their product. In the case of Tylenol, eight lives were lost through capsules being laced with cyanide. With the aim of deterring customers, companies in the UK have been blackmailed by individuals who have threatened to poison supplies or bomb shops. A large supermarket chain had its own brand of tonic water tampered with and bombs set off to extort monies, while Heinz were faced with a threat to poison jars of baby food. Whether the criminal was an individual or a group, the motive in these cases was profit. There is an undoubted cost to the target: Johnson & Johnson, in withdrawing the product from the shelves, incurred costs that took many years to recover. However, there have also been cases of disgruntled employees tampering with products, where profit was not the purpose.

Kidnapping or hostage-taking

This became a common form of corporate terrorism in the 1980s and 1990s. The motive can be one of profit, in which case there will be a substantial ransom demand to secure the release of an individual. Alternatively, the motive may be to gain international publicity for 'the cause' – whatever that may be.

The latter motive is of concern to governments and organizations alike in the wake of increasing levels of violence associated with organized crime and radical fundamentalists. It is one that should be monitored continually by all travelling senior managers and those responsible for the security of executives when travelling to Africa and the Middle East, Russia and the Former Soviet Union, certain Far Eastern countries such as Cambodia and Myanmar (Burma) and certain parts of Latin America.

Recent cases show that kidnappers have learned the art of forceful negotiation. Failure to meet a ransom demand results in a finger of the victim being sent to the family – with the promise that further failure to respond will result in the despatch of further fingers, an ear or other parts of the anatomy. These deliveries are likely to be accompanied by a rise in the ransom demand.

Political terrorism

In the 1970s and 1980s, the Bader-Meinhof Gang, the Red Brigade and the IRA sought publicity for their extreme political views by acts of violence. Elements of the latter are still active – often through the use of bombs against both government and business targets alike.

Thirty years on, these groups are far more sophisticated. Events in the UK, in connection with animal welfare, have indicated that it is a threat that should not be ignored. Terrorism still exists with Islamic groups in Malaysia, Yemen and the Philippines.

Even in Greece, groups/units are still active. A classic example is the 'November 17' Group which, in May 2000, killed, in broad daylight, a member of the British Military staff in Athens. Although they have never killed a tourist or taken one hostage, there is always a first time if they do not believe that these messages are getting through to the authorities.

All of these have been made to appear almost insignificant in the light of the events of 11 September 2001. But they matter greatly to the individuals directly affected – and, of course, to the bereaved.

These are the principal risks – and the most difficult for the individual to counter. Then, there are the lesser risks – and much depends on location and the official attitudes to policing, the judicial system and those other Grey Area Dynamics™ to which we referred earlier. We will examine the lesser risks in many overseas locations but, first, we will consider in the next chapter the defence of buildings, stock and personnel – the words contributed by experts with long experience of structure, forms of attack, stock protection and the defence and safety of personnel.

21
The defence of buildings, personnel and stock

The authors are grateful to Major Michael (Mike) Coldrick, MBE, GM, DSA, Gregory Craig, RIBA, Managing Director of EPR Architects Ltd, Gary Gillot, Chief Executive of Telepaz Ltd and Mike Hussey and Tony Partington of Canary Wharf Group plc for their contributions to this chapter. The nature and extent of their input are explained in the text.

As an indication of their skills and prescience, in July 2001, Major Mike Coldrick carried out a security survey for a firm with offices in Moorgate, in the heart of the City of London. In the section of his report under the heading 'Threat Analysis', he wrote this:

The threat from direct action groups

There are threats of violence from the following:

Provisional Irish Republican Army

The peace negotiations with the principal terrorist group, the PIRA, continue and there is little reason to anticipate a return to violence on the mainland. The use of large-scale truck bombs to target the financial centre of the City of London was instrumental in bringing the government to the negotiating table. Sadly, this example of the success of extreme violence will not be lost on other groups, existing or yet to be manifested.

The Real IRA

A rejectionist group which wishes to emulate the PIRA with large-scale bombings of prestigious targets on the mainland. On 4 March this year [2001], the BBC building in Wood Lane was bombed by this group and, on 3 April 1998, a 980 lb car bomb was interdicted on the Dublin ferry bound for the mainland. The RIRA have cells in the Home Counties but recent arrests of key members in the Republic may blunt their immediate plans.

Animal rights groups

Within the wider membership of the animal welfare and animal rights movements exist perhaps 100 radicals, and the odd maniac, who are prepared to resort to extreme violence. They comprise sub groups, for example, Animal Liberation Front (ALF), Animal Rights Militia (ALM), the Justice Department (JD), Leading Edge and Stop Huntingdon Animal Cruelty group (SHAC). Clearly, these are not all distinct groups but flags of convenience for specific actions and targets. What is evident is their demonstrated capacity to wreak severe economic damage to small and large companies with organized intimidation and physical attacks on employees, including murder, criminal damage, incendiary attacks on commercial assets and employees' homes, mail bombs, under-car bombings and hoax bomb warnings.

Islamic radicals

The current trend from Islamic radicals such as the Saudi Arabian dissident Osama bin Laden's 'Al Qaida' is for no-warning spectacular attacks on prestige targets in both the military and commercial sectors. Large buildings in financial centres, eg World Trade Center, New York, and the Seattle Spire, are typical American targets but targets in major European cities have also been earmarked. As the UK is seen by bin Laden as America's lapdog and bin Laden agents are resident in Britain, an event could take place in central London.

[In the circumstances – several weeks before 11 September 2001 – this was a remarkable piece of writing.]

Mike Coldrick is primarily a bomb technician turned security consultant – first for the military, then for the Metropolitan Police Service and currently in private practice. In April 2001, he addressed the Placemakers Luncheon Club in London – a property professionals club managed by Alan Bailey, one of this book's authors. Mike's address included much personal experience and typical humour: 'I am a bomb technician and have never been accused of being academic. Let's face it, anyone who takes bombs to pieces for a living can't be the sharpest tool in the box'.

Nevertheless, he brought together vital advice on the protection of buildings and people for the benefit of those who create structures and manage them. In 1984, the UN had a peacekeeping presence in Lebanon. America had provided a contingent of marines – and, in a single vehicle bombing, Islamic radicals killed 241 of them. How? First, a total lack of awareness: the Americans failed to react to a known threat. Second, all personnel were concentrated in one large isolated building, an attractive target. Third, the perimeter defences were weak. The suicide bomber was able to drive around security in his Mercedes truck with 5000 kg of high explosive. And, fourth, the building collapsed. The Americans left.

The Provisional IRA recognized that a major power had withdrawn its forces because of terrorism. They exploited that knowledge to bring the British government to the negotiating table. When the PIRA first tried to destroy the Canada Square buildings in Canary Wharf in London, alert guards saw the bomb vehicle being put in place before any warning was given and the bomb – 1500 kg of explosive – was defused. Subsequently, the media asked the PIRA why they had tried to destroy the building. A GHQ spokesman said 'because it is a prime economic target, symbolic of the Thatcher years. Consider, if someone was to bring down the twin towers of the World Trade Center in Manhattan, it would be a major blow to American prestige'. This comment rather surprised Mike Coldrick as he thought the PIRA were very much in bed with the Americans. But then he found an old brochure of the early building phase of Canary Wharf. In the centrefold, there was a map of the entire site – just what the terrorist needs when planning a bombing – and, at the back of the brochure, there was a photograph of the World Trade Center, apparently designed by the same architects. Three months later, Islamic radicals detonated a 4,000 lb. car bomb under the World Trade Center – and, thankfully, on that occasion, the towers did not collapse.

So what have we learned so far? Unconnected terrorist groups share a common objective – the destruction of prestigious buildings symbolic of what they despise. Vigilance is vital; poor awareness and security invite attack. Good security and police response can frustrate any attempt. Assets at risk should be dispersed. Sound architectural design can prevent catastrophic results.

In an aside during his address, Mike Coldrick assessed the typical effects of one large-scale vehicle bomb – of which five had exploded on target in the past. There was serious damage to 50 buildings and lesser damage to a further 200 – tipping many businesses into closure. Glazing damage occurred over a very wide area. At the same time, seven further truck bombs were defused on target or *en route* and a total of 21,000 kg of primed explosives were seized from bases around London – enough for another 14 truck bombs. He also reflected on what appeared to be a perfect business arrangement. Teams of Irish labourers construct buildings in London, other teams blow them up and then the first teams return to rebuild them.

Although it is virtually impossible to predict the effects of aerial attacks on tall buildings, international studies are continuing to attempt to counter the effects of large ground detonated bombs. There have been full-scale test firings in various deserts. Measures on which the studies have focused include:

- measures to mitigate blast and fragments;
- protective barriers to shield buildings from blast and fragments;
- building materials to improve resistance to bomb effects;
- equipment to detect explosives and explosive devices;
- electronic surveillance, access denial and warning systems;
- improved procedures for public safety and personnel and business security; and
- measures to control the problem of ammonium nitrate in agricultural fertilizers (an ingredient of homemade bombs).

Some interesting developments are emerging and are discussed below.

Hydro-suppression

This is a permanently installed system that throws up a dense spray of water from ground-level pumps around the building's perimeter. If a vehicle bomb is detected outside the protected building, the system produces a curtain of water spray that mitigates blast effects by up to 50 per cent. The advantages are that the system uses existing fire-fighting hardware and is a good solution for existing buildings with limited options for 'hardening' (see below). The system can be used in the event of a chemical/biological attack because it scrubs the agent out of the air. And, if demonstrators are the threat, the sprays can be turned on them.

Blast-reflecting barriers

The Israelis have worked on such barriers. They are most effective built close to the structures they are designed to protect to prevent the blast wave reforming behind the barrier. Reinforced concrete has traditionally been used but laminated materials can be just as effective with much thinner construction at lower cost.

Vehicle barriers

Much work has been done to find effective barriers to arrest the poor man's cruise missile. A speeding truck containing a ton of high explosive contains huge kinetic energy. It is vital to ensure that the security access cannot be bypassed – remember the US marines in the Lebanon.

Target hardening

The aim is to prevent blast from entering the building because, once inside, it creates havoc. There are no standard solutions for hardening existing structures and methodology varies with function, aesthetics and cost. The inside of walls can be fitted with anti-spall screens – a variety of hard and soft materials has been developed. There are steel net or Kevlar curtains and polycarbonate and plastic liners. Outer walls may be hardened with a wet retrofit concrete skin or by cladding with deformable panels that have a buffering effect.

Glazing

Glass splinters are responsible for most injuries. Blast-resistant glazing should be specified in significant new buildings. For existing buildings, there are several options – anti-shatter film and blast curtains, the fitting of laminated glass or complete replacement with custom-designed units and, for high-security zones, the fitting of anti-bandit glass. Most importantly, windows *must* stay in their frames. Blast trials indicate that a 35 mm rebate is needed. One of the benefits of using laminated glass is its ability to flex and absorb pressure created by blast. This is increased progressively by adding to the number of interlayers between the sheets of glass.

There are design options for reducing vulnerability. These include reducing the number of openings in outer walls, the placing of vital functions such as plant away from vulnerable areas, placing internal corridors around the perimeter of the building between inner and outer reinforced walls and buying adjoining land or buildings to extend the security stand-off zone. Distance is always a protection.

Ingress

Architects are now paying far more attention (or should be) to creating layers of security in entrances so that, on larger schemes, there will be an outer level of security *before* reaching Reception, with a second layer of security before reaching the main points of vertical circulation.

Protection after the blast

Building structure

Post 11 September 2001, there are many investigations and much opinion but, as yet, no hard and fast 'rules'.

As background, the design of the World Trade Center was based on the concept of an externally braced steel structure, a non-rigid centre core and floor slabs made up of lightweight steel beams with concrete planks. This system facilitated the flexing of the building under wind load and improved speed of construction. For clarity, the external structure could be viewed as a series of steel plates with holes where the windows go. Tied together, it effectively formed a column-free structural skin.

From investigations undertaken so far, it appears that the heat of the aviation fuel, which seems *not* to have been considered, relatively easily melted the lightweight floor structure and this, combined with the lack of rigidity in the central core, led to the massive progressive collapse of the floors.

In the UK, the spectacular collapse of Ronan Point (following a gas-related explosion) led to changes in regulations aimed at avoiding a repeat. Thus the UK regulations already cover protection from progressive collapse and the ability of slabs *under certain circumstances* to take the load from a partial collapse.

So where does this leave us? Gregory Craig believes that, first, there will be a move away from externally braced structures and that structural cores will be designed to create additional rigidity.

Second, there will be a review of the fire protection of structures. In the case of concrete, this is defined by the depth of concrete 'cover' to steel reinforcing and the requirements may be upgraded, or be upgraded by building owners, given their own view of risk. The same applies to steel structures, to the extent that there may be an upgrading of a combination of the fire resistance of the steel itself *and* the fire protective linings that are placed around it.

In the case of higher-rise buildings, there has been talk of hardened floors able to withstand collapse from above. This will be very difficult to achieve and it is thought that the emphasis will prove to be on preventing or minimizing collapse in the first place.

To summarize, unless legislation changes, which (in the UK) is not yet certain, the precautions will involve a judgement of risk for the building, eg political, financial, profile. In general, attention will focus on methods of upgrading design to minimize the risk of progressive collapse and minimizing the impact of partial collapse.

Control of fire, smoke and escape

In dealing with fire arising from an explosion, architects and building managers should be concerned not only with the spread of fire itself but also, and as importantly, the spread of smoke and fumes, which account for more fatalities than exposure to flames.

Design in this area is, and will remain, two-pronged: active and passive. Active systems include hand-held appliances, sprinklers and smoke extraction systems. Passive systems include compartmentalization, hard areas and means of escape.

In the UK, current legislation *requires* sprinklers for buildings of a given floor size and height. In such buildings, it should also be noted that there are specific requirements for the provision of dedicated fire-fighting lifts and lobbies. The increasing sensitivities relative to risk are likely to see the application of sprinklers to buildings not currently embraced by such regulation.

Passive measures will continue to include the compartmentalization of buildings to inhibit the spread of flame and smoke from one area to another and the increasingly robust design of cores containing escape staircases and essential services, the maintenance of which provides the means of delivery of water to fire-fighting systems, smoke extraction and communications.

Safe havens

While the safe evacuation of a building under threat or attack is of vital importance, it is equally important to recognize the danger of the 'second' bomb aimed at inflicting further death or injury following the confusion of a first strike.

With this in mind, security-minded design should consider the provision of safe havens within the building where shelter can be afforded until 'danger' is deemed to have passed.

Provision will, of course, depend upon the size of building and scale of risk. The robust core, housing lifts, lavatories and staircases, presents an obvious answer to this, given that the structural design and integrity of the area can be guaranteed. However, use of such areas will depend upon the maintenance of communications enabling those controlling security and monitoring events and the evacuation to let people know what is happening and what they should be doing – sheltering or evacuating.

To this extent, hardened or secured internal communication systems should be introduced.

Safe havens on deep floorplate lower or ground floors or basements should be considered. However, the latter must be adequately secured against illegal access into the basement and well protected from car parks or other areas of flammability.

Needless to say, any planned safe haven must be directly related to escape routes out of the building.

Plant protection

Plant can be divided into two interrelated categories: securing the protection of people and securing the vital interests of the business. The ability of life safety systems to operate throughout an emergency can do much to protect life and mitigate the worst effects of an attack.

To this extent, key plant will increasingly be placed underground or in inner secure areas with a second line of defence against bomb blast. However, much plant needs to draw in air and careful planning will be needed to ensure that air intakes and extracts are planned so they do not in themselves create unexpected points of vulnerability to the systems.

In summary, design for security is as much a matter of awareness as the application of a set of given criteria. Experience in the UK over the last 30 years of both terrorist threat and building failures has resulted in the provision of building codes and practices that take security very seriously. However, there is no room for complacency and the way these issues are considered will become more fundamental to the design process than hitherto.

The increase in robustness will involve value judgements on risk, since protection from risk has distinct design and cost implications, which must be factored in to any given set of circumstances.

It can be anticipated that regulations will be tightened and improved and the concept of resilience to technical systems expanded; the systems themselves, like the people within our buildings, being given ever greater protection in the event that 'basic' security is breached and a building successfully *attacked*.

The security of buildings and personnel does, of course, go beyond structure. It is vital to encourage total awareness among security and all other personnel – and to introduce deterrents to unauthorized entry. Electronic screening technology has become very sophisticated. We now have automatic access control systems that interrogate the individual, admit them into a closed chamber, screen them for concealed explosives and weapons and, if they fail to pass, shunt them into captivity.

Security is usually controlled from a dedicated centre. This should be in a well-protected zone to ensure that the controller is not distracted and that he survives any attack. If a control room is sited close to reception, it could be wiped out by a bomb attack – and evacuation control is lost.

Cost matters. A high level of security is likely to add 10 per cent to the cost of a new tall commercial building. For an average medium–rise corporate building it might cost an extra 2–5 per cent to achieve an adequate level of security. There is a line in a Hamas operational manual that says 'Why stalk a tiger when there are sheep to be had?'

Chemical and biological threats

The spectre of these threats is very real. Chemical and biological agents are not a threat to buildings but to their occupants. We have referred to water sprays. When he was a member of the ATB (Anti-Terrorist Branch), Mike Coldrick and his colleagues busied themselves with respirators, doing exercises at Porton Down, writing contingency plans – and even stocking up with body bags. When he left the job, Mike took with him his respirator and anti-nerve gas syringes. (He still feels guilty – because, if ever he needs them, he will have to tell his wife he doesn't have a set for her.)

These threats include the possible use of Anthrax as a terrorist weapon. The following is based on guidelines provided by the UK Public Health Laboratory Service. There has been extensive coverage in the media recently of the risk posed by Anthrax and the possible use of the mail as a means of transmission.

Anthrax is relatively difficult to catch. It occurs in three main forms – cutaneous (skin), respiratory (lungs) and abdominal (after swallowing). Of these, the respiratory form is the most dangerous. It can only be caught by breathing in a fairly large amount of contaminated material. Simply handling a letter, even if it contained Anthrax, would be unlikely to be a significant risk. The UK Public Health guidelines issued on 15 October emphasize that handling a letter or package is not considered to give rise to a risk of infection. They say: 'It is unlikely, therefore, that contact with letters or packages, which sometimes claim to be contaminated, constitutes a significant exposure risk'.

Anthrax does not spread from person to person and can be diagnosed and treated with antibiotics if someone thinks they may have been exposed. To date, the incidents in the UK causing concern have involved small packages containing sand or powder. Anyone finding such a parcel should minimize handling (place the letter or package in a plastic bag or sealed container) and seek medical advice from a GP or Casualty Unit. Obviously, any suspicious incident should also be reported to the police, who will liaise with Public Health officials if necessary.

If possible, avoid inhaling any suspect material – for example, don't smell or taste any material of which you are suspicious. If you do handle suspicious powder or sand, wash your hands thoroughly with soap and water after placing the package in a sealed bag. The risk of any serious medical illness arising from this route is extremely small – Anthrax is difficult to contract and even handling contaminated material does not always result in infection.

Measures are now being introduced to improve the protection of the occupants of buildings from chemical or biological attacks. Specialists in the USA have already modified hundreds of buildings.

Evacuation of buildings on receipt of a warning or after terrorist attack

After 11 September 2001, there was obviously concern that high-profile commercial buildings elsewhere would be targeted. In London, Canary Wharf Management Limited resolved to have a practice of total building evacuation – and chose One Canada Square for the purpose. The company issued the following brief to all persons employed in the building – well over 6,000.

CANARY WHARF MANAGEMENT LIMITED

Practice total building evacuation

Canary Wharf Management Limited, in conjunction with your employer, will conduct a practice total evacuation of One Canada Square.

There will be an announcement before the practice evacuation:

May I have your attention please?
There will be a practice evacuation of the building in 10 minutes
There will be a practice evacuation of the building in 10 minutes

The evacuation message will be broadcast over the PA system throughout the building.

May I have your attention please?
May I have your attention please?
This is a practice evacuation of the building
Please leave the building immediately using stairs and passenger lifts
Please leave the building immediately using stairs and passenger lifts
Follow the direction of Evacuation Marshals and Security
Please evacuate calmly and do not rush.

The message will be repeated until the floors have been evacuated. It is very important that you listen carefully to the message.

Method of evacuation

There is a choice of how you evacuate – passenger lifts or staircase.

Evacuation using passenger lifts
- Enter the lift lobby and press the down button.
- The passenger lifts will switch to a different programme used only for mass evacuation.
- For effective evacuation lightly loaded lifts may collect passengers from lower floors.

- If the lift is overloaded the lift buzzer will sound and the lift will not move.
- If the lift is overloaded some passengers will have to get out of the car and wait for the next lift or use the staircase.
- The lift may take a few minutes to return, remember this is a practice, you are safe to wait for the lift.
- Evacuation Marshals have been trained to assist with evacuation.
- Mobility impaired (disabled) and those with a medical condition should use lifts to evacuate, please give assistance and priority where necessary.
- Upon arrival at ground level, leave the building and immediately move away following directions given by security.

Evacuation using the staircase
- Go to your nearest staircase.
- Remember this is a practice, do not rush, but proceed in an orderly fashion.
- An Evacuation Marshal will stand at the staircase entrance to monitor the evacuation, give direction and ask you to evacuate slowly and calmly.
- A PA system has recently been installed to give information in the staircases.
- It is important that you listen to announcements in the staircase from the PA system – this is for your safety, updates and instructions may be given.
- Please keep your voices low in the staircases to ensure good communication.
- Be courteous and respectful to others evacuating.
- Staircase pressurization will be operated to supply air to the staircases for your comfort and, in the event of fire, prevent the ingress of smoke into the staircase. The fans may be noisy and you will experience air movement.
- It is vital that once out of the building, you move immediately away to ensure others still evacuating can leave safely.
- Follow directions given by security.

On leaving the building

- You will be directed to Canada Square or Cabot Square, your employer may require you to go to a prearranged assembly area.
- Do not return sooner than one hour once you have evacuated the building. Remember your security pass.

- You are not required to remain at the assembly area prior to returning to the building.

Communication

Communication is essential to ensure that evacuation is successful. The following means of communication will enable you to report an accident, request first aid or assistance and report any other emergency:

- **Emergency assistance phones** are located **every 5 floors in the staircase** for your use *only* if there is an emergency. Pick up the receiver, you will be automatically connected to the Estate Control Centre who will deal with the emergency accordingly. Please remember to replace the handset after use.
- **Red fire phones** are available in an emergency **on each floor of the building, in the lobby between the floor and staircase.** Pick up the phone, you will hear a buzzing tone, wait for an answer, this may take a minute or longer, please be patient. The call will be answered in the Fire Command Centre and the emergency dealt with. You will not be required to state the floor level or colour of the staircase as this is indicated to the person answering the phone.
- **Evacuation Marshals, Observers and Security Officers** are present to communicate with you if assistance is required. Observers and Security Officers will be equipped with radios. These people will also monitor the evacuation and report crowding and incidents.
- **Public announcements (PA) floor and staircases** Please listen carefully to announcements given to you. During the evacuation the messages may change to give new instructions, direction and updates that are important.

Medical assistance

There will be two general registered nurses, Canary Wharf Management Limited, tenant first aiders and supplemental first aiders available to give assistance.

If a person has an accident

If possible remove the injured or ill person to a safe place on the nearest floor landing, use the red fire phone or emergency assistance phone to get first aid.

First-aiders will access the floor by using a fire-fighting lift. If the person cannot be moved, use the red fire phone or emergency assistance phone to get help or to give information. The PA system can be used to ask people to stand still, slow down or follow other instructions.

Before the evacuation

- Do not plan for visitors or meetings immediately prior to the practice evacuation.
- Please familiarize yourselves with the location of the staircases.
- Be sure you understand what you are required to do and be prepared to evacuate when you hear the message sound.
- Please remember the differences between this practice evacuation and evacuation in case of fire.
- Remember to take your security pass and have appropriate clothing ready.
- Do not bring briefcases or other bulky items with you during the evacuation.

[Note: the original document contained floor plans, which have not been reproduced for security reasons.]

Following the practice evacuation, the Canary Wharf Group commented on its success and on related activity to reduce and manage risk.

1. The historic risk to tall buildings has been fire – a risk comprehensively addressed over many decades in terms of both building design and evacuation procedures. The result of the decades of study and experience of fire has been to reduce the risk of fatality due to an office fire to 1 in 14,000,000, which is approximately the chance of winning the National Lottery.

2. Building managers and the fire services have also developed contingency plans to deal with situations where the fire cannot be contained within the fire floor. Phased evacuation proceeds up the building from the fire floor. Phased evacuation allows successive evacuation of floors in a controlled manner according to the risk profile in the building.

3.   However, the tragic events of 11 September 2001 have introduced a new form of catastrophic risk where a massive flying bomb may intentionally impact a building. The subsequent biological attacks in the USA have also added further threats that are now considered credible. Compared with the many day-to-day risks to which the general public is unwittingly exposed, the risk of a catastrophic event happening again is extremely low and improbable.

4.   For comparison, some normal risks per annum are as follows:
      –   Chance of death from accident   1 : 4,200
      –   Chance of death from fire in home   1 : 70,000
      –   Chance of death in an airline crash   1 : 150,000

5.   The occupants of tall buildings, particularly prominent ones, are understandably concerned that they will have no warning of a hijacking and therefore cannot evacuate. Also, if they survive the impact, they are worried that they will not be able to evacuate the building. Good building design should ensure that the building survives to permit evacuation of survivors and good procedures should minimize the inevitable chaos and speed evacuation.

6.   Canary Wharf has taken the view that enhanced awareness of erratic behaviour of airlines or overt hijacking will permit the security services to give some warning to possible targets and that the objective of the contingency plan should be to try to minimize the casualties by the most expeditious form of evacuation before impact. The recent evacuation of One Canada Square was designed to evacuate as many people as possible from a building before impact. The fastest method would be to use lifts only but we thought that few occupants would wait 18 or so minutes for a lift to exit the building. Similarly, employees would not wait for their turn in a phased evacuation. In an extreme emergency, occupants want to do something positive to protect their safety rather than wait – so we allowed occupants to make their own choice; whether to use stairs or lifts.

7.   The practice evacuation of 30 October was very successful with a high level of participation. We believe that 85 per cent of the official employment in a building would be present at any one time in the

business day. In our case, this would be 6,375 persons and, in the test, 5,469 (86 per cent) participated. The total evacuation time was 20 minutes, determined by those using the slowest method – the stairs. Those using the lifts exited in 13 minutes. Some 2,939 (54 per cent) used the stairs and 2,530 (46 per cent) used the lifts.

8. The results of the evacuation on 30 October supported our original predictions. We have now estimated the simultaneous total evacuation on One Canada Square using stairs only at between 30 and 45 minutes, which we believe is a good predicted result.

9. However, some occupants and the press have now erroneously confused the new simultaneous evacuation drill for an imminent catastrophe with the normal fire evacuation drill and believe that occupants can evacuate using lifts in a fire. We are continuing with a hearts and minds campaign to explain the differences in the scenarios and responses and to allay any fears that they may not get out of the building post impact.

10. We believe that the evacuation procedure developed, combined with the existing building design, will be sufficient to deal with an imminent catastrophic event due to terrorism.

Defence of stock

As there is often a direct connection between terrorism and straightforward (if that is an appropriate word) crime, it would be wrong to omit reference to theft of stock. Some warehouses across the world contain transportable stock of almost incalculable value. In consequence, they are targets of both terrorists and 'straightforward' crooks, sometimes working together and sharing the spoils.

Technology has, of course, come to the aid of stock defence. Recent developments have included the systems installed by Telepaz Ltd of High Wycombe, England. These include standard systems: CCTV, sound alarms and other tricks that alert standard security and police protection. On entry, the miscreants are faced with another problem. The systems trigger jets of 'dry ice' which reduces visibility to zero. This gives security and the police the time to arrive in number and arrest whoever is inside.

Telepaz offered one example of how effective these defences can be. A warehouse in Yorkshire carrying thousands of pallets of cigarettes, worth many millions of pounds, was broken into by a gang of highly organized criminals. They broke through the roof of the building and had stolen vehicles at the ready to remove the millions of pounds worth of stock. They were, however, all caught due to the sterling efforts of the police using a number of squad cars backed up by a helicopter. Some were caught on the roof and others in their vehicles. They were all handcuffed, taken to the police station and subsequently charged. They will all serve time.

This successful outcome was the result of being able to contact the police rapidly to advise them of the break-in. This was all made possible by a network of detectors, CCTV cameras, audio verification microphones, audio-diallers and a remote monitoring centre, which could talk to the police to give them vital information while the heist was in progress. Equally important was the backup of a black-box recorder that provided necessary evidence for the police in their prosecution.

The success of systems such as these has swept through the ranks of criminals and terrorists with the result that attempts to rob well-laden warehouses guarded by the equipment have reduced dramatically – with consequent reductions in insurance premiums.

Cybercrime

The increasing sophistication of the organized crime groups has already been mentioned elsewhere in this book. It is wise to remember that sophistication can be bought or hired – and, if they need to step up their levels of sophistication, the necessary skills can be easily acquired by organized crime and terrorist groups.

It is also wise for the boards of international corporations to remember that their computers – in-country and at home – contain information of real value to competitors. Customer lists, sales records, stock levels – all of these things and more can be stolen. The introduction of viruses can destroy information vital to management, seriously disrupt business for an extended period and blunt a competitive edge.

There is also always a possibility that a competitor has organized crime connections. Details of the nature and location of stock are of real value to criminal groups – and, of course, to those political and religious activists who resort to crime to bolster their funds. Quite apart from the sale value of stolen stock, its replacement can be disruptive and time-consuming. Stock losses can create distribution voids that a competitor will be glad to fill.

Security of information is, therefore, important – just as the security of communications systems is vital to management. A vulnerable data centre – vulnerable, that is, to attack by bombs as opposed to viruses – demands continuity arrangements that will ensure that the business will survive. Such arrangements include ensuring that alternative, equipped space is available – and many international corporations have already invested in continuity in this way. Every element of a communications system has to be defended – imagine your far-flung corporate world without email facilities, for example.

The international corporate's own experts and consultants will advise on defence against what we have called cybercrime. Once again, what matters is awareness of the risks at the decision-making level.

22
Proactive and precautionary measures

Effective contingency planning is always prudent. When a crisis breaks, events are likely to move quickly and there is rarely enough time to collect thoughts. Neither is there time to think through the appropriate course of action from scratch. Therefore, a company needs to prepare plans which, at best, can be followed or, at worst, can be used as a basis for further immediate steps to deal with the situation.

At the heart of such a plan should be the selection and organization of a Crisis Management Team (CMT), which must have three main functions. These are:

- policy and planning;
- decision-making;
- on-the-spot executive action.

The problems likely to be mitigated by contingency planning and effective pre-planning in this instance are kidnaps and organized crime/terrorist action.

Formal plans should include the structure of the CMT that will handle a crisis situation, its lines of decision-making authority, its communications in the structure and the company's policies and procedures. The executive members who would be involved, and their alternates, should be identified together with necessary external advisers. Each should be aware of relevant responsibilities and the appropriate limits of decision-making capabilities. Company procedures should be tailored to meet specific circumstances and situations that may arise.

Exposure to the risks referred to will be reduced substantially and reductions will be more effective if consideration has been given to precautionary measures. If a crisis should arise, knowing how it will be best handled will improve the prospects of a safe and successful conclusion. In this respect, the advice of professional advisors can be invaluable.

Personal security

Personal security at home and abroad relies on constant awareness of your surroundings and the need to exercise care and common sense at all times. It is the responsibility of every individual to take simple and sensible precautions to enhance their personal safety when travelling or at home. This section contains guidelines to assist you when travelling to countries or areas of potential risk. In general, the risk to travellers is from opportunist crime rather than a premeditated attack, but it is important that good planning is carried out before the journey commences. Details of the journey should be known to as few people as possible.

International travel

Take some time to plan your trip.

- Request a security risk briefing.
- Establish points of contact at all stages of your itinerary.
- Familiarize yourself with the culture, local laws and political climate of the countries you intend to visit.
- Check weather forecasts before travelling for monsoon, hurricanes etc. Inclement weather disrupts travel and can be dangerous. Some areas are also earthquake prone.

- Travel anonymously without displaying the company logo or company luggage tags. Write only your name and postcode on a covered tag. Your full office address should be written on a stick-on label inside your suitcase or bag.
- Do not discuss business or your travel arrangements with fellow passengers or crew. Maintain a low profile. If asked, be vague regarding where you are staying. Do not divulge the name of your company or your position.
- In high-risk environments, ask check-in clerks at airports/hotels to write down your flight number/hotel room etc, rather than say it out aloud.
- In particularly sensitive countries, arrange to be met on arrival by someone you can easily recognize or whose identification can be verified, possibly by using a code-word. If kidnapping is of concern, ask for a photo of the company driver to be emailed or faxed to you. Do not hand over personal baggage until you have verified the identity of the recipient.
- Photocopy the details of your passport and visas and carry the copies separately. Leave a copy at home. Make sure you are aware of visa requirements and comply with immigration requirements.
- Leave a copy of your itinerary with a colleague or your secretary.
- Be aware that, in some countries, there is a risk from landmines.
- If travelling by boat, be aware that, in some regions, there is a significant piracy risk especially in the Asia Pacific region.

Documents and currency

- Do not unnecessarily carry company documents containing confidential information or documents identifying your title, position or association with particular organizations, professions or political groups.
- Memorize your passport number so as not to reveal your passport when filling in landing cards. Delay presentation until required at immigration.
- Prior to travel, obtain some local currency or US dollars in low denomination notes for unforeseen contingencies upon arrival. Have at least one reserve travellers cheque.

- Do not carry large sums of money in one wallet/purse. If confronted, drop/throw to the ground a 'sacrifice wallet' containing enough to satisfy an opportunist robber. Keep the rest in a separate pocket/ wallet/purse.

Medical

- Medication should be carried in original containers on your person. Carry medical details that a physician might need should you become ill while travelling.
- Carry an anti-infection medical kit, especially when travelling to countries with a high HIV and AIDS risk. You should familiarize yourself with all inoculation requirements, eg prophylactic treatment starts two weeks before visiting a malaria zone and continues for two weeks on return.
- Avoid intimate contact with locals in high-risk HIV and AIDS environments.
- Know your blood group.
- Upon arrival in an unfamiliar place, particularly tropical countries, familiarize yourself with any dietary precautions. You are advised to drink bottled water (ensure seal is intact). Avoid salads and fresh vegetables washed in local water and be cautious about where and what you eat and avoid food stalls.
- All travellers must have insurance cover, including full medical repatriation.

Airport safety

- If you have a connecting flight, know beforehand which terminal it departs from and how long it takes to get there.
- Do not carry packages or gifts on behalf of any other person whether known to you or not.
- Avoid public areas. Go through to the departure lounge as soon as possible.

- Keep your personal hand baggage with you at all times.
- Stay away from unattended luggage.
- Beware of distractions such as people asking questions, loud noises etc, as these may be part of a scam to distract you to allow others to steal property, especially in arrival/departure areas.

Hotel safety

- Use reputable hotels. It is worth upgrading your hotel to ensure a good level of security. In high-risk areas, it is advisable not to use the company name when making hotel reservations or hiring/renting a car.
- Keep your luggage within view or touch. It is advisable to position luggage against your leg during registration and place your briefcase or handbag on the desk or counter in front of you.
- Ask for a room between the third and eighth floors. Few cities have fire appliances that can reach above the eighth floor and walk-in thieves are less likely to venture above the lower floors.
- Have the hotel reception clerk write down the room number instead of saying it out loud.
- Don't give your room number to strangers. It is also wise for women to let men think they are travelling with a companion.
- Do not hand in your passport unless required by law. As a general rule, keep the room key with you.
- Always accept assistance upon check-in. Allow the porter to open the room, turn the lights on and check the room to ensure that it is vacant and ready for your stay.
- Before dismissing the porter, always inspect the door lock, locks on sliding doors, optical viewer, privacy latch or chain, room safe, dead-lock bolt on interconnecting doors and telephone.
- Familiarize yourself with all exit routes and fire escapes. Read the fire safety notice in the hotel room and count the number of doors (or paces) between your room and the nearest fire exit. Check the roof exit. If there is a smoke detector in the room, use the test button to ensure it is working correctly.

- Ensure that valuable and sensitive documents are kept in the hotel safe or safe deposit box facility in your room.
- Use the door chain or privacy latch.
- Keep the room door locked at all times and the curtains drawn at night. Upon entering your room, ensure nobody is in it before locking the doors.
- On leaving your room, check that sliding doors/windows are locked. Housekeepers may have unlocked them.
- Keep the TV and/or a light switched on when you are not in your room.
- Keep your room tidy so that intrusion will be more easily identified. Keep luggage locked.
- Do not open the hotel room to strangers. If someone claims to be the police or hotel staff, call the front desk to verify before opening the door.
- If you feel someone is watching you in the lobby as you board the elevator, push several buttons for floors below you and several above you. That way, no one will know at which floor you alight.
- Meet unknown visitors in public rooms in the hotel. Be extremely prudent when giving out personal information, home or hotel addresses or telephone numbers.
- Be discreet when using hotel telephones. They are not secure. Beware of eavesdroppers.
- Be careful how you open packages or envelopes sent to the hotel if you do not know the sender.
- Women should not hesitate to request hotel personnel to escort them to their rooms if returning late.

Street awareness

- Keep a low profile. Dress and behave conservatively. Do not display cash or jewellery. Avoid conspicuous behaviour that will draw attention to you as a wealthy foreigner. Be polite but cautious of people trying to engage you in political or controversial debates.
- Respect local dress codes and modes of behaviour.

- Avoid slum districts, poorly lit areas and narrow alleyways.
- Learn common phrases and/or carry a local phrase book or card for use in an emergency. A city and country road map is also useful.
- If confronted by armed attackers, always give up your valuables. Do not resist. Never carry large quantities of cash or any items that you are not prepared to lose.
- Know how to use public telephones. Carry a local phone card and small change at all times for emergencies.
- Learn to recognize the uniforms and credentials of public services, eg the police.
- In high crime rate countries, be doubly aware as elements of the police may be involved in robbery/corruption and other crimes, including kidnapping.
- Consider carrying at least one credit card separately so, if your wallet is stolen, you are still financially functional.
- Place wallets and purses in zipper, buttoned or inside pockets.
- Never display large amounts of money when paying a bill. Carry your money in a moneybag or disperse it throughout your garments. Remember that, if you have a 'sacrifice wallet', you must have some cash in it to satisfy a robber. If a credit card is used, be sure it is returned after each transaction *and that it is yours*.
- Be careful using ATMs. Use them only during the day at large protected facilities, eg inside banks. Avoid highly visible ATMs on streets where criminals can observe transactions.
- Avoid street money-changers and other offers to change money.
- Do not throw away credit card receipts. Take them home to be checked against your statement.
- Keep a separate note of telephone numbers of companies and/or agents issuing travellers cheques, travel tickets, credit cards, etc. Report any loss as soon as possible.
- Treat with caution accidents, unusual occurrences, distractions and distress calls that may be hoaxes.
- Be prepared to walk away from any situation on the street or indoors that could turn to violence or lead to the use of weapons.
- Exercise caution and common-sense when visiting nightclubs, discotheques and other late-night establishments. Arrange return

transport to your hotel or residence as reputable taxis are often difficult to find at night.

- When out at night, avoid excessive drinking of alcoholic beverages, especially if alone. Never accept a beverage in an open container from a stranger or recent acquaintance as it may be drugged. The same goes for food.
- Be aware of 'honey traps' where female/male company is used to manoeuvre one into a compromising position.
- Women should exercise extreme caution when dealing with strangers/ casual acquaintances.
- Be cautious in crowded areas such as public transport and train stations, open-air markets and popular tourist sites as pickpockets are most active in such locations.
- Avoid demonstrations and other large gatherings. If you get caught up in one, stay calm. Go with the flow. Maintain a friendly attitude and do not respond to provocation. Try to get to a safe place, eg police station.
- Maintain at least two arms' distance from an enquiring stranger, when asked for a cigarette, a light or the time etc.
- If possible carry briefcases, handbags, mobile computers, etc in a secure manner to prevent snatch-type thefts.
- When casually walking about, leave items such as credit cards, driving licence, membership cards and family photos in a hotel safe deposit or at home. Wear loose clothes and shoes that are easy to walk and run in. Women should kick off their shoes if they are too high to run in.
- The loss or theft of a passport should be reported immediately to the nearest Embassy or Consulate.
- Walk on well-lit busy streets as much as possible, face on-coming traffic. Avoid shortcuts.
- If you think you are being followed, cross the road and keep walking. If still worried, make for a well-lit public place or police station, hotel lobby, etc.
- Be careful when crossing the road. In towns, vehicles often do not obey speed limits and may not stop at traffic lights.

Security when mobile

Taxi

- Choose taxis with care. Never hire unmarked taxi cabs or enter any taxi carrying unfamiliar passengers.
- Take only licensed taxis. Normally, official taxis are paid for within the terminal and those that serve the better hotels are the safest. Ask the hotel reception to arrange a taxi for you.
- If calling for a taxi from a public place, ensure your conversation is not overheard.
- Ask for the name of the driver who will respond to your call and the taxi licence plate number.
- Always agree on the destination and fare prior to entering the vehicle. Ask the hotel concierge for an estimate of the time and fare to the destination.
- Have the address of your destination written out in local language and carry it with you.
- Watch your luggage being put into the boot. Use only official porters dressed in uniform. Do not leave the vehicle until the driver opens the boot at your destination.
- Lone travellers should use the front passenger seat. This is a precaution against child locks in the rear of the car.
- Avoid cabs waiting in front of restaurants, night clubs, bars etc.

Car

- In a risky environment, ensure that someone responsible at your hotel or office knows where you are going, whom you are visiting, times of arrival and return and action required in the event of delay.
- Keep to centre lanes where possible and maintain a manoeuvrable distance from the vehicle in front.
- Avoid narrow, quiet and unlit streets – and avoid travel after dark in the countryside.

- Keep all doors locked when driving. If necessary for ventilation, lower the front passenger window no more than two or three inches. Air conditioning is preferable.
- Make a habit of checking your surroundings at the start and finish of your journey. Do not stop if you note suspicious persons, unfamiliar vehicles and unusual occurrences.
- Know the location of police stations, fire stations, hospitals and other public buildings that may serve as 'safe havens' situated along the routes.
- Remain alert when stationary, eg at traffic lights. Keep valuables out of sight, especially handbags and mobile phones.
- Reverse into your parking position including your own garage and do not park in dark and isolated locations.
- The use of a good alarm system and a supplementary wheel lock will deter most simple vehicle thefts.
- Do not leave valuables or other articles in your car likely to attract attention. Use the boot. Keep the parcel shelf in place in estate cars and hatchbacks.
- Ensure the vehicle is locked and windows fully closed when parked or left unattended at filling stations, home driveways or when garaged.
- Make a habit of looking inside your car before entering it and then do so as quickly as possible. Have your keys ready.
- Be cautious not to accept immediately as bona fide a police officer or other officer in uniform. Ask to see his warrant card or other means of identification.
- Beware of other drivers flagging you down, signalling 'faults' on your car to you, hitchhikers and staged accident scenes.
- In the event of a minor accident, it may be prudent to let the other driver come to you. Open the window slightly and assess his/her attitude. If necessary, exchange details without leaving the vehicle.
- Be aware of being followed generally and, in particular, in the case of any staged accidents and other 'incidents'.
- Never respond to aggression on the road and never communicate with other drivers. Avoid eye contact.
- Be aware that hire cars in many countries may be in poor condition. This also goes for vehicles in general.

Transport – general

- Try to stick to main roads/highways.
- Exercise caution on all roads. The incidence of road traffic accidents will generally be higher in less developed countries.
- Try to avoid bus travel.
- Any bus travel should be during daylight hours on first-class transport where possible.
- Do not hitchhike or accept rides from, or offer rides to, strangers anywhere.
- Be aware that rail travel is dangerous in many countries.
- On trains, search your compartment for possible contraband prior to crossing borders. Keep your baggage with you and secure your compartment door at night.

Confrontation
- If you believe you are being followed, confirm by making a detour or by accelerating, braking or changing lanes in a moderate fashion.
- Note details of suspect vehicle and occupants.
- Do not stop or get boxed in.
- Drive to the nearest 'safe haven' such as a police station. Do not drive to your home/hotel or to the office.
- Inform the police, if you have not already done so by mobile phone.
- If directly threatened – keep moving.
- Check that all doors and windows are locked and closed respectively. Try to avoid travelling alongside the attacking vehicle.
- Switch on headlights and hazard lights or sound the horn to gain attention.

Motorway breakdown
- In the event of motorway breakdown, go to an emergency telephone to pinpoint the exact location. This will often result in a faster response than using a mobile phone.
- Switch on hazard lights. Deploy warning signs if applicable.
- If it is necessary to walk to the emergency telephone, make sure all doors are locked and windows are closed.

- Do not accept a lift.
- Face oncoming traffic while telephoning.
- When with your car, leave the passenger door wide open (if not central locking) and secure all other doors and windows. Wait on the embankment, close to the car, unless unsafe to do so. If an unidentified vehicle draws up, return quickly to the car and lock it.
- Speak to approaching strangers through a narrow gap in the window. Tell them that the police have been called.
- It is advisable for women travelling alone to carry a mobile telephone for use in an emergency.

Portable computer and mobile telephone security

- Portable equipment must be kept secure at all times and not left unattended. You should be particularly vigilant in the office or other places such as airport lounges and hotel lobbies.
- If equipment is left overnight in the office, then lock it away out of sight.
- Beware of walk-in thieves. Challenge strangers.
- When at home, use the equipment out of view from external observation. When not in use, ensure it is kept secure.
- At hotels, use safe deposit facilities.
- When mobile, conceal all equipment in your car boot. Remember to lock your vehicle when unattended even for the shortest period, for instance, while paying for petrol.
- While using the computer in public, beware of inquisitive strangers overlooking the screen.
- Carry your laptop in something less conspicuous than a normal carrying case.
- Power-on and other passwords must be used and changed regularly.
- Remember to back up data regularly. It may be useful to copy any essential files on to disk in case of laptop loss. Alternatively, email essential files to your contact abroad.
- Report loss of company property without delay.
- Users should record serial numbers and full descriptions of equipment.

- Users should consider use of locking devices and marking equipment with an invisible spray, which has a unique identifiable code.
- Analogue mobile phones are not secure and are increasingly rare. Ensure your cellular phone (including any you are renting locally) uses a digital system. Even then, remember that any landline you call may not be secure.
- In public places, speak quietly and use veiled speech.
- In some circumstances, encryption may be appropriate.

Security at home

- Know your neighbours and their telephone numbers.
- Fit mortise deadlocks to outer doors, which slow down forced entry.
- Fit window locks on ground floor windows and on upper floors to which access can be obtained, especially those hidden from view of passers-by. Any window not normally used should be permanently secured. Where fire escape is possible through locked windows, keys should be kept handy but not in view.
- Keep strict control of house keys. Ensure duplicate keys are made only with your knowledge. Keys should not be labelled. You should avoid making them identifiable by an outsider.
- Avoid leaving keys under the mat, in the letterbox or other obvious hiding places.
- Fit a new lock if a key is stolen or lost in suspicious circumstances.
- Make a safety check each night before retiring to ensure that doors and windows are locked. Close all curtains and blinds before dusk.
- Illuminate the approaches to your house and garage with exterior lights using light sensors.
- Avoid leaving the house in darkness and consider the use of a time switch for lifts, radio or television in the house.
- Leave on a courtesy light that illuminates the front door during the hours of darkness and avoid switching on the inside light when answering the door.
- Keep torches in handy locations known to all occupants.

- Check visitors before opening the door by using a peephole or, if possible, from an adjacent window. If appropriate, ask for proof of identity. Fit strong chains on outer doors and use them.
- Beware of those we are conditioned to recognize as friendly, eg policemen, clergymen, a well-dressed person or anyone who protests at your extra caution.
- Arrange fixed times for workmen, meter readers, etc to call. Check their identity and never leave them in the house on their own.
- Treat late callers, whether known or unknown, with caution.
- If a stranger asks to use your telephone, offer to make the call for him/her.
- Always answer the telephone by saying 'hello'. Do not immediately identify yourself or the telephone number. If necessary, ask for caller's name and number.
- If a telephone is out of order, report it at once. Locate nearest public phone. Pick a cellular network that suits your area.
- Maintain a list of emergency numbers and procedures close to your telephone.
- Report all anonymous or threatening calls to the police. Consider using an answerphone to monitor calls.
- In high-risk environments, civil unrest, etc, stock up on food and water. Keep petrol tanks topped up. Keep a reasonable amount of hard and local currency at home to meet any sudden needs. Buying an open airline ticket in advance saves the trouble of getting one at the airport, but does not guarantee a seat.

Child safety

- Inform the school authorities that your children must not be collected by anyone else without prior authority.
- Ensure that you are well acquainted with baby-sitters, who should be instructed in the door opening and telephone answering procedures. Make certain that they know where you can be reached and the location of emergency telephone numbers.

- Advise children of two 'safe houses' in the neighbourhood they can always go to for help.
- Discourage young children from answering the door or telephone.
- Make sure members of the family, particularly children, keep each other informed as to where they are going, whom they are with and when they will be home.
- Ensure older children who do not have pagers or cellular phones carry phone cards and inform you when they change their plans or location.

Leisure

- Do not hike alone in remote areas, on remote beaches, trails and ruins.
- Use only officially approved tour guides and groups. Even then, be aware of what is going on in the country. If in doubt, stay at home/hotel etc.

Women travellers

- In developing countries and male-dominated societies, dress conservatively. Avoid provocative, form-fitting clothing.
- Women should always dress conservatively if visiting a religious site.
- A lone woman may be considered fair game. Understand this and prepare yourself mentally for any propositions, suggestive comments or catcalls. Ignore them.
- In some cultures, it may be considered incorrect for a woman to travel alone.
- In some cultures, making eye contact with a man is a signal that you want company.
- Behave confidently. Try to look as if you know exactly what you are doing and where you are going.
- Copy local women. If they don't sit alone in cafes, go out alone at night or wear sleeveless shirts, then neither should you.
- Some men will use the opportunity offered by crowded trains or buses to touch/pinch females next to them. Try to avoid this with reserved

seating or avoid these modes of transport altogether. In some countries, make use of female-only sections in buses and trains.

Attack and kidnap for ransom

The chances of attack and kidnap for ransom are extremely limited. In some parts of the world, kidnap for ransom has become a popular form of criminal activity – but, in numerical terms, cases are few. Nevertheless, if it happens, the primary objective is self-preservation – and your reactions, both immediate and long-term, will affect the outcome.

Personal reactions

In a direct attack, your reactions, assessments and decisions are critical. If you are certain that the intention is to kidnap or rob you, it is probably best to surrender gracefully. Your attackers will be excited and nervous and aggressive resistance on your part is likely to make the situation worse than it need be. They could kill you, injure you or hold you in far worse conditions than might otherwise be the case.

If you are uncertain what your attackers' aims are, if they are shooting at you and/or you are not yet at close quarters, then there are limited options open to you:

- Take cover, either instantly by dropping to the ground or crouching on the car floor, or by moving at speed to nearby cover affording better protection.
- Break contact by headlong flight, controlled retreat or forcing your way out through the attackers.
- Raise the alarm or call for assistance by shouting, pressing panic buttons, setting off personal alarms or using a radio.

If a bomb is thrown at you, there is only one option open to you: drop flat behind whatever cover is available. There is seldom time to run.

Reaction skills

Even your most rigorously applied and well-thought-out protective measures can fail by chance or against a determined and able attacker. Your next layer of defence, after your protective measures, must be your ability to react.

This ability should be based on a lead from your earlier preparatory measures.

The most important reaction quality in a fast-moving crisis, such as an ambush or bombing, is a decisive mind. To freeze or hesitate is often fatal.

A sudden crisis can put you in a state of stunned shock or excited hyper-activity. Neither condition is likely to produce an effective result. Being prepared for this reaction should help you overcome it. The other alternative is the use of well-rehearsed drills and prior analysis of all the possible options and eventualities.

In a slower-moving emergency, clear and logical thinking is more important. You should then have time to gain some appreciation of the situation facing you, consider the options and establish priorities.

Certain skills are not easy to learn systematically but, if you have the time and the inclination, you could take instruction in evasive driving techniques. It is important to remember that their potential for use is low, while the time and effort needed to master them are considerable.

Reaction drills

These drills involve automatically carrying out pre-planned, rehearsed sequences of action, which vary according to the type of incident, the local situation and the calibre and experience of those involved. An example of what to do if your car is ambushed is given below.

In all car attacks, your reaction should be an immediate action drill. This should allow your mind to unfreeze and start assessing the situation without wasting valuable time.

● Brace for impact.

- If you have a radio, call out 'Ambush' and try to say where you are. If you are being driven, crouch on the floor; if driving, hunch down as low as possible. If it is dark, put your headlights on full.
- Watch your mirror.
- Prepare to smash the windscreen.
- If your car has smoke dispensers, prepare to fire them.

After you have gone through this drill, you have three choices:

1. Continue forward at speed, ramming through any obstruction in the way.
2. Withdraw by carrying out a fast reverse to cover, a fast reverse into a J or U-turn or a 180-degree turn.
3. Get out of the car (but only if you have been stopped or exposed) into cover of the engine block, into nearby cover by a fast sprint or into an available rescue car.

If a car draws up alongside you, and one of the occupants attempts to shoot you, stamp on the brakes suddenly. This will cause the attacker to overshoot, then use one of the methods outlined above to effect an escape.

Coping with captivity

If, in spite of all your precautions and abilities, you are captured by attackers, there are several ways to improve your chances of survival in the face of extreme provocation and hardship.

Conduct as a prisoner – sensible routines

Your captors may well be nervous and jumpy so do not make the situation worse by attempting to antagonize or alarm them. Co-operate as best you can, be polite and do not argue with them or provoke them. Also be careful not to make erratic or suspicious movements that could cause a violent reaction.

It is important to keep faith in yourself and the outside world; remember that you will not be forgotten and you are not wrong.

Try not to relax or be taken in by apparently good relationships with your captors. Remember that they are deadly enemies. Instead, set yourself tasks that will help you to remain positive. Turn the situation around by attempting to build human relationships with your captors.

Make an effort to manage yourself, your time and your personal environment. The objective of these activities is to maintain your morale and self-discipline.

Remember that security forces are probably trying to rescue you. Try to anticipate their actions or requirements and be ready to help or exploit any situation. For example, keep clear of any doors or windows if you think that a rescue is imminent, drop flat on the floor and lie still if one does take place.

Do not try to negotiate with your captors, as this may result in prolonging your confinement. Remember that everything they say or do is generally designed to increase your dependence on them. They will almost certainly attempt to dispirit you; try to ignore such attempts without upsetting them if possible. Do not get drawn into political arguments that could create anger, but do try to show them that you are a human being. Eat and drink whatever you are given, as you must remain as strong as possible under the circumstances.

Take whatever exercise you can and organize your day around a strict routine. Doing this will alleviate stress. Also, try to keep contact with events in the outside world. Ask to be given newspapers or a radio. If possible, devise 'mind games' to stimulate your mental powers; these will also help to pass the time. For example, plan your life story or redesign your house.

Human relationships

Building human relationships with your captors must be done carefully. It means you should:

- project an image of a reasonable, intelligent, person who will not cause trouble and accepts his/her lot with dignity, equanimity and without malice;
- avoid arguments, disputes and taking sides in your captors' internal disputes;

- carefully demonstrate the superiority of your beliefs and lifestyles by means of your attitude, manner, high standards of personal conduct and your self-discipline;
- take a genuine and sympathetic interest in your captors as human beings and attempt to establish a rapport;
- show gratitude for favours and use opportunities to return them;
- use the word 'we' in order to encourage the concept of a common cause or interest.

Managing the situation

Managing yourself is the maintenance of personal standards, incentives and alertness. It is vital that you keep clean, repair clothes, take physical exercise, exercise your mind by reading, writing, memory exercises and problem solving. Above all, keep your sense of humour. John McCarthy has said that he and Brian Keenan only remained sane during their captivity by telling each other jokes and making light of their situation.

Managing your time means keeping track of time and, as far as possible, maintaining a regular schedule for personal hygiene, housekeeping, work tasks, exercise, mental stimulation and sleep. It is recognized that this will not necessarily be an easy task but it will benefit you if it can be done.

There are many indications of passing time; try to become alert to them. For example, maintain a crude calendar and mentally celebrate birthdays, holidays and any other special occasions.

Managing your personal environment means personalizing your area of confinement and treating it like a home. If your captors allow it, rearrange it to your individual taste, display any photos that you might have, create specific places for certain activities and keep it clean. Ask for the things that you need but do not expect all requests to be granted.

Conveying intelligence

With regard to helping/anticipating security force action, note everything you can about your captors. Pass any information that you can without jeopardizing your safety. Useful information will include:

- their numbers, weapons, appearance, characteristics, unusual words or phrases, accents, behaviour traits, relationships with each other and potential weaknesses;
- determining who is in charge and keeping track of what is happening. This information will be very useful after your release, especially if there are other persons still being held hostage;
- taking note of furniture, objects or walls that would provide cover in a fire fight.

Duration of captivity

The length of time that you might be held hostage can range from a few hours to a few years. Do not anticipate a quick release as morale may decline if this does not occur. Rather, be prepared to withstand lengthy imprisonment.

Your employers, security forces or government have three basic options open to them. They can capitulate to your captors, negotiate or attempt a rescue.

Rescue attempts and escape

The techniques and procedures used for rescue and negotiation are well developed and have been proven in a great many scenarios. A vital ingredient for a successful outcome is information; the more the security forces can find out about your situation and confinement, the better the chances of a safe conclusion.

Rescue will probably involve one or more of the following techniques:

- stand-off sharp shooters;
- gas and/or other incapacitating agents;
- a clandestine or covert approach by an assault team;
- diversions with a fast close-quarter assault.

Whichever method is chosen, you should bear in mind that a rescue attempt is going to be a dramatic and potentially dangerous event and a captive must be prepared for it to be successful. A rescue attempt will only be undertaken when the security forces are confident of success or if it is felt that you are in far greater danger from remaining in captivity.

Before making a rescue attempt, those concerned will make absolutely sure that they can distinguish you from your captors. It is for this reason that inactivity is used as a means of 'buying time'.

It must be pointed out that an attempt to escape is an extremely risky strategy. The best chances of an escape would be early in the period of captivity. However, the opportunity rarely arises in a hostage situation. Also, attempting to overpower any of the captors will be dangerous and potentially deadly.

Surviving after escape or release

A comforting thought in the circumstances is to remember that statistics indicate that, if kidnapped, your chances of survival are good. But, what if you do manage to escape, or are released into a strange environment?

It is possible that you find yourself stranded in an inhospitable place with no available assistance. Surviving an aircraft crash-landing in a jungle, escaping from captors or the complete break-down of law and order are all events that would leave you dependent on your own resources and skills.

As a precaution, try to familiarize yourself with some of the more extreme areas of your city or town, so that you know what to expect. This should obviously be done with the greatest care as this process could be dangerous in itself. A safer method would be to study maps of the area. Certainly, it would be very useful to learn the main techniques for wilderness survival.

Many people have survived against very high odds. The essential requirements for survival in any situation are food, water, fire and shelter. To these can be added the secondary concerns of your state of health and a means of navigation.

Safeguarding your family

The procedures and drills so far described will be useful not only to you but also to those around you: your family, colleagues and staff. As a general rule, you should involve others as much as is possible – or sensible – so that they are also protected. Children can be particularly at risk and it is vital that they are made aware of the risks; without causing too much distress and anxiety. It should be remembered that this will cause as much major change in their lifestyles as it will in yours.

General security procedures

Ensure that you always know the whereabouts of your family and other close dependants. Never leave young children unattended anywhere, even at home. If you have to leave children with others, make sure that they are left with people known to you and whose backgrounds have been carefully vetted.

Instruct servants not to admit strangers into the house, especially if there are no adults present to keep a check on them. Make sure that children's rooms are not accessible directly from outside the building. Also, keep the children's doors open at night so that noises can be easily heard.

Security of children away from the home

Do not let children use taxis or public transport unaccompanied. Encourage children to travel in pairs or groups wherever possible.

As previously mentioned, avoid routines for children as well as yourself; vary times and routes of travel, etc. Unfamiliar drivers or escorts must be treated with suspicion and ask questions in order to confirm their identity to your satisfaction.

All play and recreation areas used by children should be strictly super-vised by trustworthy adults.

Security at schools

Make sure that children are escorted to and from school by official school transport or by people known to you. If necessary, use an escorted car pool. Try to vary routes and timings wherever possible.

Schools should be asked to report to the relevant security forces any suspicious persons loitering in or around the school.

If the school should receive a request, either in person or by telephone, for the early release of any children from school, they should act in accordance with previously agreed, written instructions given by you. In doing so, the school should:

- discover the identity of the caller and whether he/she is calling from your home;
- ring back on a previously agreed number, not one supplied by the caller;
- ensure that the voice of the caller is verified by the child or one of the children;
- ensure that the caller uses a previously agreed 'duress' and 'all OK' code;
- ensure that the caller can give full details of the child or children.

All of the above steps should be included in agreed procedures.

Additional instructions
Teach your children any routine security procedures and how to contact the emergency services or security forces. They should be instructed:

- how to call the police if strangers or prowlers are spotted around the home;
- to keep doors and windows locked when they are at home and not to admit strangers;
- not to leave home without informing you where they will be and with whom;
- to use busy, well-lit streets;
- to refuse lifts from strangers and not to accompany strangers on foot;
- to be suspicious of anyone walking alongside them;
- to refuse any gifts from strangers or slight acquaintances – however tempting;
- not to answer questions about themselves, their family or their home;
- not to open mail.

Teenage children
Teenage children are the most vulnerable to kidnap attempts because they tend to resist parental and other supervision. Also, they are easier than very young children to handle as captives.

If you have teenage children, you must make them aware of these facts. They should be discouraged from making 'blind dates' or from going to parties given by strangers, unless they are in the company of several friends.

Response to a kidnap call

During the call

Establish the following details:

- who the victim is, together with a code name for the victim;
- where and when the victim was seized;
- the state of the victim's health – inform the caller of any special medical condition;
- what the kidnappers want, when and how this is to be delivered; and ask to speak to the victim in order to establish state of health and that the caller really does have the victim. If this is not allowed, attempt to gain other indisputable evidence.

After the call

Check your written notes and make sure that you recorded as many details as possible. Then write notes under the following headings:

- source of call (eg local, long-distance, call-box etc);
- sex and approximate age of the caller;
- details of voice (eg high, low, husky, loud, soft, fast, slow etc);
- accent and, if disguised, natural or assumed;
- manner (eg calm, nervous, excited, confident, emotional etc);
- language (eg cultured, uneducated, abusive etc);
- distortion (eg coughing, wheezing, stuttering etc);
- background sounds (eg quiet, noisy, trains, people, aircraft, music, animals etc).

Dealing with bombs

Letter bombs

Letter bombs have been used regularly to harm people and it is important that you know what to look for. Mail bombs in envelopes have certain characteristics.

Oil or other stains on the outside of the envelope are key indicators. Similarly, signs that the envelope has been opened and re-glued or taped should draw your attention.

Care should be taken if the envelope seems heavier than its size or postage would suggest or, if it is unusually rigid – especially along its centre length. Care should be exercised if the postage paid is in excess of the size of the envelope or if the thickness of the envelope or package is not uniform.

Other key signals include a lack of return address, envelopes addressed to high-ranking officials, incorrect titles, poor typewriting or handwriting, or a postmark from abroad or from an unusual place.

In short, exercise extreme caution at all times.

Car bombs

The nature of vehicle checks will depend on the circumstances. A routine vehicle check should be carried out every time you, or your driver, returns to the car. A routine check is unlikely to spot a well-concealed bomb but it might spot a hastily improvised one. In any event, some precaution is better than none.

As the car is approached, look for obvious signs: footprints, finger marks, dropped objects, disturbed surroundings. When you reach the vehicle, stoop down carefully and look underneath for evidence of disturbed soil or dust, any wires hanging down or other suspicious objects.

Walk around the car, checking by eye and touch, the windows, doors, wheel arches, bumpers, engine, exhaust and fuel cap.

Finally, check inside for anything suspicious, eg packages that have been moved or wires jutting out from seats etc.

You should discipline yourself and your driver to check quickly and instinctively. However, extreme caution must be exercised as it might be that an attacker has planned to attack you while you are undertaking the check. Therefore, be aware of any parked cars and do the check as quickly as possible. Remember, your car is a useful pointer to potential assailants.

A longer check must be done if the car is left unattended for some time, eg first thing in the morning. If a bodyguard or driver is employed, he should be responsible for this task. A routine search of this kind will take between 10 and 20 minutes and should be performed two or three times every day.

It is sensible to follow a set system and use such aids as a torch, a mirror, a probe and a checklist.

The routine should be followed rigorously. Check the car from the rear forwards and from the bottom to the top. Do not forget to look in less obvious places such as the headrests, radio/cassette speakers, clocks, air conditioners etc.

A full vehicle search should be carried out by experts and should be performed when you suspect that there is a bomb in the vehicle. Specially trained personnel will have specialist equipment and any search will take up to two hours. In the meantime, all others should be kept away from the car.

As with all elements of security awareness, common sense and extreme vigilance should be applied at all times.

Part Four

Conclusions – So Where Do We Stand Now?

23
Conclusions

So where do we stand now?

'Besides the habit of analysis, what marks the mind
of the strategist is an intellectual elasticity or flexibility
that enables him to come up with realistic responses
to changing situations, not simply to discriminate with
great precision among different shades of grey.'

(Kenichi Ohmae, 1992)

There is no simple correlation between good intelligence and success in non-domestic markets. There is only the high probability of failure, given that there are so many different risk variables with high potential impacts and probabilities of occurrence. Good intelligence leads to better knowledge of non-domestic markets and better strategic planning. Putting a monetary figure to it, however, is impossible, unless one asks how much was lost by not knowing about something important. How much was lost by not getting a contract? Did the competition get it unfairly and how? Could one have avoided having the company's reputation muddied and the ensuing financial loss? Could one have avoided going into business with organized crime and losing control of money and assets?

Some senior executives will read *The Financial Times* and *The Wall Street Journal*, skim a trade publication or two, and then think that they know everything that's going on in their particular industry. Even if they do, this will not help them overseas, where the very nature of competition is distorted by GADs. Coupled with Western superiority complexes, this creates blindness as to the realities of doing business abroad. Their very education precludes most of them from coming to grips with reality. Most Western business schools do not teach any kind of competitive or non-domestic market intelligence, with the exceptions of some in France and Sweden.

Research on non-domestic markets will be *ad hoc*, with inappropriate resources and inadequate funding. Companies often rely on their accountants and bankers who may be biased anyway, and can only go so far in their research. They will not know much about a particular market except what they might be told by potential business partners, distributors or suppliers, where appearances should definitely not be taken at face value. The problem with advisors is that there is too much subjectivity. Most of them have not spent any time in-country and do not know about the soft passive-legal issues that impact businesses far more than they realize. Banks often have a conflict of interest, giving a one-dimensional view of a country and then passing this on to the client. The banks as well as the ratings agencies were caught out in South-East Asia and Russia. The fact is that banks need deals to go ahead and their motivation is success fees. Consultancies and banks involved in advisory roles will also sometimes be subject to bureaucratic conflicts of interest in their own organizations, which can colour the advice they give.

The same is true of M&A specialists, who will be working on fees upfront plus a percentage on completion of the deal. There is a need for these people to complete the deal, because jobs and commissions are on the line. There is therefore a conflict of interest. There may also be a 'hands off' of responsibility throughout the M&A process, from pre-acquisition due diligence, through to the actual signing of the deal and post-merger integration, which means that advisors will be concerned with their part of the deal only. The smaller company does not have much money to spend on research, while the larger company will not want to spend any, either because it thinks that it does not need to, because it is dealing directly with a government, or because it does not want to have to write off large sums if the deal does not go ahead.

'Short-termism' is a problem both within and outside the corporation. The outside advisors are short-term in their outlook for obvious reasons, but executives suffer from it too. Given limited budgets and timescales, they may rush to complete projects, often cutting corners, and, in the process, either missing or ignoring the grey issues which others will have to deal with in the future. Much of the blame lies with investors and shareholders demanding results in a success or failure culture that reflects on the individual.

The corporations that are successful in non-domestic markets will invest time and resources, so that they are aware of GAD issues likely to impact on their business operations. Ideally, they will have a corporate intelligence function co-located with the strategic planning units, at the strategic level (see Figure 23.1). The strategic planning unit reports directly to the senior executives at board level on non-domestic market strategy, with the intelligence function providing the intelligence required for the strategic planners. What usually happens is that the strategists do their own research (as described in Chapter 2) before putting the plan together, which is why, although the two functions should be co-located, they should report to the board separately.

This way, there can be no fitting the facts to suit the plan, making for much more objective strategic decision-making. If the strategy team is drawn from a particular line of business or strategic business unit, then it is even more important that the intelligence team be drawn from 'outsiders', that is, from different parts of the company, to mitigate against conflicts of interest. A standing intelligence function reporting to the board, as opposed to one drawn up *ad hoc* on a project basis, would be an advantage, providing for continuity and experience.

There are three main tasks for the intelligence function:

1. To make the strategy planners and board aware of the likely GAD factors present in a market at macro and micro levels, thus providing for insightful decision-making.

2. To provide the same intelligence on competitors (as well as general competitor intelligence).
3. To force the planners continually to reappraise and assess the appropriateness of their strategy in the light of changes in the environment, and to act as a check and balance against falling into a mindset of misconceptions, superiority and complacency.

There could also be a competitive intelligence unit attached to each business unit, but this will obviously vary according to the corporation. This unit, together with the strategic intelligence function, should be most closely involved with research both in-country and at corporate headquarters,

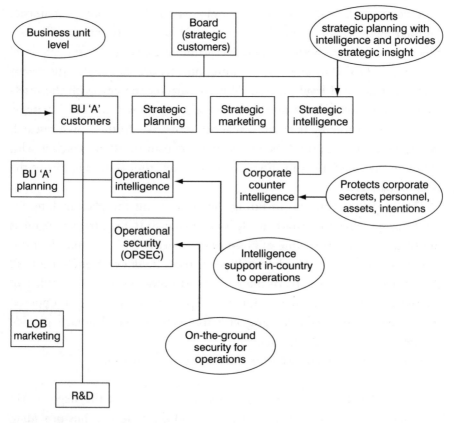

Source: F Milburn/MIG
Figure 23.1 Sustainability – audit and approach

collating, analysing and challenging all the information provided by the so-called 'experts', as well as conducting research of their own.

What one doesn't want to see is each information-gathering function such as sales, R&D and marketing conducting its own market research, unless they talk to each other and share information effectively, which can be very hard to achieve in some companies due to bureaucratic politics. The effective intelligence unit should be close to the prime customers for its 'product', but accessible to everyone in the corporation who needs it.

Good intelligence will be a huge asset in such strategic activities as M&A, by increasing the range of possible candidates, finding true fits between the companies, and showing the true worth of potential acquisitions and their contribution to overall strategy. Intelligence will help choose candidates for their future potential rather than past performance, help with price negotiations and, most importantly, compensate for being an outsider when carrying out such activities overseas. Non-domestic markets present unconventional risks and so require an unconventional approach.

One of the ways in which grey areas can be identified and planned for is war gaming (see Figure 23.2). This is a way of testing scenarios 'real time', and is useful for helping executives and planners break out of a particular mindset and prepare for what might happen when things go wrong. The concept involves teams of people taking on the roles of competitors, company executives, government regulators and other key players. Scenarios can be run in different ways, but a common one is the 'Red team/Blue team' approach. This involves two competing teams as the name suggests, with the Red team drawn from the intelligence function, and the Blue team made up of strategists.

The Red team's job is to play devil's advocate, whether as a competitor, government regulator or other key player. The intelligence analyst, for example, should try to put himself mentally in the place of a strategic planner in a rival company, and so ferret out the key perceptions and assumptions on which a competitor's strategy is based. The Red team throws in 'wildcards', which could include new legislation, foreign policy initiatives, political and security upheavals, new entrant companies not normally considered part of the landscape, and GADs that can spring surprises on the players. By doing this, a host of 'what if' scenarios are created. These can then be evaluated, the three or four most likely scenarios chosen and then planned for. It is important to have a range of scenarios from 'worst case' to the ideal business environment.

Examples of 'what if' scenarios could be: 'what happens if China block-ades Taiwan?' or 'what happens if we make substantial investment and the industry is re-nationalized in the future?' War gaming helps identify information requirements and critical success factors, as well as probable moves by competitors, and evolving conditions in a market. It can also show probable competitor or governmental responses to your own actions and help identify weaknesses. War gaming increases teamwork, helps people to understand the interplay of GADs and limits surprise: in non-domestic markets, it is the surprises that cost money.

It should be clear from the preceding analysis of the risks in non-domestic markets that the only certainty is uncertainty, for the unwary that is. Complacency, over-confidence and arrogance are all fatal traps that will sink the unprepared. The costs of failure can literally be fatal, and not just in financial terms. It is ironic that companies will prepare non-domestic strategies in order to make money, but are not willing to spend money on doing their homework for those strategies. The 'lean and hungry' approach often precludes investigation of the facts prior to disaster. Non-domestic market intelligence should be seen not simply as a cost centre but as a valuable safeguard against losses. It is also a useful tool that will help to

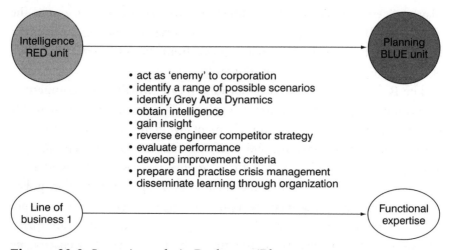

Figure 23.2 Scenario analysis: Red team/Blue team concept or war gaming

generate future profit, by identifying opportunities. The value of good market intelligence can be quantified in terms of profits gained, and profits not lost.

There is clearly a need for a regular and accurate flow of intelligence, and continual reality audits of the Grey Area Dynamics™ in non-domestic markets. Cutting corners to save money can make one look good in the short term only. As Frederick the Great once said, 'It is pardonable to be defeated, but never to be surprised'.

The events of 11 September 2001 showed the impact of surprise. With the vast number of terrorists trained in Sudan and Afghanistan now back in the West, we cannot afford to be surprised again.

Whether we like it or not, there is no substitute for objective intelligence. However, the conventional approach, utilizing traditional due diligence practices, are inadequate. Today, the decision-making board member has to look out at the world differently.

References

Bowden, M (1995) *Black Hawk Down: A Story of Modern War*, Penguin.

Hubbard, N (1999) *Acquisition Strategy and Implementation*, Macmillan Press.

Ohmae, K (1992) *The Mind of The Strategist*, McGraw Hill.

Regester, M and Larkin, J (1997) *Risk Issues and Crisis Management*, Kogan Page, London.

(1999) *The Price of Oil, Human Rights Watch*.

About the authors

Stuart Poole-Robb is the Chief Executive of the Merchant International Group founded in 1982. Now 57, he joined the RAF at 15½ as a boy entrant. After four years in the RAF, which saw him serve in Aden, Bahrain, Germany, Muscat and Sharjah, he was transferred to the RAF Regiment (Special Investigations Branch). In 1964, he was selected for special training at Hereford and, subsequently, completed hot weather training in Borneo. Following further training in counter-insurgency and counter-terrorism, he served in Egypt, Germany, Libya, Nigeria, Oman, the Yemen and other hot spots until he left in 1971 – although his connection continued through the Operations Research Unit at Century House where he saw service in the GDR (East Germany) and elsewhere.

As a civilian, he worked for the Rank Organisation, Sperry Rand Inc, Alders International and Corals plc where he was Group Special Projects Director. His work with MIG began in 1982.

Stuart Poole-Robb maintains a high level of fitness – skiing, gliding, tennis, running and martial arts – and is currently completing a four year programme for a Black Belt in Shotokan Karate.

Alan Bailey claims to be on the wrong side of most ages and has followed a range of careers simultaneously. He was conscripted into the army straight from his public school. Commissioned as a gunner, he transferred to the Intelligence Corps and served until 1964. He spent time in the public service and then became an Under Secretary with the Royal Institution of Chartered Surveyors. Between 1969 and 1979, he was the first chief executive of the World of Property Housing Trust (now Sanctuary), building homes for those in social need. He was then invited to join and manage a property services group, the profits of which were devoted to charitable endeavour, and became a trustee director of several charities – including Help the Aged and ActionAid. He was also a columnist for *The Times, The Guardian, Illustrated London News, Director, Estates Gazette, Property Week* and *New Law Journal*. He also became a national cartoonist. Between 1995 and 1998, he was Chairman of the Merchant International Group Ltd and recently re-joined the board of that company. He serves on the boards of other companies as a non-executive director but is the Executive Chairman of City & West End Clubs Ltd (Placemakers), ABS Communications and Alastor Ltd. He is a graduate member of the Communications, Advertising and Marketing Foundation, and a member of the Chartered Institute of Marketing, the Chartered Institute of Journalists and the Institute of Public Relations. He is a member of the Wig and Pen Club and the Special Forces Club.

About MIG

Merchant International Group Ltd (MIG) is a leading strategic research and corporate intelligence company. Established in 1982, MIG specializes in identifying, monitoring and analysing the risks, weaknesses and threats encountered by companies investing and operating in non-domestic markets. To this end, the concept of 'Grey Area Dynamics™' – a collective description of passive and non-passive, legal and illegal factors such as corruption, bureaucracy, organized crime, tribalism and cultural integration, xenophobia and corporate espionage – was created.

The company's expertise lies in creating total transparency and advising its clients on the ramifications of Grey Area Dynamics™ impacting on their business outside their home market. With 20 years of knowledge and experience through in-country projects for FTSE 100 and Fortune 500 companies, publications such as *Risky Business* clearly illustrate the vital intelligence required by companies, which is so often ignored.

MIG hopes this book will act as a business guide to help corporate decision-makers avoid subjectivity, conflict of interests and inadequate research prior to embarking in an overseas market.

Chief Executive Officer:	Stuart Poole-Robb
Head of Global Risks:	Dr Rashna Writer

75–79 Knightsbridge
London SW1X 9HL
Tel: +44 (0)20 7259 5060
Fax: +44 (0)20 7259 5090
www.merchantinternational.com
email: headoffice@merchantinternational.com

MERCHANT INTERNATIONAL GROUP (MIG)
PUBLICATIONS

MIG regularly produces a range of publications designed to assist those whose task it is to identify, analyse and measure risk before deciding on recommending or maintaining investment in non-domestic markets. There are two publications:

		Prices per year in £	
		Hard copy by post	By email
RISK UPDATE	12 issues per year	300.00	265.00
GLOBAL RISK TRENDS	12 issues per year	750.00	600.00

Individual copies are available on request, via post or email as follows:

RISK UPDATE	£25.00 by post	£20.00 by email
GLOBAL RISK TRENDS	£75.00 by post	£60.00 by email

No VAT is levied. Special reduced terms apply if subscribers want several copies of all or any of the publications. Prices quoted are valid to June 2002.

✄ ————————————————————————————————

To:

The Publications Director, MIG, 75–79 Knightsbridge, London, SW1X 9HL

I wish to subscribe to your publications. Please ring me with full details.

NAME:..

DESIGNATION: ....

COMPANY: ....

ADDRESS:...

TEL: .... FAX: .... EMAIL: ....

Index

DATE DUE

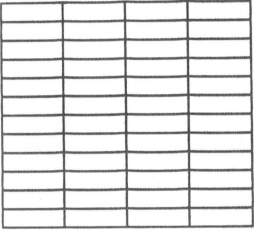